D0231105

San Antonio Cookbook II

San Antonio Cookbook II

collected by the

SAN ANTONIO SYMPHONY LEAGUE

Copyright 1976

SYMPHONY SOCIETY OF SAN ANTONIO

First Edition	April 1976	5,000 Copies
Second Printing	September 1976	10,000 Copies
Third Printing	June 1978	10,000 Copies
Second Edition	August 1980	13,000 Copies
Second Printing	December 1983	10,000 Copies

Library of Congress Number 80-53214

ISBN 0-9612470-0-2

Frontispiece - PASEO DEL RIO - Ivan McDougal

The culinary arts contained herein are dedicated to the
musical arts made a living part of our community culture
by the

San Antonio Symphony

THE WOMEN'S COMMITTEE OF
THE SYMPHONY SOCIETY OF SAN ANTONIO

PRESIDENT   Mrs. F. Daniel Foley

THE CREATORS OF
San Antonio Cookbook II

EDITOR & CHAIRMAN   Mrs. Geoffrey P. Wiedeman

CO-CHAIRMAN   Mrs. Gerald W. Massy III

Mrs. H. Randolph Brown
Mrs. Clifford J. Buckley
Mrs. J. Robert Burkhart
Mrs. Gilbert L. Curtis
Mrs. Robert G. Dawson
Mrs. Leo F. Dusard, Jr.
Mrs. John T. Dyer
Mrs. Richard E. Eddleman
Mrs. Clarence A. Fey
Mrs. Lyman R. Fink
Mrs. Kenneth R. Gaarder
Mrs. Robert Galbreath
Vivian M. Gersema
Mrs. Michael J. Kaine
Mrs. John M. Kefauver
Mrs. Charles L. Kenward
Mrs. Johnson Lewenthal
Mrs. Lawrence A. Martin, Jr.

Gerald W. Massy III
Mrs. Mike Montgomery
Mrs. Eugene Nolte, Jr.
Mrs. Carlos J. G. Perry
Mrs. H. H. Phillips, Jr.
Mrs. Ralph Rowden
Mrs. E. Morgan Schmidt
Mrs. Alexis Shelokov
Mrs. Charles Shield III
Mrs. Richard D. Small, Jr.
Mrs. McGregor Snodgrass
Mrs. William L. Starnes
Mrs. George C. Viney
Mrs. Thomas A. Wachsmuth
Mrs. Joel W. Westbrook III
Geoffrey P. Wiedeman, M.D.
Mrs. Willard Woodring
Colonel Jack C. Young

ART LEAGUE LIAISON — Mrs. H. Randolph Brown

ILLUSTRATIONS — Members of the San Antonio Art League

COVER ILLUSTRATION — Mrs. John M. Kefauver

RESTAURANT EDITOR — Mrs. Gerald W. Massy III

RESTAURANT ILLUSTRATIONS — Florida Booth

PUBLICITY — Mrs. Carlos Montemayor

NARRATIVE — Mrs. Geoffrey P. Wiedeman
Mrs. Carlos J. G. Perry
Mrs. Robert Galbreath

San Antonio Cookbook II

points with pride to its predecessor

THE SAN ANTONIO COOKBOOK
1962 - 1976

RECIPIENT OF SAN ANTONIO CONSERVATION SOCIETY AWARD

1962

"For capturing — figuratively and literally — the flavors of San Antonio in *The San Antonio Cookbook.*

"The recipes contributed by San Antonio gourmet cooks reflect the broad and varied aspects of San Antonio life and culture as the book includes examples of all our foods from caviar to roasted doves and tacos.

"A vivid picture of the City's personality is painted by the text and is augmented by the accompanying beautiful drawings of San Antonio scenes and landmarks."

Your purchase of SAN ANTONIO COOKBOOK II is an expression of your interest in, and devotion to, the continuation of fine music.

San Antonio

A Star of Texas

What is San Antonio? So many things! San Antonio is fiestas, freeways and football; tourists and conventions; opera, theater and art; symphonies and sunshine; beauty and bustling big business; pageants, parades, and pictures out of the past.

San Antonio is the gaiety of the Paseo Del Rio on a summer evening — cafes, shops, paddle boats and barges; dixieland jazz, flamenco rhythms, strolling singers and mariachi guitars.

San Antonio is the soft sounds of Spanish together with a Texas twang; as American as the cowboy, as continental as a quaint European village.

San Antonio is the look of leafy pecans along the river, the beauty of blue bonnets in the spring, the feel of the first "norther" in the fall.

San Antonio is a special place. A place of which the residents are fiercely proud and a place with which all visitors fall in love.

Founded in 1718 by Spanish missionaries and settlers from the Canary Islands, San Antonio has lived under six flags. It was the scene of historic battles of great significance to our country. Its past was one of a roisterous "Wild West" town where drovers assembled for the long, dangerous Chisolm Trail ride to Kansas. But despite its

THE ALAMO — Margaret Putnam

romantic, storybook beginnings, San Antonio has always been a regional center of culture.

Along with Boston, New Orleans and San Francisco, San Antonio is considered to be one of America's four "Unique Cities". Today, it is the 10th largest in our country and each year, tourist and convention activities attract millions more to explore its beauty. It is an ever-growing medical and educational center, an international gateway for travelers and a market terminal for the great Southwest.

Cooled by gulf breezes in summer, the city is lush with palm fronds, banana leaves and mesquite. Stately, ancient live oaks stand a hundred feet tall or hug the ground in serpentine fashion. Gardens are a sea of color where zinnias, marigolds and roses bask in the sun and share honors with tomato plants, okra and parsley.

With the advent of fall, the first "norther" blows in, bringing chilly mornings, sunny days and crisp, clear nights. Chrysanthemums bloom and hunting season gets underway.

Nature's traditional red and green of Christmas time heralds the arrival of winter. Pyracantha bushes are laden with bright red berries, and poinsettias — as tall as trees — are topped with their own Christmas ornaments.

San Antonio stands today as a magnificent blend of colorful history and diverse cultures. Each gave its best to her heritage. The Alamo symbolizes that great heritage where the past, present and future are linked together. The old stands by the new, and even the most casual observer will feel the silent drama of history joining the modern march of progress in a great metropolis.

In our SAN ANTONIO COOKBOOK II, we have attempted to meld together all the backgrounds of our historic old city. We offer a variety of recipes. Some are typically southern, some Mexican in flavor. Others are typically Texas or internationally haute cuisine. But most of all, they are typically San Antonio.

Please enjoy our contribution to your kitchen and share with us our special shining STAR OF TEXAS — SAN ANTONIO.

Salud!

The Scenes of San Antonio

We gratefully acknowledge our appreciation to the talented artists of the San Antonio Art League for their contribution to San Antonio Cookbook II.

Table of Contents

ARNESON RIVER THEATER — Clay McGaughy

The Spice of San Antonio

Fiestas & Flavors from Old Mexico

"Bienvenidos, amigos, a San Antonio—nuestra ciudad de fiestas."
(Welcome, friends, to San Antonio—our city of festivals.)

In the Alamo City, from January through December, there is usually a festival in progress. German, Greek and Mexican Fiestas compete for our attention with Israeli, Lebanese, Polish and Texas Folklife Festivals. Each one is unique in its presentation of food, dance and fun.

The greatest festival of all occurs in the springtime. The magic date is April 21 — San Jacinto Day. On that day in 1836, General Sam Houston, commanding the remnants of the Army of Texas after the fall of the Alamo, defeated the poorly supplied Mexican Army and established for all time the future history of Texas.

Each year during the week of the 21st of April, San Antonio comes alive with "Fiesta Week". The night sky glows with reflections from the "King's River Parade" as thousands of people line the banks of the San Antonio River. They await the arrival of "King Antonio" and his parade of beautifully bedecked floats — which truly float — down the winding river through the heart of San Antonio and the Paseo Del Rio, located one level below the city streets.

Everyday traffic makes way for the magnificent daylight street parade — hours long. The city sparkles with America's greatest nighttime flambeau parade. There are solemn ceremonies of history and heritage at the Alamo, and the crowning of "The Queen of The Order of The Alamo" is a glittering spectacle to recall the fairytale fantasies of our childhood.

"Fiesta Week" also brings "A Night In Old San Antonio" which is sponsored by the San Antonio Conservation Society. La Villita, the historically restored original Spanish settlement, becomes a fiesta unto itself. It's a tiny area, a few blocks square in the center of town, where for four nights thousands of people, elbow to elbow, savor the fun of Fiesta.

MEXICAN PLAZA — Ed Willmann

But San Antonio's intertwined history and heritage with Mexico does not stop at the Alamo or with fiestas and celebrations. From the beginning, the flavors of Mexico were subtly woven into the life-style of everyone who passed this way.

These flavors were not all pure Mexican in origin. They were a blend of foodstuffs available west of the Mississippi and south of the Red River Valley; from the desert lands of New Mexico and Arizona to the heart of Latin America.

Today, flavors from Old Mexico are some of the SPICE OF SAN ANTONIO. Tortillas, tacos, frijoles and chili, peppered with the inimitable jalapeño, are as natural to San Antonio as gumbo is to New Orleans and baked beans are to Boston.

But — if Mexican seasonings are new to you, take care — *Muy Picante!*

ENCHILADAS

12 tortillas, fresh
6 to 8 pisado chiles
  (dried red chiles)
1 cup beef broth
1 garlic clove
1/4 cup onion, chopped

shortening
3 tablespoons flour
1 large onion, chopped
2 cups sharp cheese, grated
water

Wash chiles and remove seeds. Simmer them in water until tender and remove the peel. Transfer the chiles to a blender with the broth, garlic and 1/4 cup onions and blend together. In a skillet large enough to hold a tortilla without bending, heat the shortening. In another skillet melt 4 tablespoons shortening and add the flour. When the mixture is slightly brown, add the chile sauce from the blender and add enough water to make a medium thick gravy. Place a tortilla in the hot oil skillet just long enough to heat it. Immediately place it in the skillet with the sauce and then to a plate. Fill with onions and cheese then roll and place in a greased baking dish. Repeat the process until all tortillas are used. Sprinkle the top with onions and cheese and pour remaining sauce over the enchiladas. Place in a 200° oven until ready to serve. Serves 6.

LBJ RANCH ENCHILADAS

chili of your choice with some
of the meat separated
from juice

1 onion, chopped fine
3 cups American cheese, grated
corn tortillas

In a 2 quart pot, 3/4 full of boiling water, dip tortillas, one at a time, for 1 second. Remove and place 1/4 teaspoon of onion, 1 tablespoon chili meat and 1 tablespoon of grated cheese on each softened tortilla. Roll the tortilla and place side by side in a baking dish with rolled edges on the bottom. Pour about 1 cup of chili juice over the enchiladas. Bake 10 to 12 minutes in 350° oven. Remove from oven and sprinkle with 1 1/2 cups of grated cheese. Return to the oven for 5 more minutes. Serve immediately.

MRS. LYNDON B. JOHNSON
LBJ Ranch, Stonewall, Texas

ENCHILADA SPINACH CASSEROLE

2 lbs. ground chuck
1 large onion, chopped
1 package frozen spinach
1 (1 lb.) can tomatoes
1 can mushroom soup
1 can golden mushroom soup
1 (8 oz.) carton sour cream
1/4 cup milk

3 garlic cloves, minced
16 fresh or frozen tortillas
1/2 cup melted butter
2 (4 oz.) cans chopped green
chiles
1/2 lb. Longhorn cheese, grated
salt and pepper

Brown meat and drain off liquid. Stir in onions, tomatoes, spinach (cooked and drained well), salt and pepper. In another bowl combine soups, sour cream, milk, garlic, chiles and mix well. Dip 8 tortillas in melted butter and arrange on the bottom and sides of a large, shallow casserole. Spoon the meat mixture on the tortillas and add a layer of cheese. (Reserve 1/2 cup of cheese). Arrange the other 8 tortillas, dipped in melted butter, on top and pour the mushroom soups sauce over the top. Sprinkle with the remaining cheese. Bake 35 minutes in 325° oven. To make in advance, cook only 25 minutes, cover and refrigerate. Before serving, heat 30 minutes. Serves 12.

YVONNE BROWN TANNER (MRS. VAN NESS)

CHICKEN ENCHILADAS WITH GREEN TOMATO SAUCE

4 cans (8½ oz.) Tomatitos
  Verdes, drained
1 clove garlic, minced
1 large onion, chopped
½ teaspoon coriander, heaping
1 teaspoon salt

1 pint sour cream
2 dozen tortillas
2 cups cooking oil, heated
1 lb. American cheese, grated
2 cups cooked, diced chicken

Put tomatoes, garlic, onion, coriander and salt into blender; puree; pour into sauce pan and simmer for 30 to 40 minutes. Remove from heat, stir in sour cream. Dip each tortilla in very hot oil, then in sauce. Remove and put 1½ tablespoons chicken and 1 tablespoon cheese on top and roll the tortilla. Place in shallow pan side by side. Pour sauce over enchiladas, sprinkle with cheese. Bake at 325° 20 to 30 minutes.

MRS. CHARLES STANLEY PRICE (JOY)

CHICKEN ENCHILADAS

4 whole chicken breasts
1 tablespoon butter
1 large onion, chopped
5 large jalapeño peppers,
  chopped and seeded
1 pint sour cream
10 oz. Monterey Jack cheese,
  grated
1 teaspoon oregano

garlic powder, onion powder
  and black pepper to taste
¼ to ½ teaspoon salt
4 tablespoon stuffed green
  olives, chopped
Tabasco, to taste
½ cup cream sherry
3½ dozen tortillas

Remove skin and place chicken breasts in a baking pan and sprinkle generously with garlic powder, onion powder and black pepper. Sprinkle a generous dash of Tabasco on each breast. Add cream sherry and cover with foil. Bake for about 45 minutes at 350° or until chicken is done. Remove bone and cut chicken breasts into cubes. Set aside. (Should be about 3½ cups.)

Saute onions and jalapeños in butter until onions are transparent. Remove from heat and add cubed chicken and sour cream. Stir thoroughly until chicken cubes begin to break up slightly. Add cheese and the remaining seasonings. Place 1 tablespoon of this mixture on each tortilla. Roll up the tortilla and place in a baking dish. Cover with your favorite enchilada sauce. Bake at 350° for 20 minutes. Remove from oven and cover with more grated cheese. Return baking dish to the oven for about 10 minutes or until cheese is melted and sauce is bubbly. Makes 3½ dozen.

COLONEL JACK C. YOUNG

TAMALES

2 dozen dried corn husks	1½ teaspoons salt
⅓ cup lard	1½ teaspoons baking powder
2 cups masa harina	1½ cups warm stock

Soak the corn husks in hot water until softened. Cream the lard until it is light and fluffy. Mix masa harina with salt and baking powder and beat into lard, bit by bit. Gradually beat in enough stock to make a rather mushy dough. Shake excess water from softened corn husks. Spread 1 tablespoon dough on the center part of the husk, leaving room to fold over ends at top and bottom. Place a tablespoon of filling in center of dough and fold like a jelly-roll so that the filling is completely covered by dough. Fold ends of husks over at top and bottom. Put tamales in a steamer with the bottom end of the corn husk down and steam for about one hour, or until the dough comes away from the husk. Sheets of kitchen parchment, about 8 inches by 4 inches, can be substituted for corn husks.

Tamales may be filled with a variety of meats and sauces. Mole Poblano made with either turkey or chicken and Adobo Rojo made with pork or chicken are among the most popular fillings. Picadillo also makes an excellent filling. Meat and poultry for tamales should always be boneless and either shredded or cut into small pieces. In Texas, ground venison is often added to pork for filling. Makes 2 dozen.

TOSTADOS

Cut corn tortillas in sixths and fry in hot shortening until brown. Drain thoroughly on paper towels. Sprinkle with salt while hot.

CHILEQUILES

1 medium onion
1 garlic clove
1 (No. 2) can tomatoes
1 package tortillas
salt and pepper

1 can Ortega chile peppers
2 cups grated yellow cheese
1 pint sour cream
2 tablespoons oil

Chop onion and garlic and fry in oil until clear. Add tomatoes, salt and pepper to taste. Simmer 15 minutes. Remove seed from peppers and cut each into 4 strips. Cut tortillas in ¼ and dip in hot fat. Remove at once. Drain well. Place layer of tortillas in baking dish, add sauce, peppers and cheese, ending with cheese. Make at least 2 layers of each. Place in hot oven for 45 minutes or until just bubbling. Before serving remove from oven and top with 1 pint of sour cream. Place under broiler until top is slightly brown. Must be piping hot when served.

MRS. LOUIS J. KOCUREK

NACHOS

Fry corn tortillas in hot fat until crisp and drain. Break into 3 or 4 pieces, cover with grated cheese and top with a thin slice of jalapeño. Put under the broiler until cheese melts. (You may use commercial corn chips. Doritos work quite well.)

PICADILLO

½ lb. beef, ground
½ lb. pork, ground
4 tomatoes, peeled and sliced
3 green onions, chopped
3 medium potatoes, diced
1 jar pimiento, diced
¾ cups toasted almonds, slivered

2 to 3 cloves garlic
¼ teaspoon pepper
1 teaspoon salt
1 (6 oz.) can tomato paste
2 jalapeños, chopped
¾ cup raisins
¼ teaspoon oregano

Cover meat with water; add salt and pepper. Simmer covered 30 minutes. Add remaining ingredients, and cook until potatoes are tender. Drain excess liquid. Serve in chafing dish with tostados.

MRS. ROBERT KELSO

PICADILLO II

3 lbs. beef, ground
3 onions, finely chopped
3 garlic cloves, minced
  (minced instant garlic
  may be used)
2 green peppers, finely chopped
1 package Wick Fowler's
  3 Alarm Chili Mix
1 tablespoon oregano

1 large can tomatoes or 2 small
  cans tomato sauce
1 can water chestnuts, finely
  chopped
1 cup white raisins
2 (4 oz.) cans mushroom stems
  and pieces
1 cup green olives, chopped

Combine first 4 ingredients in skillet and brown in small amount of olive oil. Add remaining ingredients (except for package of masa in Fowler's mix) and simmer for about 2 hours. Add masa. May be prepared in advance and heated just before serving. Serve with firm dip chips. May be refrigerated for several days. Freezes well.

MRS. MICHAEL J. KAINE (ETHEL)

TACOS

Tacos are small tortillas rolled and stuffed with various mixtures and fried crisp in lard. They may also be served soft, without frying. In the United States the taco is not rolled, but simply folded in half. In Mexico they are always rolled.

For a taco party, set out bowls of various hot sauces, canned chiles, chopped lettuce and tomatoes, sauteed ground beef or chorizo (Mexican hot sausage), shredded cooked chicken or pork, guacamole, frijoles refritos or whatever filling suits your fancy. Serve the taco soft or crispy and allow your guests to assemble their own.

BEEF TACOS WITH A DIFFERENCE

1 lb. ground beef
1 potato, chopped
1 onion, chopped
1 garlic clove, chopped

1/2 teaspoon cumino
10 taco shells
salt and pepper
lettuce and tomatoes, chopped

Brown the ground beef. Blend the potatoes, onion, garlic in a blender with a small amount of water to liquify and stir into the browned meat. Cook until the potato mixture is thoroughly cooked. (The addition of the potato will make the ground beef stick together.) Season with salt and pepper and add cumino. Divide mixture into 10 taco shells, and place on a baking sheet. Bake in 350° oven for a few minutes. Serve immediately with chopped lettuce, tomatoes and your favorite taco sauce.

MARILYN B. PAGE (MRS. CAREY)

HENRY B.'S FAVORITE SOFT TACOS

10 corn tortillas
8 green peppers
2 tablespoons shortening
½ teaspoon garlic salt
½ cup onions, minced
1 (1 lb.) can tomatoes

⅓ teaspoon black pepper
1 cup American cheese
  grated
½ cup jalapeño cheese,
  grated (optional)

Remove seeds from green peppers and boil until soft. Drain and allow to cool. Remove the skins and mash with a fork. Heat the shortening and saute onions. Add tomatoes, garlic salt and pepper. Add the green peppers and stir. Simmer for 2 minutes. Add cheese and stir until cheese melts. Heat oil in frying pan and dip corn tortilla in the hot oil. Remove quickly to a baking dish. Add 2 tablespoons filling and roll. Continue until all tortillas have been filled. Add remaining filling on top of the tacos and sprinkle with more grated cheese. Serve immediately. This is a favorite with vegetarian friends.

HENRY B. GONZALEZ
United States Representative, State of Texas

CHILE CON QUESO

½ lb. pasteurized cheese   ½ can tomatoes with green chiles

Melt tomatoes with chile peppers and cheese in top of a double boiler. Serve as a dip with corn chips, spread on toast or crackers, or as a filling for hard boiled eggs and celery. May be served warm over broken corn chips or toasted tortillas.

MRS. LYNDON B. JOHNSON
LBJ Ranch, Stonewall, Texas

GUACAMOLE

2 large avocados
1 medium tomato, peeled
1 tablespoon onion, minced
1 or more canned serrano chiles

1 tablespoon fresh cilantro
salt and pepper
juice of 1 lime

Peel and mash the avocados. Remove seeds and chop chiles and tomatoes. Chop cilantro and combine all ingredients. Pile in a serving dish with the avocado pit in the center to help prevent discoloration. Use as a sauce, a dip, a salad or to make Chalupas Compuestas. Makes about 2 cups.

FRIJOLES — MEXICAN BEANS

1 cup dried pinto or
   kidney beans
1 whole onion, peeled

1 whole clove of garlic
1 teaspoon leaf oregano
salt to taste

Soak the beans in water to cover overnight. Drain the beans and put them in a saucepan. Add water to cover to a depth of 1 inch above the level of the beans. Add the onion, garlic and oregano and simmer 1 hour. Add salt to taste and continue to cook for 1 hour or longer until the beans are tender. (Small piece salt pork may be added to beans when cooking.) Makes 2 cups.

MRS. EUGENE NOLTE, JR. (MARGARET)

FRIJOLES REFRITOS — REFRIED MEXICAN BEANS

2 lbs. pinto or kidney beans
3 tablespoons chili powder
1 lb. salt pork, cut into
   small pieces
1 garlic clove, sliced
1 tablespoon salt

2 tablespoons lard
   or bacon grease
1 cup American or Longhorn
   cheese, grated
12 green onions, sliced thin

Cover the frijoles and salt pork with boiling water. Add chili powder, garlic and salt. Simmer for several hours until tender, adding more boiling water as needed. When frijoles are tender, put lard or bacon grease in a large skillet and add frijoles, a spoonful at a time, and mash well. Cook over low heat for several hours, stirring occasionally. Frijoles should become a rich, dark brown color. To serve, mound high in a large Mexican bean bowl and cover with grated cheese and onions.

MRS. NEVILLE MURRAY

CHALUPAS

6 tortillas or commercial
  Chalupa shells
1 cup cooking oil
½ cup frijoles refritos
  (refried beans)
2 cups grated cheese
salt and pepper to taste
6 onions, chopped fine
¾ cup tomatoes, chopped fine
3 cups finely chopped lettuce

Fry tortillas in cooking oil until crisp. Spread each tortilla with refritos (see Index) and cheese. Place on a cookie sheet and bake at 350° until heated and cheese melts. While piping hot, place on 6 individual plates. Sprinkle each Chalupa with a little salt and pepper. Add 1 teaspoon onion, 2 teaspoons tomato and ½ cup lettuce. Serve immediately. Serves 6.

Add Guacamole (see Index) on top of the Chalupa and you have "Chalupas Compuestas."

MRS. CHARLES STANLEY PRICE (JOY)

MENUDO

6 lbs. tripe
1 small red pepper, dry
2 onions
¼ lb. red chile pods or
  ½ cup chili powder
salt and pepper to taste
1 pig hock
1 bay leaf
1 teaspoon oregano
1 soup bone
2 cloves of garlic
1 teaspoon comino seed
2 cans golden hominy

Cut tripe into bite-size pieces, wash and cover with water. Add soup bone, pig hock, bay leaf, red pepper and boil until tender (about 4 hours). Add garlic, onion, oregano and comino and boil until onion is tender. Add chile pods and boil 30 minutes longer. Add hominy and cook another 30 minutes. Add salt and pepper to taste. If you use chile pods, remove seeds, wash and boil for 10 minutes, cool and put them through sieve. To serve: Fill soup bowl with Menudo, sprinkle with chopped onion and oregano with lemon on the side. Serves 12.

CEYLON R. KIDWELL

CABRITO — Baby Goat

1 cabrito	1 stalk celery
salt	$\frac{1}{2}$ cup water
pepper	$1\frac{1}{2}$ cups dry white wine
oregano	1 tablespoon lemon juice
garlic salt	optional seasonings: thyme,
2 slices onion	parsley, bay leaf
2 slices carrot	

Rub meat well with salt, pepper, oregano and garlic salt. If the kid has been fed in Mexico, the taste of the oregano and wild marjoram is already in the meat and it is not necessary to add more. Roast at 500° until brown; then reduce heat to 375°. Add onion, carrots, celery and water. Cook 18 to 20 minutes per pound. One half hour before serving, uncover cabrito and pour off all the collected fat except $\frac{1}{4}$ cup. Add dry white wine and lemon juice. Baste several times before serving. Cabrito is generally cooked split in half. For smaller servings it can be cut into quarters with the two sides of ribs making 6 pieces in all.

MRS. HAMILTON BONNET

CEVICHE

1 lb. raw corbina fillets, or	1 jalapeño pepper,
any firm white fish	chopped and seeded
lime juice	1 clove garlic, minced
1 large onion, chopped	$\frac{1}{4}$ teaspoon salt

Cut fish into cubes or in strips $1\frac{1}{2}$ inch by $\frac{1}{2}$ inch. Layer with onion and chile pepper. Salt. Add lime juice to cover. Stir every 15 minutes for 1 hour. Refrigerate for 24 hours. Stir occasionally. Serve chilled with crackers. Makes 1 quart.

PEG ZIPERMAN

TOMATO CEVICHE

1½ lbs. mild fish (mahi-mahi, flounder, sole, turbot, scallops)
1 teaspoon sugar
2 teaspoons salt (may use part garlic salt)
pinch oregano
4 dashes Tabasco
1 or 2 canned jalapeños, finely chopped
1 medium onion, finely chopped
1 teaspoon white pepper
juice of 4 large limes or ½ cup Realime
2 cups ripe tomatoes, chopped

Cut fish into small strips or cubes. Place in a bowl with all other ingredients except tomatoes and marinate in the refrigerator for at least 4 hours. (The lime will cook the raw fish.) Add tomatoes and mix well. Will keep for several days in the refrigerator.

To serve as an appetizer, place on a serving plate and surround with Triscuits. To serve as a salad, peel and cut 4 avocados in half. Remove seed, fill with fish mixture and serve on lettuce leaf. Serves 8.

MRS. ROYCE MOSER, JR. (LOIS)

FISH IN ESCABECHE SAUCE

2 lbs. any white fish, cut in 2 or 3 inch pieces
flour
oil for deep frying
4 cloves garlic, minced
2 large onions, thinly sliced
½ small can jalapeño chiles or 2 fresh ones, diced
½ cup olive oil
2 green peppers, chopped
¼ teaspoon cumin seed
½ teaspoon oregano
½ teaspoon peppercorns, crushed
2 teaspoons salt
2 bay leaves
1½ cups white wine vinegar
sliced pimiento and ripe olives

Roll fish in flour lightly, fry quickly and arrange in a large casserole. In stainless skillet, heat olive oil and saute onion, garlic, green pepper. Add seasonings (Fiesta Brand) and wine vinegar. Bring to a boil, simmer 10 minutes. Pour over fish; cool, refrigerate at least 24 hours. Allow to come to room temperature and garnish with pimiento strips and olives. Serve with crackers. (You may break up and flake the fish after it has been fried, if you prefer.) Serves 25.

MRS. CLIFTON BOLNER

PESCADO A LA VERACRUZANA

2 lbs. red snapper
1/4 cup olive oil
1 onion, chopped
5 large tomatoes, peeled
  and chopped

1 (3 oz.) jar green olives
1 small hot green pepper, minced
salt and pepper to taste

Saute onions in olive oil. Add tomatoes, olives, hot peppers, salt and pepper. Cook about 20 minutes. In a large skillet, heat a little oil and brown fish on both sides. Add the tomato sauce and cook about 15 minutes or until fish is thoroughly cooked. Serves 4 to 5.

VERA SERGEANT

OLIVIA'S ASADO EN CRUDO

8 to 10 ancho or pisado chiles
  (dried red)
3 garlic cloves
1/8 teaspoon comino
2 or 3 clove stems

1 teaspoon orange rind, grated
2 tablespoons shortening
3 lbs. cubed pork
3 lbs. cubed beef
1 quart water

Boil chiles until tender. Remove skin and seeds. Grind chiles in a molcayete or blender with garlic, cominos, cloves and orange rind. Melt shortening in a large Dutch Oven, add chile mixture and water. Simmer for 20 minutes. Bring to a boil, add pork and beef and simmer until the meat is tender. Add salt and pepper to taste. Serve with Spanish Rice (see Index), pinto beans and tortillas.

MRS. OLIVIA GARZA

TAMPIQUENA STEAK

2 lbs. sirloin steak, cut in
  1 1/2 inch wide strips
salt and pepper
2 tablespoons oil
1 large tomato, chopped

2 green peppers, sliced
1 onion cut in rings
3 garlic cloves
1 cup water

Fry meat in oil until done; remove from pan. Add tomato, green peppers, onion, garlic, salt, pepper and water to the same skillet. Simmer 15 minutes, add meat, heat and serve. Serve over cooked plain rice. Serves 4 to 6.

LAURIE RICHLEY

PEPPER STEAK MEXICANA

1½ lbs. round steak, cut
  ½ inch thick
¼ cup all-purpose flour
½ teaspoon salt
⅛ teaspoon pepper
¼ cup oil or shortening
1 can (16 oz.) tomatoes
1¾ cups water

½ cup chopped onion
1 small clove garlic, minced
2 small whole green chiles
  (Serrano)
1 tablespoon beef flavor gravy
  base (optional)
1½ teaspoons Worcestershire
2 large green peppers

Cut green peppers and steak in strips. Combine flour, salt and pepper. Coat meat strips with flour. In a large skillet, saute meat in hot oil until browned on all sides. Drain tomatoes, reserving liquid. Add tomato liquid, water, onion, garlic and gravy base to meat in skillet. Cover and simmer for 1¼ hours until meat is tender. Uncover. Stir in Worcestershire sauce. Add green pepper strips and chiles. Cover and simmer for 5 minutes. If necessary, thicken gravy with a mixture of flour and water. Add drained tomatoes and cook about 5 minutes more. Serve over hot rice. Serves 6.

ALICE TREVINO

MEXICAN LAMB ROAST

6 lb. leg of lamb, boned,
  rolled and tied
1 cup Beaujolais
¾ cup orange juice
¼ cup hot chile sauce
¼ cup water
1 onion, finely chopped

1 teaspoon crushed comino
2 tablespoons brown sugar
2 tablespoons olive oil
1 tablespoon chili powder
¾ teaspoon dried oregano
salt and pepper to taste

Place lamb in a deep glass or enamel pan. Combine remaining ingredients, pour over meat and refrigerate for 24 hours. Drain meat, place on rack in open roasting pan. Roast in very hot oven, 450°, for 15 minutes; reduce temperature to 350°. Pour marinade over meat and continue roasting for about 2½ hours. Serve pan drippings as sauce with meat. Serves 12.

MRS. EUGENE NOLTE, JR. (MARGARET)

ANTICUCHOS

1 large beef tenderloin
1½ cups red wine vinegar
1 cup water
2 teaspoons salt
½ teaspoon pepper

2 garlic cloves, crushed
4 serrano chiles, chopped fine
1 teaspoon oregano
1 teaspoon cumin
1 teaspoon paprika

Blend chiles with a little water in a blender to make a paste. Combine chile paste and all other ingredients, except meat, in a large bowl. Cut meat into 1½ inch cubes and add to the bowl. There must be enough liquid to cover the meat. Allow to marinate 8 to 10 hours or overnight. Place 6 or 8 pieces of meat on skewers and cook over hot coals, basting frequently with the marinade. Serves 5 or 6.

MOLE DE GUAJALOTE
A Classic Mexican Turkey or Chicken Dish

1 small turkey or large chicken,
   cut in serving pieces
4 tablespoons lard
3 ancho chiles
3 pasilla chiles
3 mulato chiles
2 onions
4 garlic cloves
4 oz. blanched almonds

½ cup raisins
½ teaspoon each clove,
   cinnamon, coriander
1 sprig cilantro (optional)
1 lb. tomatoes, peeled and seeded
1 tortilla or slice of toast
2 oz. bitter chocolate
salt and pepper to taste
reserved stock

Cook turkey or chicken in salted water for 1 hour or until done. Drain, reserving 2 cups of stock. Heat lard in a large skillet and brown the meat. Remove from the skillet and set aside. Wash chiles, remove stems, seeds and veins. Soak in 2 cups of hot water for 1 hour. Blend to a fairly coarse mixture in a blender the onions, garlic, almonds, raisins, clove, cinnamon, coriander, cilantro, tortilla or toast, tomatoes and chiles with the water in which they were soaked. (This will be too much for the blender at one time, so blend it bit by bit.)

Heat the lard remaining in the skillet, adding a little more if necessary to make 3 tablespoons. Cook the blended mixture in the lard for 5 minutes, stirring constantly. Thin this mixture with 2 cups of the broth and add chocolate, salt and pepper. Cook over low heat to melt the chocolate. The sauce should be quite thick. Return the turkey or chicken to the sauce and cook over the lowest possible heat for $\frac{1}{2}$ hour. (You may use all ancho or pasilla chiles if desired.) Serves 6 to 8.

MRS. EUGENE NOLTE, JR. (MARGARET)

ARROZ CON POLLO

salt and pepper
1 chicken, cut in serving pieces
3 tablespoons olive oil
1 garlic clove
1 cup raw rice
2 cups chicken broth

$\frac{1}{2}$ teaspoon saffron
1 small jar pimiento
1 package frozen peas
3 tomatoes, chopped
sprig fresh cilantro (optional)
1 teaspoon salt

In a deep, heavy pot, brown seasoned chicken in olive oil. Add garlic, cook for a few minutes and discard garlic. Add rice and brown slightly. Add tomatoes, chicken broth, saffron, salt and peas. Bring to a boil. Reduce heat, cover tightly, and simmer until all liquid has been absorbed and chicken is tender. Put rice in the center of a platter and surround with chicken pieces. Garnish with pimiento strips and cilantro. Serves 6.

FRAN GOODMAN

POLLO CON CALAVACITA

1 fryer or selected pieces
3 lbs. zucchini or calabassa
4 ears corn
3 tomatoes or 1 (12 oz.) can
1 green pepper, cut in strips

1 large onion, chopped
1 or 2 garlic cloves, chopped
generous pinch of comino
2 or 3 serrano or jalapeño
   peppers

Brown chicken lightly in a small amount of butter. Add onion, garlic, tomatoes, comino and hot peppers and a small amount of water. Simmer about $\frac{1}{2}$ hour. Add squash, corn from the cobs, green pepper strips and simmer about another $\frac{1}{2}$ hour. There should be very little moisture left, but it should not be dry. This is a delicious dish made with lean pork or a combination of pork and chicken. It is also better made the day before and reheated at serving time. Serves 6.

CLEO LUX DE ARRENDONDO

YUCATAN CHICKEN BREASTS

6 chicken breast halves
3 tablespoons butter
1 tablespoon oil
salt and pepper to taste
⅓ cup Cognac, heated
2 garlic cloves, chopped fine
1 (4 oz.) can green chiles,
   chopped and peeled

1 (16 oz.) can frozen
   orange juice concentrate
½ green pepper
6 crosswise orange slices with
   rind, cut in half
½ cup almonds
dash Tabasco

Heat butter and oil in a large skillet and saute chicken breasts until just golden. Do not brown. Season with salt and pepper and pour in Cognac. Ignite Cognac and allow flame to burn out. Add garlic, chiles and Tabasco. Add orange juice concentrate and blend well. Simmer 15 to 20 minutes, or until chicken breasts are just tender and cooked through. Remove breasts to a hot platter and pour sauce over the breasts. Garnish with thin sliced green pepper, orange slices and almonds. Serves 6.

ANN BENEDICT

CHICKEN SALPICON

10 chicken breast halves
3 garlic cloves
1 bay leaf
1 (14 oz.) can tomatoes
¼ cup fresh cilantro, chopped
salt and pepper to taste
1 cup canned green chiles,
   chopped
1 cup cooked garbanzo beans,
   drained

½ lb. Monterey Jack cheese,
   cut in ¼ inch cubes
2 avocados, cut into strips
3 tomatoes, cut into thin
   sliced wedges
8 oz. Wishbone Italian dressing
8 to 10 large dried red chiles
8 oz. canned chicken broth
2 large onions, chopped
¼ cup oil

Place chicken pieces in a heavy pot and cover with water. Add 2 garlic cloves, bay leaf, canned tomatoes, cilantro, salt and pepper. Simmer until chicken is tender. In another pot, cover dried chiles with cold water and simmer 10 to 15 minutes. Cover and allow to stand for 2 hours. Place the chiles, onions and 1 garlic clove in a blender with 4 oz. chicken broth. Blend until smooth. Strain this mixture and combine with oil and the rest of the chicken broth. Simmer for 45 minutes. Add more broth if necessary. Remove the cooked chicken from the bone and shred. Place the shredded chicken in a 9 x 11 inch pyrex dish. Add the salad dressing to the hot chile mixture and pour over the chicken. Cover and allow to marinate overnight.

At serving time, scoop out the chicken and place on a serving dish. Drain off the remaining liquid and discard. Layer the garbanzo beans, chopped chiles, cheese, avocado and tomatoes on top of the chicken and garnish with parsley. Serve cold as a buffet meal with plenty of tostadas. Serves 6 to 8.

MRS. WILLIAM K. DOUGLAS (MARIWADE)

CHILES RELLENOS

6 fresh or dried poblano chiles
  (green peppers may be
  substituted - but not as good)
1 medium onion, chopped fine
1 tomato, peeled and coarsely
  chopped
1/4 cup olive oil
3/4 lb. ground pork
3/4 lb. ground beef
1/4 cup raisins

1/4 cup pineapple, coarsely
  chopped (optional)
2 bananas, sliced (optional)
1/4 cup chopped pecans
salt and fresh ground pepper
2 eggs, separated
flour
oil for frying
seasoned tomato sauce
Mexican hot sauce

If using fresh green peppers or chiles poblanos, hold the peppers on a fork over a gas flame or electric burner until the skin blisters. Wrap in a damp cloth and leave 30 minutes, then peel, cut off cap with stem, and remove seeds. Slit lengthwise. If using dried poblanos, slit and remove seeds and veins.

Saute onion and tomato in olive oil until onion is golden. Add pork and beef and saute until brown, crumbling the meat with a fork. Drain off excess fat. Add raisins, pineapple and simmer 5 minutes. Remove from fire and add bananas and pecans. Season to taste with salt and pepper. Stuff the peppers with the mixture and replace caps. Secure with toothpicks.

Beat egg yolks until thick and egg whites until they form stiff peaks. Fold the whites into the yolks. Dip peppers in flour, then into the egg batter and fry in oil. Keep warm in a 250° oven until serving time. Serve with seasoned tomato sauce and Mexican hot sauce, (see Index), Serves 6.

CHILES RELLENOS SOUFFLE

2 or 3 fresh poblano peppers or 1 (7 oz.) can whole green chiles
1 lb. sharp Cheddar cheese, grated
½ lb. Monterey Jack cheese, grated
4 eggs
2 tablespoons flour
½ teaspoon salt
1 (13 oz.) can evaporated milk
1 small can tomato sauce
½ package taco seasoning mix

Remove veins and seeds from chiles and lay them on the bottom of a buttered 8 x 13 inch baking dish. Spread the cheeses on top of the chiles. Beat the eggs, milk, flour and salt and pour over the cheeses. Bake for about 25 minutes at 350°. Combine tomato sauce and taco seasoning and pour over the dish. Bake 5 more minutes. Serve immediately. Fresh poblano peppers are better for this dish than canned green chiles. Serves 8.

MRS. GEORGE F. WROTEN

CALAVACITA MEXICANA

3 lbs. calavacita (Mexican squash)
3 lbs. lean pork, cut in cubes
1 medium onion, chopped
2 tablespoons oil
2 cloves garlic, minced
1 teaspoon comino seeds
1 lb. can tomatoes, whole
¾ cup water
1 green pepper, chopped
1 lb. can corn, whole kernel
salt and pepper to taste
corn tortillas
hot chile sauce (see Index)

Brown pork meat and onions in oil. Remove excess oil after browning. In a Molcajete or dish, crush garlic and cominos and mix with tomatoes. Add tomato mixture, plus water and green pepper to the meat. Add salt and pepper to taste. Simmer 10 minutes. Wash and dice calavacita, exclude some of the seeds, and add to the meat and tomato mixture. Simmer 5 minutes or until calavacita is tender. Add drained corn and heat 3 to 5 minutes longer. Serve with hot corn tortillas and hot chile sauce. Serves 6.

MRS. JOE BERNAL (MARY ESTHER)

MEXICAN EGGPLANT

1 eggplant, peeled, sliced
  1/4 inch thick
2 cloves garlic, chopped fine
1 large green pepper,
  chopped fine
2 to 4 green chile peppers,
  chopped

1 can tomato paste
1 can of water
2 eggs, beaten
grated yellow cheese
salt and pepper
olive oil

Saute garlic, green pepper and green chile peppers until soft in olive oil. Add tomato paste, water, salt and pepper to taste and simmer until sauce thickens. Dip eggplant into the eggs and saute until golden brown in olive oil. Place eggplant slices in a baking dish and cover with the sauce and grated yellow cheese. Bake at 350° for 30 minutes. Serves 6.

MRS. BEN FOSTER

SOPA PICANTE — Thick Mexican Soup

2 medium size zucchini, grated
1 large onion, grated
2 cups V8 juice
1 cup beef broth, or 2 beef cubes
  in cup hot water
1½ teaspoons chili powder
  (Gebhardt's)

1 teaspoon cumin seeds
3 corn tortillas, chopped fine
salt and pepper
1 chile pequin (more if
  desired)

Heat V8 juice and beef broth. Add grated zucchinis and onion. Boil for 5 minutes. Add seasonings and chile pequin. Add the chopped tortillas. Serve hot or cold. Serves 3 or 4.

MRS. HERBERT W. WORCESTER

SOPA DE FIDEO — Vermicelli Soup

1 (4 oz.) package vermicelli or
  very thin spaghetti
2 cups fresh, ripe tomatoes,
  chopped
2 cups chorizo (Mexican sausage)
1 large onion, minced

2 cups chicken consomme (may
  use bouillon cubes dissolved in
  water)
½ cup fresh cilantro or parsley,
  finely chopped
¼ cup olive oil or vegetable oil

Heat oil, break vermicelli into small pieces, and stir-fry until light golden brown. Add remaining ingredients and simmer for 20 minutes. Add more consomme if necessary. Serves 8.

EMPANADAS

pie dough
½ lb. pork, beef, or chicken
3 tablespoons butter
1 tablespoon parsley
1 green pepper, minced
½ tomato, chopped
1 small onion, chopped

2 tablespoons olives, green or black, chopped
2 tablespoons currants
2 tablespoons mustard pickles, chopped
½ teaspoon sugar
½ teaspoon salt

Make your favorite pie dough. Roll out, but not too thin, and cut into 3 inch circles. Saute onions and meat in butter. Add remaining ingredients to meat mixture and mix well. Fill circle of dough, making moon by folding over one half of the circle and pinch to close. Bake in a 400° to 450° oven or fry in deep fat. Makes 18.

MRS. BEN FOSTER

JOSEFINAS

1 loaf thin sliced bread
½ lb. soft butter
1 cup canned green chiles, chopped

½ lb. shredded Cheddar cheese
1 cup mayonnaise
1 clove garlic, crushed

Cut bread slices into quarters and spread with a mixture of butter and chiles, flavored with the crushed garlic clove. Top this with cheese and mayonnaise mixture, spreading the mixture to the edges. Broil until brown and fluffy. Makes about 5 dozen Josefinas.

FLOUR TORTILLAS

4 cups flour
2 tablespoons lard
1 tablespoon salt

1 teaspoon baking powder
1¼ cups tepid water
2 tablespoons shortening

In a large bowl, mix flour with salt and baking powder. Cut in the shortening and lard. Slowly add tepid water. Knead the dough and roll into balls (golf ball size). Roll out flat and thin. To cook, brown slightly in dry frying pan. Makes approximately 3 dozen 5 inch tortillas.

MRS. HERBERT KELLEHER

HUEVOS RANCHEROS

1 tablespoon bacon drippings
  or butter
1 small onion, chopped
2 canned green chiles, chopped
4 eggs

1 cup canned tomatoes with
  liquid or 3 fresh tomatoes,
  chopped
salt and pepper to taste
4 flour tortillas, warmed

Saute onion and chiles in bacon drippings or butter. Add tomatoes and seasonings and bring to a boil. Poach the eggs in this sauce. To serve, place an egg on each tortilla and cover with sauce. This recipe may be simplified by adding 2 tablespoons of Pace's Picante Sauce to canned tomatoes and omitting the onions and green chiles. Serves 4.

MRS. WILLARD WOODRING (ALYNE)

HUEVOS RANCHEROS II

1 large onion, finely chopped
1 clove garlic, chopped
1 lb. tomatoes, peeled and
  chopped
salt, pepper to taste
1/2 teaspoon sugar

1/4 teaspoon oregano
5 tablespoons lard
3 or more canned serrano
  chiles, chopped
12 tortillas
12 eggs

Heat 2 tablespoons lard in a skillet and fry onion and garlic until limp. Add tomatoes, salt, pepper, sugar, oregano and chiles. Simmer this sauce gently for about 15 minutes. Heat 3 tablespoons lard in a skillet and fry the tortillas on both sides until limp or, if preferred, until quite crisp. Place 2 tortillas, side by side, on each plate and keep warm. Fry eggs in lard or butter. Slide an egg onto each tortilla. Pour sauce over eggs and serve. Serves 6.

LAURIE RICHLEY

EGGS FIDELIO

6 large eggs
2 tablespoons Pace's Picante
  Sauce
1 small can button mushrooms
5 tablespoons dry Vermouth

2 tablespoons cream
butter
salt and pepper
oregano

Saute mushrooms in butter, 4 tablespoons Vermouth, a pinch of oregano, and salt and pepper to taste. Place 1 tablespoon Vermouth and Picante Sauce in a cup and set aside. Beat eggs with cream and add salt and pepper to taste. Place 2 tablespoons butter in frying pan, and when melted add eggs. Cook over slow heat. When eggs begin to harden, add Picante mixture and scramble. Just before eggs are scrambled to your liking, drain mushrooms and add to eggs. Serve with hot, buttered English muffins and very cold champagne. Serves 2.

FIDEL G. CHAMBERLAIN, JR.

JALAPENO CORN BREAD

3 cups yellow cornmeal
1 cup creamed corn
1 teaspoon sugar
2 teaspoons salt
1 cup chopped onions
1⅓ cups grated Cheddar cheese

1½ teaspoons baking powder
1 cup salad oil
3 eggs
1¾ cups milk
½ cup canned jalapeño peppers, chopped

Mix all ingredients well and pour into a greased 9 x 16 inch baking dish. Bake for 40 to 50 minutes in 350° oven. Serves 16.

MRS. GILBERT L. CURTIS (LORRIE)

JALAPENO CORNBREAD WITH GROUND MEAT

1 cup yellow corn meal
1 cup milk
2 eggs, beaten
¾ teaspoon salt
½ teaspoon soda
½ cup bacon drippings

1 (17 oz.) can cream style corn
1 lb. ground beef or pork
1 large onion, chopped
1 lb. yellow cheese, grated
4 or 5 jalapeño peppers, canned

Preheat oven to 350°. Combine corn meal, milk, eggs, salt, soda, bacon drippings and corn. Mix well and set aside. Brown ground meat until crumbly and drain well on paper towels. Pour half of batter into a well greased baking dish that has been dusted with corn meal. Sprinkle grated cheese over batter and sprinkle meat on top of the cheese. Sprinkle chopped onion and jalapeño peppers over the meat. Top with remaining corn bread mixture. Bake at 350° for 50 minutes. Serve 6 to 8.

VERA SERGEANT

STUFFED JALAPENOS — CRISPY FRIED

12 canned jalapeño peppers
1 large package cream cheese
1 egg
1 cup milk

salt and pepper to taste
bread crumbs
flour
deep fat for frying

Slice jalapeños in half lengthwise, remove the seeds and put seeds in a bowl. Mix ¼ of the seeds with the cream cheese. Stuff the peppers with cheese and place in the freezer. Combine milk, egg, salt and pepper. After jalapeños are frozen, roll in flour, dip in milk mixture, and roll in bread crumbs. Dip again in milk mixture and once more roll in bread crumbs. Press the mixture firmly around the jalapeños, and return to the freezer until ready to fry. At serving time, drop frozen in deep fat, 325°, until they are crispy and brown. Serve hot.

BROOKS AIR FORCE BASE OFFICERS' OPEN MESS

JALAPENO CHEESE PIE

jalapeño peppers, canned
10 oz. sharp cheese, grated

4 eggs

Slice jalapeño peppers and remove seeds. Pat dry with paper towels and line the bottom of a shallow baking dish with the peppers. (Use as many or as few as desired.) Spread grated cheese on the peppers. Beat the eggs until foamy and pour over the cheese. Bake at 350° for 35 minutes. Cool, slice and serve. Serves 6 to 8.

MRS. HARRY C. BAYNE (MELBA)

STUFFED JALAPENOS

12 canned jalapeño peppers
1 (16 oz.) can salmon in oil
1 large onion, minced

½ cup vinegar
dash of black pepper
3 tablespoons salt

Cut jalapeños in half, remove seeds, and place in glass or plastic bowl. Cover with cold water and 3 tablespoons salt. Refrigerate at least 3 hours or overnight. Remove from salt solution and towel dry the jalapeños. (Soaking removes the "hot".) Mash salmon; add minced onion, vinegar and black pepper. Generously stuff the jala-peños. Tuna may be substituted for salmon. Serves 12.

MRS. EUGENE NOLTE, JR. (MARGARET)

JALAPENO SHRIMP SALAD

2 lbs. small shrimp
2/3 cup salad dressing
4 avocados
8 tomatoes, peeled and chopped
8 canned jalapeños, minced

1/2 cup onions, chopped fine
1 cup celery, chopped fine
1/2 teaspoon fresh ground pepper
1 tablespoon salt
juice 1 large lemon or lime

Cook, peel and devein shrimp. Make a french dressing of oil, vinegar, garlic, salt and pepper and marinate shrimp in the dressing for several hours. Combine vegetables, seasonings (Fiesta Brand) and lemon juice and add to shrimp. Refrigerate for at least 2 hours. At serving time, mix gently. May be used as an appetizer or as a salad. If used as a luncheon salad, cover 8 dishes with large lettuce leaves, then finely chopped lettuce or other greens. Cover with the shrimp mixture and garnish each plate with 4 spears of asparagus, 2 hard boiled egg slices, a pitted olive and a lemon wedge. Serves 4 to 6.

MRS. CLIFTON BOLNER

MEXICAN CHILE PEPPERS AND HOT SAUCES

In San Antonio, Mexican hot sauces are served over almost all Mexican dishes—and some that are not Mexican. The "hot" comes from the chile peppers. The seeds are the hottest part of the pepper and are usually discarded. It is advisable to wear gloves when using fresh chiles to avoid burning the skin on your hands. In many instances, canned chiles may be used and are less trouble.

There are three kinds of "hot-hot" chiles used to make Mexican sauces. Chiles serranos, a small, bright green chile about 1½ inches long; chile pequin, a tiny red berry; and jalapeños, a small bell-pepper-like chile. (Poblano chiles are long green peppers used primarily to make "Chiles Rellenos.") All three hot chiles make excellent sauces with a combination of fresh or canned tomatoes, onions, garlic, oregano, cilantro or parsley, and a little oil. They will keep for weeks covered in the refrigerator.

SALSA VERDE — Green Tomato Hot Sauce

1 (10 oz.) can Mexican green
  tomatoes, drained
1 small onion, chopped
6 sprigs fresh cilantro, chopped

2 canned serrano chiles,
  chopped (Ortega brand are
  the mildest)
salt to taste

Combine and whirl in a blender. Makes 1 cup.

MEXICAN HOT SAUCE — Cooked

4 canned or fresh serranos,
  chopped fine
1 garlic clove, minced
1 tablespoon oil

1 (14½ oz.) can tomatoes,
  coarsely chopped
½ teaspoon salt

Saute the chiles and garlic in oil. Add tomatoes, salt and simmer about 5 minutes. To this basic sauce, you may add finely chopped onions, cilantro or parsley. The seeds are the hottest part of chile peppers so include or discard them according to the "hot" desired.

MEXICAN TACO SAUCE

⅓ cup onion, chopped
3 cups fresh or 1 (16 oz.)
  can tomatoes
½ teaspoon oregano

2 tablespoons olive oil
salt to taste
1 teaspoon cilantro or parsley
1 hot chile pepper

Combine onion, tomatoes, oregano, salt, cilantro and hot chile. Blend just a moment, using chop cycle of a blender. Heat oil in a sauce pan, add the mixture and simmer 10 minutes. This is a good, all-purpose hot sauce.

SALSA CRUDA — Mexican Hot Sauce

2 large, ripe tomatoes, peeled
   and chopped or 1 small can
   tomatoes, chopped
2 canned serrano chiles, chopped
1 small onion, chopped

1 tablespoon cilantro or
   parsley, chopped
salt to taste
pinch of sugar

Combine all ingredients. This is an uncooked, all-purpose sauce.

BRISCOE PICOSO SAUCE

22 fresh green chiles
4 cloves garlic, chopped
juice of 1 lemon

1 teaspoon salt
2 large cans Hunt's whole stewed
   tomatoes, drained

Boil chiles in plain water until they lose their bright green color. Peel and place in blender with garlic, lemon juice and salt. Blend until it is a smooth paste. Add tomatoes, turn on blender, then immediately turn it off. The tomatoes should still be pulpy and bite size. This is an all-purpose, super-hot Mexican sauce.

DOLPH BRISCOE
Governor of the State of Texas

JALAPENO HOT SAUCE

6 canned jalapeños, sliced
   including the seeds
2 large onions, cut into chunks
1 tablespoon garlic,
   coarsely chopped

1 small can tomato paste
1 scant tomato paste can vinegar
1 tablespoon sugar
1 (10 oz.) can tomato sauce
1 tablespoon salt

Put all ingredients in a blender and blend until it is the consistency of catsup. Bring to a boil in a saucepan and pour into jars and seal. Makes 1 quart. This will keep for months in the refrigerator. Use it alone as a dip for tostadas; a teaspoon peps up stews, soup, meat sauces; mix with cottage cheese; and, of course, serve with Mexican dishes. If fresh Jalapeños are available, the sauce is even better.

RUTH WHITE

BUNUELOS

1 tablespoon white vinegar ½ cup orange juice
4 cups flour   warm water
2 teaspoons baking powder   oil for frying
1 egg   sugar and cinnamon
3 tablespoons shortening

Combine flour, vinegar, baking powder, egg, shortening and orange juice. Add water to make a dough. Slice chunks of dough and roll very thin into the desired circle size. In a skillet large enough to hold the rolled circle of dough without bending, melt oil. Drop circles of dough, one at a time, into the hot oil and fry until crisp. Remove from oil, drain on paper towels and sprinkle with sugar and cinnamon.

MRS. THOMAS C. SPENCER

SOPA DE PLATANO — Mexican Banana Dessert

2 lbs. ripe bananas   1 teaspoon salt
4 cups orange juice   ½ teaspoon cinnamon
1 tablespoon lemon juice   2 egg whites, beaten stiff
2 cups cold water

Mash together the bananas, orange juice and lemon juice. Add the cold water, salt, cinnamon and simmer the mixture for 10 minutes. Chill. Fold egg whites into the mixture. Serve with fresh strawberries or raspberries. Serves 6.

TOCINO DEL CIELO — Custard Flan

1 cup of sugar   1½ cups ground blanched
3 tablespoons water   almonds
3 egg yolks   cinnamon
2 teaspoons grated lemon rind

Combine sugar and water in a saucepan. Bring to a boil and cook for 2 minutes. Remove from heat and allow to cool slightly. Beat egg yolks until thick and light and stir in lemon rind, almonds and add to sugar syrup. Cook over low heat stirring constantly, about 20 minutes. Remove from heat and beat until pale. Turn into a buttered shallow baking dish about ½ inch thick. Sprinkle lightly with cinnamon. Bake in oven at 350° for 7 minutes. Allow to cool.

SOPAIPILLAS

1 package dry yeast	1 tablespoon melted butter
½ cup warm water	1 teaspoon salt
1 teaspoon sugar	1 egg
3 cups flour	additional warm water

Dissolve yeast in ½ cup warm water and add sugar. Mix flour, butter, salt and egg. Pour in yeast mixture, and add enough additional water to make a thick bread-type dough. Knead dough for several minutes, and let rise until doubled in bulk, about 20 to 30 minutes. Roll out to ¼ inch thickness, and cut into pieces about 2 inches square. Drop into hot fat, and fry briefly until brown. Serve with honey.

MRS. JAMES A. EARL

MEXICAN KAHLUA SOUFFLE

1 tablespoon cornstarch	1 tablespoon unflavored gelatin
1 cup evaporated milk	½ cup Kahlua
3 eggs, separated	¼ teaspoon vanilla
5 tablespoons sugar	pinch of salt

Mix cornstarch with a little water and add to milk. Cook over low heat, stirring constantly until thickened. Beat egg yolks lightly with 4 tablespoons of the sugar. Soften gelatin in ¼ cup of water. Add yolks and gelatin to milk and cook for 5 minutes, stirring constantly. Allow to cool slightly and add Kahlua and vanilla. Add salt and 1 tablespoon of sugar to egg whites and beat until standing in peaks. Fold into the yolk mixture, pour into souffle dish and chill until set. Serves 6.

MARGARET PACE

The Toast of Texas
Buffalo, Birds, Barbecue, Beans
and other Beautiful Things

Hunting is a way of life in Texas. Game is close at hand and abundant. With the arrival of the deer season, intrepid hunters bring home venison which fill freezers to overflowing, often to the dismay of the hunter's wife.

Backstrap of venison, well prepared, is the choice bounty at the hunter's table. It is hoarded and served only on special occasions. Dove, succulent and tender, vie with wild duck and quail in popularity.

The Texas Barbecue is also a way of life. Although the need of the chuckwagon to follow the cowboy for months on end up the long Chisolm Trail to Kansas is a thing of the past, barbecue beef and beans remain a regional favorite. It is typical Texas fare for any large, relaxed gathering.

The next time you prepare game, wild birds or other such beautiful things, try a TOAST OF TEXAS.

BACKSTRAP OF VENISON

1 venison backstrap
  (tenderloin)
4 tablespoons butter
garlic salt

fresh lemon juice
Worcestershire sauce
pepper

Slice backstrap into filets and pound with a meat mallet. Squeeze lemon juice on both sides of meat and season with pepper, garlic, salt and Worcestershire sauce. Melt butter in a heavy skillet and saute the filets over high heat until brown on the outside and medium rare inside. Remove from the skillet and pour the pan juices over the meat before serving. Serve with Bearnaise sauce (see Index), if desired.

MRS. SCHREINER NELSON (SHAWN)

VENISON STEAK IN WINE SAUCE

1½ lbs. venison steaks, cut thin
seasoned flour
grated Parmesan cheese
  (optional)
4 tablespoons butter

1 bouillon cube
¼ cup boiling water
3 tablespoons Sherry, Marsala
  or Madeira Wine

Pound the steaks with a mallet until very thin. Dredge them in seasoned flour. If desired, cheese may be added at this time. Saute the slices in heated butter until golden brown on both sides. Remove meat and place on a hot serving platter. Dissolve the bouillon cube in boiling water and add to the pan drippings. Stir in the wine while scrapping the pan well. When thoroughly mixed, pour the hot sauce over the meat. Serves 4 to 6.

KING ANTONIO L — A. ROANE HARWOOD

VENISON STEAK WITH MARINADE

Venison should be aged for no less than 7 days and preferably 3 to 4 weeks. Broiling or roasting on a rack are the best methods for cooking venison. The choicest portions are the hind quarters and the saddle.

To prepare venison steaks, slice into serving portions and remove all fat as this retains the gamey flavor. Wash thoroughly before broiling or roasting. These steps are absolutely necessary if your venison steak is to be the tasty treat it should be.

6 tenderloin venison steaks or
  ¾ to 1 inch steak, large
  enough for 6
½ cup beef consomme
½ cup dry red wine
⅓ cup soy sauce

1½ teaspoons Lawry's
  Seasoned Salt
¼ cup onion, chopped
1 tablespoon lime juice
2 tablespoons honey or
  brown sugar

Mix all ingredients and marinate the venison overnight in the refrigerator. Broil on a rack in the oven or over a charcoal grill until done to your taste. Venison tenderloin is good medium rare. Serves 6.

MRS. WILLIAM L. STARNES (MARY DEE)

DEER STEAK MAGIC

1 venison steak   ½ can water
1 can celery soup   salt and pepper

Salt and pepper venison steak. Place it in a cast iron skillet. Pour soup and water over the steak. Cover with foil, sealing the top tight. Place in a 350° oven for 2 hours. Do not stir, uncover or touch it for the 2 hours. The steak and gravy will be ready for the table

This recipe is so amazingly simple they call it "Deer Magic" on the Ziegler I-Bar Ranch.

MRS. THAD M. ZIEGLER

WINE VENISON ROAST

1 venison roast   2 cloves garlic
1 large onion   Burgundy wine
½ green pepper   carrots, peeled
3 chiles verdes   potatoes, peeled

Make small incision in meat and stuff with small slivers of green pepper, chiles verdes, salt, pepper and lightly flour the meat. Brown in heavy covered skillet or dutch oven, with enough bacon grease to cover the bottom. Add quartered onions, carrots and potatoes. Remove from heat and pour in enough wine to half cover the meat. Roast in 350° oven until tender, basting frequently. A little flour may be added to liquid for gravy.

MRS. LESLIE NEAL, JR.

DEER-SAUSAGE CASSEROLE

1¾ lbs. deer meat, ground or   1 (8 oz.) can sliced mushrooms
  cut into small pieces   ¼ lb. elbow macaroni, uncooked
¼ lb. pork sausage   ¼ cup olive juice
1 garlic clove, crushed or minced ½ cup ripe olives sliced
1 onion, chopped   2 large cans tomatoes
pepper   1 small can whole kernel corn
sweet basil   ½ lb. American cheese, grated
1 green pepper, chopped   Parmesan cheese

Brown deer meat and sausage in large heavy skillet. Crumble the meat and pour off excess fat. Add garlic, onion, pepper, basil and all remaining ingredients except Parmesan cheese. Mix well. Place in a

12 x 14 x 3 inch baking dish and cover generously with Parmesan cheese. Bake at 350° for 45 minutes covered with foil. Remove foil and bake until a brown crust forms on the top, about 15 minutes. The casserole may be made ready for the oven in advance. Serves 8.

MRS. FRANK E. ROUSE (WIN)

VENISON STROGANOFF

2 lbs. venison sirloin
4 tablespoons butter
1/2 lb. mushrooms, sliced
1/2 cup tomato juice
1 garlic clove, minced

2 teaspoons salt
1 teaspoon pepper
1 can mushroom soup
1 cup sour cream

Cut venison into 3/4 inch cubes and brown in butter. Add mushrooms and tomato juice. Cover and simmer for 30 minutes. Add remaining ingredients, except the sour cream. Simmer for 1 hour. Add sour cream just before serving. Serve over brown rice. Serves 6.

MRS. FRANK E. ROUSE (WIN)

VENISON STEW AND DUMPLINGS

1 lb. venison
1/4 cup water
1 tablespoon flour
1 tablespoon butter
1 onion, sliced
2 tablespoons parsley, minced

1 cup wine vinegar
1 tablespoon pickling spice
1 teaspoon salt
1 bay leaf
1 cup biscuit mix
6 tablespoons buttermilk

Clean meat thoroughly. Combine onion, parsley, vinegar, pickling spice, salt and bay leaf in a large bowl. Cut meat into cubes and immerse in marinade. Cover and set in refrigerator for 24 hours. Place meat and marinade in a large cooking pot. Add water and bring to a boil. Reduce heat, cover and simmer until meat is tender, about 3 hours. Combine flour and butter and add to stew. Cook, stirring constantly for 5 minutes. Blend biscuit mix and buttermilk and spoon into stew. Cook approximately 5 minutes with the lid on. Serves 4.

MAJOR GENERAL LOUIS COIRA

VENISON CHILI

½ lb. sirloin, ground fine
½ lb. venison, ground coarsely
1 lb. venison, cubed
beef suet, size of an egg
1 (8 oz.) can tomato sauce
1 cup water
1 (12 oz.) bottle beer
4 large jalapeño chiles, chopped,
  with seeds

6 tablespoons chili powder
1¾ teaspoons cayenne
1 teaspoon paprika
2½ teaspoons cumino
¼ teaspoon oregano
1½ teaspoons salt
2 tablespoons onion, chopped
1½ tablespoons masa harina

Sear venison and sirloin in a heavy skillet until light grey in color. Add tomato sauce, water and ½ bottle of beer. As mixture begins to heat, add chili powder, cayenne, paprika, cumino, oregano, salt and onions. Cook over high heat for 15 minutes. Reduce heat to just above a simmer for about 1 hour and 15 minutes. (As the chili thickens, add more beer.) Cook 15 more minutes and add masa, mixed with a little beer. Continue simmer for another hour, or until chunks of venison may be cut with a spoon. Total cooking time 2½ to 3 hours. Makes 1½ quarts.

COLONEL JACK C. YOUNG

TEXAS BUFFALO STEAKS

8 buffalo round steaks, cut
  ¾ inch thick
2 cloves garlic, chopped
flour
olive oil for browning
4 green peppers, sliced

6 large onions, sliced
1 lb. fresh mushrooms, sliced
canned tomatoes or red
  wine marinade
salt and pepper to taste

Cut buffalo steaks into small pieces. Saute garlic in oil and brown the meat on all sides. In a large casserole, alternate layers of meat, green peppers, onions and mushrooms. Pour in enough canned tomatoes to cover. Add salt and pepper. Bake for 4 or 5 hours, or until tender in a 250° oven. The buffalo steaks may be marinated in any red wine marinade of your choice, using the marinade in place of the tomatoes in cooking. Serves 25 to 30.

ROAST RABBIT

2 rabbits cut into
serving pieces
1/4 cup butter or margarine
4 slices bacon, chopped
2 sprigs parsley, chopped
6 onions, chopped

1/2 lb. mushrooms, chopped
1 teaspoon salt
1/4 teaspoon pepper
3 cups Burgundy wine
1 chicken bouillon cube
    dissolved in 1 cup of hot water

Melt butter in a large skillet and brown rabbit pieces on all sides. Place rabbit and bacon in a 2 quart casserole. Cover and bake in a 300° oven for 1 hour. Combine other ingredients and simmer slowly over low heat for 1 hour or until liquid is reduced by half. Serve as a sauce over roasted rabbit. Serves 6.

ELLEN COIRA (MRS. LOUIS)

WILD DUCK

4 small wild ducks
salt and pepper
1 apple, unpeeled
1 orange, unpeeled

1 onion
2 stalks celery
8 slices bacon

Salt and pepper dressed ducks, inside and out. Quarter apple, orange, and onion; cut celery stalks in half. Stuff each duck with mixture of 1 section each of apple, orange, onion and celery. Cover each breast with 2 slices raw bacon. Bake uncovered in hot oven, 425° to 450°, for 30 minutes to 1 hour. Test with fork to determine whether breast is tender. Remove filling before serving. Serves 4.

MRS. JOHN T. DYER (NANCY)

ORANGE AND WINE ROAST DUCK

1 large wild duck
3 onions, quartered
2 bay leaves
1 stalk celery
1/2 teaspoon salt
1/8 teaspoon pepper

1 tablespoon salad oil
3/4 cup water
3/4 cup orange juice
1/4 cup sherry
1 whole orange, peeled

Clean duck, place in a deep pan, cover with water. Add onion, bay leaves, celery, salt and pepper. Bring to a boil. Reduce heat, cover and simmer for 20 minutes. Remove duck from the pan and drain. Brush the duck with oil, put the orange and onions inside the bird and set duck on a roasting pan, breast side up. Add ¾ cup water. Roast for 1 hour, uncovered, in 350° oven, basting often with mixture of orange juice and sherry. Serves 4.

MRS. LOUIS COIRA (ELLEN)

SPICED DUCKS A LA MEXICANA

Rub the birds, both inside and out with salt, pepper, ginger and paprika. Place half an apple and half a raw onion in the cavity of each bird, dredge with flour and brown in butter or bacon drippings. When the ducks are browned, remove them from the roasting pan and in the pan juices brown slightly some chopped onions, celery and green pepper. After this, add about 1 quart of water and 2 table-spoons of chili powder, dissolved in a little water. Replace the birds in this gravy and roast slowly in a 350° oven until the birds are very tender.

DUCKS WITH OLIVES

Follow the directions for the Spiced Ducks a la Mexicana, except instead of adding chili powder, add ripe and green chopped olives and a cup of Sauterne. Cook the ducks in this gravy, basting often.

MRS. JOE STRAUS

EASY TEXAS WILD BIRD RECIPE

2 to 3 birds per serving   paprika
flour   1 cup chicken broth
salt and pepper

Shake the birds in a bag with flour seasoned with salt, pepper and paprika. Be generous with the paprika for the color. Place in a shallow glass baking dish with chicken broth. Cover tightly with foil and bake in 300° oven for at least 4 hours. If liquid evaporates, add more broth. Do not uncover, otherwise, until ready to serve.

LEE MORGAN (MRS. W. M)

QUEEN ANNE'S QUAIL

4 quail
2 cups chicken stock
4 tablespoons butter
½ cup Sherry
3 tablespoons flour
salt and pepper to taste

Wash and truss 4 quail, place them in a heavy frying pan and brown in butter. When browned, place them in an oven dish. Make sauce by adding flour to remaining butter in frying pan and stir in the chicken stock. Add sherry, blend well, salt and pepper to taste. Pour over quail. Cover tightly and cook in oven 350° for approximately 1 hour. Serve with Wild Rice. Serves 4.

GRILLED QUAIL

6 quail
small pinch of powdered
Marinade:
juniper berry
2 tablespoons finely chopped
4 peppercorns, freshly crushed
onion
½ cup dry white wine
generous pinch of ground
2 tablespoons lemon juice
allspice
bread crumbs
2 ground bay leaves

Marinate the birds, salt and peppered, in marinade for 2 hours. Roll in bread crumbs and brown under low broiler flame for 18 to 20 minutes. Garnish and serve hot with melted butter on toast.

WHITNEY QUAIL FARMS, AUSTIN

STUFFED DOVES

Mix together, equal parts of dry toast and corn bread. Cook 1 lb. of sausage slowly in a large skillet until almost done, but not crisp. Drain off most of the grease, add diced onion to taste, and cook with sausage about 1 minute. Add sausage and onion mixture to bread mixture and blend well. Add milk or canned mushroom soup, to make a firm mass. Add salt and pepper to taste (take into consideration seasoning in sausage) and stuff doves as full as possible. Put doves in a large skillet, brown until browned on breast. Add 1 can mushroom soup and a little water. Cover and simmer over very slow fire for 1 to 1½ hours.

When birds are almost ready to fall apart, add a small can of mushrooms and 1 cup Sherry (or ½ cup Brandy), ⅓ cup at a time and let simmer. If there is too much liquid, simmer with lid off.

A covered electric skillet is ideal for these birds and any extra dressing can be cooked in ramekins and turned out of ramekins into liquid around birds just before serving.

BEN FOSTER

YANKEE DOVE

12 doves	2 bay leaves
¼ cup butter	1 garlic clove, crushed
1 medium onion, chopped	1 teaspoon oregano
1 lb. fresh mushrooms, sliced	2 cups red wine
2 teaspoons salt	1 (15 oz.) can tomato sauce
1 tablespoon black pepper	1 package spaghetti sauce mix

Saute the doves in a large dutch oven in butter. Remove the birds and add onion, mushrooms, salt, pepper, bay leaves, garlic and oregano. Saute until the onions are tender. Return the birds to the pot and add the wine. Simmer for 10 minutes. Add tomato sauce and spaghetti sauce mix. Place covered in a 325° oven and bake for 1½ hours. Serve with buttered noodles. Serves 6.

KING ANTONIO LI — JAMES W. GORMAN

DOVE JALAPENO

8 doves	⅓ cup sherry
flour	1 teaspoon Beau Monde
salt, pepper and thyme to taste	Seasoning
bacon grease	dash Worcestershire
beef consomme	1 whole jalapeño

Dredge dove in flour mixed with salt, pepper and thyme. Saute in bacon grease until lightly brown. Use part of the bacon grease to make a brown gravy with the consomme. (Do not use any extra flour.) Add sherry, Beau Monde, Worcestershire and whole jalapeño. Cover and simmer over low heat for 1½ hours.

ANNE ARMSTRONG (MRS. TOBIN)
Armstrong Ranch, Texas
American Ambassador to The Court of St. James

STUFFED ROAST PHEASANT

1 pheasant
½ lemon
3 slices bacon
½ cup salad oil
1 cup cranberries, chopped
1 onion, chopped
¼ cup ripe olives, chopped

1 cup stale bread crumbs
½ lb. liverwurst
¼ cup sugar
1 tablespoon parsley, minced
1 teaspoon salt
¼ teaspoon pepper

Set oven at 350°. Clean bird, rub inside and outside with lemon. Weigh bird. Combine cranberries, onion and olives in a bowl with the bread crumbs, liverwurst, sugar, parsley and seasonings. Blend thoroughly. Fill pheasant and truss. Place, breast side up, in a roasting pan. Put bacon slices over the breast. Roast 15 minutes per lb., basting occasionally with salad oil. Serves 4.

MRS. LOUIS COIRA (ELLEN)

TEXAS BARBECUED CHICKEN

1 frying chicken or 6 breasts
1 cup catsup
2 tablespoons lemon juice
1 tablespoon Worcestershire
2 tablespoons melted butter

¼ teaspoon salt
¾ cup water
1 medium onion, minced
2 tablespoons brown sugar

Dust the fryer pieces or the breasts with flour seasoned with salt and pepper. Brown slowly in a skillet. Transfer chicken to a casserole or roasting pan. Combine remaining ingredients and pour sauce over the chicken and cover pan with foil. Bake in oven at 325° for about 1½ hours, basting occasionally. Serves 4 to 6.

MRS. JAMES W. LAURIE

KING RANCH CHICKEN

3 to 4 lbs. chicken breasts
12 fresh tortillas
1 can cream of mushroom soup
1 can cream of chicken soup
1 cup green pepper, chopped

1 cup onion, chopped
1 tablespoon chili powder
1 lb. Cheddar cheese
1 can Rotel tomatoes

Simmer chicken breasts until tender; bone, dice and save stock. Line bottom and sides of well-greased 3 quart casserole with 6 tortillas, cut up. Sprinkle with 2 or more tablespoons chicken stock. Combine soups, onion, green pepper, and chili powder. Pour half of this mixture, half of chicken, and half of cheese on tortillas. Make a second layer of tortillas, chicken, soup mixture and cheese. Top last layer of cheese with can of Rotel. Bake at 350° for 1 hour, until hot and bubbly. May be prepared in advance and reheated. Serves 12 to 15.

MRS. JOHN WILLIAM RAULSTON

SAN ANTONIO DELIGHT — Tortilla Pie

1 lb. ground beef
1 medium onion, chopped
¼ teaspoon garlic salt
1 can cream of chicken soup
1 can cream of celery soup

½ cup water
3 large jalapeño peppers,
   chopped fine
12 tortillas, cut in half
1 cup cheese, grated

Saute the ground meat, onions and garlic salt in a little oil. Add soups, water and jalapeño peppers. Pour some of the beef mixture into a greased casserole and then add tortilla halves. Continue, alternating sauce and tortillas, ending with sauce. Cover and bake for 30 minutes. Add the cheese and bake for 15 minutes at 350°. Serves 6 to 8.

HENRY B. GONZALEZ
United States Representative, State of Texas

TEXAS BEEF NECK BONES

4 lbs. beef neck bones
2 medium onions, coarsely
   chopped; or leeks with
   some of the green
1 garlic clove, minced fine

2 teaspoons peanut oil
3 tablespoons flour, heaping
3 teaspoons Gaylord Hauser
   Veg-All
1½ cups beef bouillon

Wipe the neck bones well with a damp towel. Combine flour and Veg-All in a plastic bag. Add neck bones and shake well. Heat peanut oil in a Dutch Oven and brown the neck bones slowly with onions and garlic. Add bouillon. Cover and cook over low heat until tender, about 2 to 3 hours. Serve with Kasha, (see Index), or rice. Potatoes, carrots, beans, onions may be added. As a short cut, brown the cleaned neck bones in the oil in a Dutch Oven. Omit the onions, leeks, garlic and Veg-All and add 1 package Knorr Leek Soup Mix. Serves 4.

Mrs. Leonard Stern (Jeannette)

TEXAS CHILI

3 lbs. chili meat
1 (15 oz.) can tomato sauce
1 cup water
1 teaspoon Tabasco
3 heaping tablespoons chili powder from ground chile peppers
1 heaping tablespoon oregano
2 onions, chopped

1 heaping teaspoon comino powder
garlic to taste, chopped
1 teaspoon salt
1 teaspoon cayenne pepper
1 level teaspoon paprika
12 red peppers
4 or 5 chile pods
2 heaping tablespoons flour

Saute meat until grey in color and combine all ingredients, except flour, in a heavy pot. Simmer for 1 hour and 15 minutes. Thicken the chili with a mixture of flour and a little water and simmer an additional 30 minutes. Serves 6 to 8.

John G. Tower
United States Senator, State of Texas

PEDERNALES RIVER CHILI

4 lbs. chili meat (coarsely ground round steak or well-trimmed chuck)
1 large onion, chopped
2 garlic cloves, chopped
1 teaspoon oregano
1 teaspoon comino seed

6 teaspoons chili powder or to taste
1½ cups canned whole tomatoes
2 to 6 generous dashes hot sauce
salt to taste
2 cups hot water

Saute meat, onions and garlic in large heavy fry pan or dutch oven until light colored. Add oregano, comino seed, chili powder, tomatoes, hot pepper sauce, salt and hot water. Bring to a boil, lower heat and simmer about 1 hour. Skim off fat during cooking. Serves 8.

Mrs. Lyndon B. Johnson
LBJ Ranch, Stonewall, Texas

WESTERN MEAL-IN-ONE

1 lb. ground meat
1 tablespoon oil
1 clove garlic minced or ¼
  teaspoon mashed garlic
1 teaspoon salt
1 large onion, chopped
1 green pepper, seeded
  and chopped

1 teaspoon chili powder
  or to taste
1 medium size can tomatoes
1 can cream corn
¼ cup chopped ripe olives
¾ cup uncooked rice
¾ cup grated cheese

Brown meat in oil, add garlic, salt, onion, green pepper and chili powder. Saute for 5 minutes. Add tomatoes, corn and rice. Turn into a 2 quart greased casserole. Bake uncovered at 350° for 45 minutes. Sprinkle olives and cheese on top and continue baking 15 minutes longer. Serves 8.

MRS. LYMAN R. FINK (FRANCES)

TEXAS BEEF CASSEROLE

1 (12 oz.) package noodles
1 to 1½ lbs. ground beef
½ onion
1 can Campbell's tomato soup
1 large can cream style corn
3 to 4 tablespoons catsup
2 to 3 dashes Tabasco

pinch chili powder
Cheddar or Parmesan cheese,
  grated
paprika
salt and pepper
Lawry's seasoned salt

Cook noodles for 5 minutes; rinse with cold water, drain well, and season with salt, pepper and Lawry's seasoned salt. Set noodles aside. Brown meat and onion; drain off excess fat. Season with salt, pepper and Lawry's seasoned salt. Add tomato soup, corn, catsup, Tabasco and chili powder. Combine noodles and meat mixture. Pour into large buttered casserole dish; sprinkle with Cheddar or Parmesan cheese and paprika. Bake uncovered at 350° for 1 hour. Casserole may be frozen before adding cheese, and thawed overnight in refrigerator. Serves 8.

JEAN ABEL

TEXAS TAMALE PIE

1 pound hamburger
1 medium onion, chopped
1 can (16 oz.) tomatoes
1 can (8 oz.) tomato sauce
1 can (14½ oz.) red
  kidney beans
1 package frozen succotash
1 small package of corn
  muffin mix
salt, pepper and chili powder
  to taste

Brown hamburger and onion in a small amount of oil. Add tomatoes and tomato sauce. Simmer. Add kidney beans and succotash. Cook 10 minutes. Season to taste. Mash a few of the kidney beans against side of skillet for thickening. Pour into casserole. Mix corn muffin mix according to directions on package, adding extra milk so it is thinner than usual. Spoon on top of hamburger mixture. Bake at 375° until cornbread is done, about 25 or 30 minutes. Serves 6.

MRS. ROBERT DAWSON (JEANNIE)

GOOD LUCK BLACKEYED PEAS

6 (15 oz.) cans blackeyed peas
2 cups bacon, chopped
1½ cups ham, chopped
3 cups onions, chopped
2 cups green peppers, chopped

Fry bacon and ham until slightly brown. Add onions and saute about 15 minutes. Add green peppers and saute about 10 minutes. Pour in blackeyed peas with liquid and simmer for 1 hour. Cover for the last ½ hour. Serve with Hush Puppies (see Index).

JOHN HERWECK

"JOHN WAYNE" CASSEROLE

1 (2¼ oz.) can jalapeño peppers
1 lb. Monterey Jack cheese,
  coarsely grated
1 lb. Cheddar cheese,
4 egg whites
4 egg yolks
1 (8 oz.) can evaporated milk
1 tablespoon flour
½ teaspoon salt
⅛ teaspoon pepper
2 medium tomatoes, sliced

Dice peppers and combine with cheese. Pour into well greased shallow 2 quart casserole. Beat egg whites until stiff. Combine egg yolks, milk, flour, salt and pepper. Fold in egg whites. Pour this mixture on top of cheese, gently moving it into bottom mixture. Bake 30 minutes in 325° oven. Remove from oven, put sliced tomatoes on top and bake an additional 30 minutes, or until a knife inserted in the center comes out clean. Serves 8.

MRS. J. R. REED (KATIE)

BEANS AND BEEF

1 (No. 2) can pork and beans
1 lb. lean ground beef
1 onion, chopped
½ cup catsup
grated Longhorn or Cheddar
cheese (optional)

Saute onion in small amount of cooking oil until tender. Brown meat, and add beans and catsup. Bake in moderate oven for 30 to 35 minutes. For added flavor, top casserole with grated cheese. Serves 4.

MRS. ROBERT N. CAMPBELL, JR.

BARBECUE BEANS

1 can dark red kidney beans
1 can baked beans
1 garlic clove, mashed
1 medium onion, chopped
3 tablespoons bacon drippings
½ cup catsup
1 tablespoon dark brown sugar
1 tablespoon dry mustard
salt and pepper to taste

Mix all ingredients and bake in 350° oven for 1 hour.

BARBECUE BEEF BRISKET

1 large beef brisket
6 tablespoons butter or
    margarine, softened
3 tablespoons dry mustard
4 teaspoons salt
4 teaspoons sugar
1 teaspoon paprika
½ teaspoon pepper
3 tablespoons Worcestershire
6 tablespoons olive or salad oil
3 tablespoons catsup

Combine butter or margarine, dry mustard, 3 teaspoons salt, 3 tablespoons sugar, paprika and pepper. Rub the paste into the meat on both sides. Using a heavy skillet, sear the meat quickly on both sides on a hot fire over coals or high heat on the stove. Combine Worcestershire, olive oil or salad oil, catsup, 1 teaspoon of sugar and 1 teaspoon salt. Brush meat with a portion of the sauce. Grill at least 1 hour over hot coals or medium heat in the oven until done. Baste frequently with sauce.

CLARENCE A. FEY

BARBECUED SPARERIBS

2 lbs. spareribs
½ cup chopped onions
2 tablespoons shortening
1 cup water
3½ tablespoons vinegar
1½ tablespoons Worcestershire
½ cup lemon juice
3½ tablespoons brown sugar
1¾ cups chili sauce
1 teaspoon salt
½ teaspoon paprika

Place spareribs in pan. Cover with waxed paper and bake in 500° oven for 15 minutes. Reduce heat to 350°. Saute onions in shortening. Add water, vinegar, Worcestershire, lemon juice, brown sugar, chili sauce, salt, paprika and simmer 20 minutes. Remove waxed paper from ribs and pour sauce over top. Bake ribs for 1 hour, basting frequently with the pan liquid. Serves 4.

MRS. JOEL W. WESTBROOK, III (ELAINE)

KRAWITZ RANCH BARBECUE SAUCE

1 teaspoon chili powder or 1
   chile pepper pod, finely
   chopped
2 minced garlic cloves
1 large chopped onion
2 tablespoons paprika
2 teaspoons salt
¼ teaspoon pepper
4 tablespoons brown sugar
1 cup water
½ cup vinegar
2½ cups tomato juice

Simmer ingredients together for 30 minutes, preferably in a heavy cast iron pot. This is a South Texas ranch's cherished traditional recipe for barbecue sauce, with the origin dating to the early 1800's. Good for beef steaks, ribs, etc. Sufficient for several medium sized steaks.

MRS. PETER STANLEY KRAWITZ

UNCLE CHARLIE'S BARBECUE SAUCE

4 large onions, finely chopped
2 teaspoons cayenne pepper
2 teaspoons cinnamon

2 teaspoons sausage seasoning
1 small bottle catsup

Cook onion in water until done and add other ingredients. Simmer for 10 to 15 minutes.

MRS. WILLIAM BRADFORD BUGG

SOMBRERO SPREAD

2 teaspoons salt
2 lbs. ground beef
2 cups chopped onion
1 bottle (14 oz.) Heinz
  Hot Catsup
5 teaspoons chili powder

1 teaspoon comino seed
1 lb. cooked pinto beans, or
  1 to 2 cans
2 cups shredded American cheese
1 cup chopped stuffed olives
corn chips or tostados

Spread salt in frying pan and heat. (Oil may be used, if preferred). Add beef, stirring with fork. When moist, add 1 cup of onions. Continue stirring until beef and onions brown. Stir in catsup, chili powder and comino seed. Mash and add pinto beans. Heat until blended. May be refrigerated or frozen. More salt, Tabasco, Worcestershire, or sugar to taste may be added. When ready to serve, heat and place in a large chafing dish. Pile olives in the center and surround with a large ring of onions and an outer ring of cheese. Olé — a sombrero. Serve with corn chips or tostados. Serves 40.

MRS. GERALD W. MASSY III (DOROTHY)

CHILI-BEEF DIP

1 (11 oz.) can chili (no beans)
1 cup dairy sour cream
¾ cup canned beef consomme

1 teaspoon Worcestershire
1 teaspoon chili powder
pinch hickory smoke salt

Mix all the above ingredients together and chill 2 to 3 hours. Serve with corn chips. Makes 3 cups.

MRS. EUGENE NOLTE, JR. (MARGARET)

JALAPENO CHEESE SPREAD

4 or 5 jalapeño peppers, seeded   4 garlic cloves, chopped
1 lb. sharp cheese, cubed   1¼ cups mayonnaise
1 large onion, sliced

Put jalapeño peppers, cheese, onion and garlic through a food grinder. Add mayonnaise and mix well. Cover and chill in the refrigerator until ready to serve.

COMPUESTA WITHOUT CHALUPA!

1 lb. ground beef   4 avocados, halved
1 medium onion, chopped   fresh tomatoes, sliced
1 can taco sauce   lettuce, chopped

Brown meat and onion in skillet. Add taco sauce and simmer for a few minutes. Place lettuce with sliced tomatoes around edge of 4 plates. Place avocado halves in the center. Pour hot meat mixture over the avocados. Serve with extra Mexican hot sauce. (1 package of dry taco seasoning mixed with 1 small can of tomato sauce may be substituted for the taco sauce.) Serves 4.

MRS. RICHARD D. SMALL, JR. (MARGE)

SAN ANTONIO SUMMER SQUASH

2 lbs. yellow summer squash   1 small can green chiles,
1 small jar (8 oz.) Cheese Whiz,   chopped
   plain or with jalapeños   1 medium onion, chopped
2 eggs   1 can cream of celery soup
salt and pepper to taste

Cut squash in small rounds and cook 15 minutes in small amount of water. Drain. Place Cheese Whiz in the bottom of a baking dish with squash on top. Salt and pepper to taste. Beat eggs slightly and add onions and chiles. Pour mixture over squash. Top with the celery soup. Bake for 30 minutes at 350° or until brown. Serve immediately. Serves 6 to 8.

CAROL R. HABERMAN
Judge, Bexar County, State of Texas

SOUTH OF THE BORDER RICE

1 cup rice
2 cans cream of celery soup
2 (8 oz.) cartons sour cream

3 (4 oz.) cans green chiles
10 oz. Cheddar cheese, grated

Cook rice. When dry and fluffy, add soup, sour cream and juice of chiles. Place 1/3 of mixture in a large, flat, greased baking dish. Add a layer of chiles and a layer of cheese. Repeat twice. Refrigerate overnight. Bake with cheese layer on top in 350° oven for 35 to 40 minutes. Serves 6.

MRS. H. M. TURNER (DOROTHY)

SAN ANTONIO ASPIC

1 large or 2 small packages
  lemon Jello
1¾ cups boiling water
1 (8 oz.) can Hunts Tomato
  Sauce

¾ to 1 (8 oz.) can Herdez
  Chile Salsa
2 tablespoons white vinegar
1 tablespoon lemon juice

Dissolve Jello in hot water. Cool slightly, then add the two sauces, vinegar and lemon juice. Pour into a greased quart mold or 12 muffin tins. Serves 12.

MRS. LAWRENCE A. MARTIN, JR. (DOLORES)

KATY KORNETTES

The Katy Railroad, famous for fine foods when train travel was in its prime, produced many unique and memorable dishes. Perhaps, none was more popular than the Katy Kornette.

2 cups fine white corn meal
1 tablespoon sugar

¼ lb. margarine
1 quart boiling milk

Bring milk to a boil and add sugar and margarine stirring with a large wire whisk. Add corn meal gradually to boiling milk, stirring constantly. Mixture will be quite thick. Remove from fire and allow to stand 5 minutes, but do not allow it to get cool. Squeeze through a large pastry bag onto an ungreased, Teflon cookie sheet. Make dough about dollar size. Let stand 5 to 15 minutes before baking in a 400° oven for 15 to 20 minutes. Makes 36 Kornettes.

MRS. WILLIAM TERRY O'DANIEL (BILLIE)

TEXAS HUSH PUPPIES

1½ cups yellow corn meal
½ cup flour
2 tablespoons baking powder
½ teaspoon salt

2 teaspoons sugar
2 eggs
⅔ cup milk
4 tablespoons chopped onion

Sift together corn meal, flour, baking powder, salt and sugar. Beat eggs, add milk and onion. Stir into corn meal and drop by tablespoonfuls into deep hot shortening at 375°. Fry a few minutes until golden brown, drain and serve.

JOHN HERWECK

SOD CAKE

1 stick margarine
1 box light brown sugar
4 eggs
2 cups Pioneer Biscuit Mix

1 cup pecans, chopped
1 can coconut
1 teaspoon vanilla

Cream margarine and brown sugar. Add eggs, biscuit mix, pecans, coconut and vanilla. Bake in greased 9 x 13 inch pan, 30 to 35 minutes, in 350° oven. Top with whipped cream. Serves 6 to 8.

MRS. MIKE CUMMINGS (SHERRY)

COFFEE CAN BREAD

4 cups unsifted flour
1 package active dry yeast
½ cup water
½ cup milk
½ cup butter
¼ cup sugar

1 teaspoon salt
½ cup ground pecans
½ cup chopped raisins
2 eggs, slightly beaten
2 (1 lb.) coffee cans

Mix yeast with 2 cups of flour. Stir, over low heat, water, milk, butter, sugar and salt until the butter melts. Cool for 5 minutes. Add flour and yeast mixture. Add remaining 2 cups of flour, nuts, fruit and eggs. Dough will be stiff. Knead on floured board until the dough is smooth and raisins are well distributed. Lightly oil the insides of each coffee can. Divide dough in half and place in coffee cans. Cover with plastic tops. Let rise in a warm place (85°) until the dough reaches the top of the cans. Remove plastic tops and bake at 375° for about 35 minutes or until the tops sound hollow when tapped. Do not freeze.

MAJOR GENERAL JOHN H. McCORMICK

SAN ANTONIO PRALINES

1 cup white sugar
½ cup brown sugar
¼ cup milk

1 tablespoon butter or margarine
1 teaspoon vanilla
1 cup pecans, chopped

Mix sugars, milk, butter and pecans in a saucepan. Bring to a boil and boil a minute or two. Remove from heat, add vanilla and beat until creamy. Working very quickly, drop by spoonfuls onto waxed paper. Allow to cool.

HOW TO COOK ONE'S GOOSE

1. Obtain a goose.
2. Thaw if frozen. Wash well and rinse out the cavity.
3. Sprinkle garlic powder, onion powder and black pepper inside the cavity.
4. Stuff with chunks of apple and onion.
5. Rub the outside with soy sauce and the entire breast area with butter or margarine. Sprinkle the breast with onion powder, garlic powder and black pepper.
6. Cover the breast with bacon slices cut in half and place goose, breast side up, in a roasting pan 1½ to 2 inches deep. Pour in 1 cup dry white wine and ⅓ cup water. Add 2 slices of onion, 3 or 4 shakes of Tabasco, 1 tablespoon Worcestershire, and a small jalapeño pepper, chopped. Bake, uncovered, for 30 minutes at 400°
7. Reduce oven to 325° or 350° and baste goose with the sauce. Make sure the bacon remains on the breast. Cover tightly with foil and continue baking for 2½ hours, basting every 30 or 45 minutes. At the end of this cooking time, the breast meat should have begun to fall away from the bone. It should be fork tender.

If you don't like wild game, throw the goose away and drink the sauce. It's delicious!

COLONEL JACK C. YOUNG

The Symphony Season of San Antonio
Favorites from Visiting Artist Friends & The San Antonio Symphony

Modern technology captured sound on tape and gave us beautiful music at the turn of a dial. But — a live concert of a masterfully directed Symphony Orchestra, a talented solo instrumentalist, or a perfectly trained human voice still offers man a joyous experience.

In San Antonio we are able to indulge ourselves often in such an experience. The San Antonio Symphony, under the distinguished direction of Dr. Victor Alessandro, brings great music to thousands of San Antonians and residents of Texas and Mexico. It travels extensively, from the Rio Grande Valley to the West Coast, attracting enthusiastic music lovers wherever it appears. Other than the regular Symphony Season, it offers matinee Family Concerts and a yearly season of "Pops". It performs for over 200,000 San Antonio school children each year — the largest student audience in the nation. The San Antonio Department of Parks and Recreation sponsors "Music for the City" concerts throughout the city to the delight of thousands of citizens.

We are fortunate to have two outstanding new concert halls — the acoustically perfect Theater for the Performing Arts, and the greek amphitheater, Laurie Auditorium at Trinity University.

Maestro Alessandro is an internationally renowned conductor and the Symphony has been guided by his musical talents since 1951. For 25 years he has also directed the San Antonio Grand Opera Season, with some of the world's greatest voices singing its most outstanding operas. These operas are backed by our widely acclaimed concert choral group, the "Mastersingers", under the direction of Roger Melone. Mr. Melone is also the associate conductor of the Symphony.

For the past nine years the San Antonio Symphony was fortunate to have had the late John Corigliano as its Concertmaster. Mr. Corigliano had been Concertmaster for the New York Philharmonic Orchestra under the baton of its famous conductor, Arturo Toscanini.

THEATER FOR THE PERFORMING ARTS — Yvonne Schlichenmaier

In this section we are privileged to present recipes from some of the great guest artists and Symphony members who have performed recently for us in San Antonio. We are extremely grateful for their contribution to the SAN ANTONIO COOKBOOK II.

EGGS MEDICA

This recipe is from the wife of our distinguished Director, Dr. Victor Alessandro, whose musical genius and dedication has made our Symphony one of the ten major orchestras in America.

When Dr. Alessandro is conducting, he fasts from noon to keep his senses keen. But after an evening of music and the last notes of a concert have been dissolved in applause, the Maestro delights in this dish.

1 medium onion, coarsely chopped
2 tablespoons butter or margarine
¾ cup Medica (see Index)

1 small bunch celery hearts, coarsely chopped
3 eggs, beaten

In a heavy skillet, saute onions until transparent. Add celery and cook 2 minutes. Add Medica and stir gently. Add eggs, cover and cook over very low heat until firm, about 15 minutes. Serves 2 or 3.

MRS. VICTOR ALESSANDRO (RUTH)

UNIVERSITY CLUB CHEESE PUFFS

1 lb. cream cheese
1 egg yolk
1 teaspoon onion, grated

1 teaspoon MSG
1 teaspoon baking powder

Mix cheese, egg yolk, onion and MSG. Add baking powder, mix well and refrigerate. When ready to serve, mound on Ritz crackers and bake 5 to 7 minutes in a 375° oven. Chopped chives, shrimp, clams or chipped beef may be added.

OLIVIA STAPP
Mezzo Soprano, "Die Meistersinger" - 1974

CLASSIC QUICHE LORRAINE

1 (9 inch) pie shell, baked
½ lb. bacon
2 cups heavy cream
3 whole eggs
3 egg yolks

1½ teaspoons salt
¼ teaspoon cayenne pepper
½ cup chopped chives
½ cup Swiss cheese, grated

Cut bacon into 1 inch squares and fry crisp. Spread bacon evenly over the bottom of the pie shell. Sprinkle chives and cheese over the bacon. Beat the cream with the egg yolks, whole eggs, salt and cayenne pepper. Pour mixture over bacon, chives and cheese. Place in 400° oven and bake for 20 minutes or until the quiche rises and the top is brown. Shake lightly to insure the eggs are firm. Serves 4 to 6.

Miss Armstrong sends one of her favorite dishes - the classic Quiche Lorraine.

KARAN ARMSTRONG
Soprano, "Pagliacci" - 1973; "Tales of Hoffman" - 1975

BITTERBALLEN - Crispy Deep Fried Cocktail Snacks

3 lbs. lean stew meat
2 cups milk
1 large onion, chopped
1 bunch green onions, chopped
curry powder, to taste
soy sauce

20 medium mushrooms, canned
flour
2 eggs
bread crumbs
¼ lb. butter

In a large pan, brown stew meat on all sides in the butter. Pour enough cold water into the pan to make a nice gravy. Cook on medium heat for 1 to 1½ hours. In a separate pan, saute onion and green onions until golden brown. Add salt, soy sauce, mushrooms and curry. Add this to meat and gravy and heat for 5 or 10 minutes.

Mix milk and enough flour to make a heavy batter. It must be heavy and pour slowly out of the bowl. Pour into the meat sauce and stir well. Heat, stirring constantly until substance does not stick to the side and bottom of the pan. It must be so thick that a wooden spoon will remain upright in the ragout.

Spoon the ragout onto 2 large, flat plates and spread out as thin as possible. Put plates in the freezer for ¾ hour or until absolutely cold but not frozen.

Beat the eggs in a small bowl. Pour bread crumbs in a small bowl. Roll the ragout mixture into bite size balls. It should not stick to your hands. If it does, it needs more cooling. Dip the balls into bread crumbs, dip in the egg batter and in the crumbs again. Drop balls into deep, hot oil and fry until just golden brown.

Mr. Boerlage says, "This is a typical Dutch snack to eat with an aperitif."

FRANS BOERLAGE
Stage Director, "Die Meistersinger" - 1974; "Flying Dutchman" - 1976

SU-KI-YA-KI A LA SILLS

1 package fresh spinach
⅓ cup tomato juice
⅓ cup Worcestershire
⅓ cup bleached almonds
2 tablespoons chopped beef suet
3 cups onions, thin sliced
1 bunch green onions, minced
1 can bamboo shoots
1 can water chestnuts

1 can bean sprouts
1 bunch celery, chopped
1 cup fresh mushrooms, sliced
2 lbs. London Broil
⅓ cup sugar
1 lb. bean curd
¾ cup chicken stock
½ cup soy sauce

Cut London Broil into ⅛ inch thick serving pieces. Coat a Chinese wok with suet and heat over a hibachi. (Outdoors in the summer or in the winter, place the hibachi in a fireplace or on a well-insulated card table). Stir in onions, bamboo shoots, almonds, spinach, chestnuts, celery and bean sprouts. Cook 5 minutes. Add mushrooms, mix and stir for 5 minutes. Add meat, sugar, soy sauce, tomato juice, Worcestershire and bean curd. Mix and cook 15 minutes, stirring frequently. Pour in chicken stock. (Canned broth may be used.) Allow to cook another 8 to 10 minutes. Serve with rice. Serves 8.

Miss Sills says "I really like this recipe. It's off-beat enough to make an 'event' of the meal. Providing you've opened all cans, washed, sliced and diced everything ahead of time and put them in attractive bowls covered with plastic paper, it can be cooked in full view of everyone so that you don't have to leave the party yourself. An unusual meal with a cast of friends to share it is as much a production as any opera. This one gives the hostess a chance to be star as well as producer, for the one who does the actual cooking is usually the target of all eyes."

BEVERLY SILLS
Soprano, "Evening of Opera" - 1968; "Daughter of the Regiment" - 1972; "La Traviata" - 1973; "Barber of Seville" - 1976

SOUR CREAM BEEF FILET

1½ lbs. filet of beef
smoked bacon strips
salt and pepper to taste
1 medium onion, sliced
3 to 4 carrots, sliced
2 turnips, sliced
3 to 4 tablespoons shortening

2 tablespoons flour
1½ cups beef stock
1 bay leaf
20 black peppercorns
1 to 2 tablespoons lemon juice
1 cup sour cream
red wine

Lard the beef with bacon strips and rub with salt and pepper. Place in a pan and roast in 350° oven until not quite done, basting with own gravy. A little water or stock may be added. Remove the meat from the pan and pour off excess fat. Sprinkle the vegetables with a little flour and brown in shortening until golden brown. Add beef stock or well-diluted consomme, enough to make a medium-thick sauce. Place meat back into the sauce, add bay leaf, peppercorns and lemon juice. Simmer slowly until done. Remove the meat again, place on a serving dish and keep warm. Mix sour cream with the sauce and put through a coarse sieve. Add wine, heat and pour sauce over the meat. Serves 4 to 6.

RUDOLPH FIRKUSNY
Pianist - 1973

BEEF TOMANOFF

1½ lbs. beef filet
3 tablespoons butter
¾ tablespoon grated onion
¾ lb. mushrooms, sliced

salt and pepper to taste
dash of nutmeg
½ teaspoon basil
½ cup sour cream

Slice beef into ½ inch slices. Pound with a mallet until thin and re-cut into strips about 1 inch wide. Melt 1 tablespoon of butter in a pan and saute onions for 2 minutes. Add beef, saute quickly for 5 minutes, turning so the meat will brown evenly. Remove meat and keep warm. Add 2 tablespoons of butter to pan and saute mushrooms. Return beef to the pan and season with salt, pepper, nutmeg and basil. Add sour cream and heat very gently. Do not boil. Serves 4.

Miss Lear and Mr. Stewart share the cooking chores in their household and this is one of their original recipes.

EVELYN LEAR
Lyric Soprano - 1972
THOMAS STEWART
Baritone, "Die Meistersinger Excerpts" - 1973

HIRTE OXTAIL RAGOUT

4½ lbs. chopped oxtails
2 cups wine vinegar
2 bay leaves
1 teaspoon thyme
3 cloves
3 pepper corns and 3 turns
  of the peppermill
1 lemon rind, grated
1 cup red wine
1 onion, chopped fine
lemon juice

1 garlic clove, chopped fine
  (optional)
1 onion, sliced
1 bunch scallions
3 oz. smoked ham
2 tablespoons flour
2 cups beef consomme
salt and pepper to taste
pinch of sugar
mushroom essence

Cook wine vinegar with bay leaves, cloves, pepper, thyme and lemon rind. Allow to cool and add red wine, chopped onion and garlic. Add oxtails and marinate overnight. Remove oxtails and place in pottery type pot (it must have a tight cover). Add sliced onion, scallions and 2 cups of marinade. Fry smoked ham with flour until brown and stir in consomme. Add salt and pepper to taste. Cover and cook in 400° oven for 4 hours. Adjust seasoning with salt, pepper, lemon juice, sugar and mushroom essence. Serve with buttered noodles. Serves 4.

KLAUS HIRTE
Baritone, "Die Meistersinger" - 1974

HOT PICKLED POT ROAST

3 to 5 lb. roast
salad mustard
2 tablespoons wine vinegar
2 tablespoons soy sauce
1/3 cup dry Vermouth
1/4 teaspoon garlic powder
1 teaspoon seasoning salt
1/4 teaspoon thyme
1/2 teaspoon basil leaves

1/2 teaspoon rosemary
1 1/2 cups water
4 medium potatoes peeled and
    quartered lengthwise
8 small boiling onions
8 small carrots
4 small yams peeled and halved
celery seed, seasoning salt,
    coarse black pepper, paprika

Brush sirloin tip or pikes peak roast with salad mustard using a pastry brush and arrange in roasting pan. Combine next 8 ingredients and pour over roast. Add water and place vegetables around meat. Sprinkle seasoning salt, pepper, celery seed and paprika over all making sure potatoes have plenty of celery seed and paprika. Place uncovered in 500° oven for 20 minutes then reduce heat to 350°, cover and cook for 1 1/2 to 2 hours or longer until tender. Pan juices may be thickened or left as is for gravy. Serves 6 to 8.

BARBARA FAUGHT
Viola, San Antonio Symphony

PARMESAN MEAT LOAF

2 lbs. ground beef
1/2 to 3/4 lbs. hot pork sausage
1 large onion, chopped fine
1 teaspoon salt
1 cup Italian cracker crumbs

2 eggs, beaten
1 cup tomato sauce
1/2 teaspoon Accent
black pepper to taste

Mix all ingredients together with half of the tomato sauce. Place meatloaf in well greased loaf pan. Bake at 350° for 1/2 hour. Remove from oven and pour remaining sauce over the loaf. Bake for another 1/2 hour. Remove from pan and serve with Parmesan cheese.

KARAN ARMSTRONG
Soprano, "Pagliacci" - 1973; "Tales of Hoffman" - 1975

LAMB CHOPS WITH HORSERADISH

4 loin lamb chops

1 package frozen green beans,
   partially thawed

2 tablespoons butter

2 tablespoons flour

1 cup milk

salt and pepper to taste

4 tablespoons horseradish

2 egg yolks

¼ cup bread crumbs

3 tablespoons Parmesan
   cheese, grated

Saute lamb chops on one side only. Place the chops in a baking dish with the sauteed side down. Surround the chops with the beans. Melt butter in a saucepan and blend in flour. Cook a few minutes and gradually add milk, stirring constantly, until sauce is thick and smooth. Add salt and pepper. Cool slightly and stir in horseradish and egg yolks. Pour the sauce over the chops and beans and top with breadcrumbs mixed with grated cheese. Bake in 350° oven for 45 to 55 minutes. Serves 4.

Miss Caldwell thinks "most foods can be enhanced by the addition of either whipped cream or horseradish". She offers us a delicious example.

SARAH CALDWELL
Guest Conductor, "War and Peace" - 1975

HONEYED WELSH LAMB
(OEN CYMREIG MELOG)

3 to 4 lbs. lamb, (leg or
   shoulder)

1 cup honey

1 teaspoon ground ginger

1 tablespoon rosemary

1 cup dry cider

salt and pepper

Rub the lamb with salt, pepper and ginger. Line a baking dish with foil and place lamb in the dish. Sprinkle with rosemary and spoon honey over the top of the meat. Pour the cider all around the lamb. Place in 450° oven for 30 minutes, then lower the oven to 400°. The lamb should cook a total of 25 minutes per pound, plus 20 minutes. Baste occasionally, adding more cider as juices are absorbed. More rosemary may be used as garnish after cooking. Serves 6 to 8.

"Being a Welsh soprano, I wanted to send you a favorite Welsh recipe of mine, and I do hope that people will enjoy cooking and eating it as much as I do!"

JANET PRICE
Soprano - 1974

CHICKEN WITH CRUMBS

1 fryer cut in serving pieces
2 tablespoons melted butter
1 garlic clove, crushed
2 sprigs parsley, minced

1 teaspoon rosemary, crushed
salt and pepper to taste
1 cup corn flakes, crumbed

Wash chicken and dry with paper towels. Place skin side up in a shallow baking pan. Sprinkle chicken evenly with salt, pepper and rub with garlic. Sprinkle with parsley and rosemary. Pour butter evenly over the chicken and then sprinkle with corn flakes. Place in the center of oven and bake for 1 hour and 20 minutes to 1½ hours, until crust is brown. It is not necessary to baste or turn the chicken pieces. Serves 3 to 4.

"This is a favorite in the Rudel household from super-chef Rita."

JULIUS RUDEL
Director, New York City Opera

BAKED CHICKEN BREAST

6 whole chicken breasts
bread crumbs

Parmesan cheese
butter or margarine

Bone each whole chicken breast. (They should not be split.) Lay breasts, skin side down and spoon on 1 heaping tablespoon of bread-crumbs to which a generous amount of Parmesan cheese has been added. Add a pat of butter. Close the chicken breast around the crumbs, cheese and butter and turn upside down so they resemble a closed fist. Butter the outside of each breast, sprinkle with bread crumbs and cheese and bake in a 325° oven for about 50 minutes, basting occasionally. Serves 6, and "add a few extras for hearty eaters".

EVE QUELER
Guest Conductor, 1975

TWO SEASONS CHICKEN HARBIN

3½ lb. fryer, boned, skinned and cut into 1 inch cubes

Light Sauce - Combine the following:

2 tablespoons sherry
¼ cup chicken broth
½ teaspoon sugar
juice from 1 garlic clove

½ teaspoon salt
1 teaspoon fresh ginger, minced
1 tablespoon cornstarch

Dark Sauce - Combine the following:

2 tablespoons red wine
¼ cup soy sauce
2 tablespoons oyster sauce

¼ teaspoon sugar
¼ teaspoon five seasons powder
1 tablespoon cornstarch

Marinate white meat cubes in light sauce and dark meat cubes in dark sauce for at least 2 hours.

Light Ingredients

½ lb. fresh mushrooms thinly
sliced through cap and stem
8 to 10 water chestnuts, sliced

4 to 6 scallion bulbs, sliced
2 tablespoons cooking oil

Heat oil in wok or heavy skillet until it smokes. Add white meat cubes and Light Sauce and cook over high heat 3 to 5 minutes, stirring constantly. Add Light Ingredients and cook about 2 more minutes or until mushrooms are tender to taste. Remove all ingredients and place on one side of a heated platter in a warm oven.

Dark Ingredients

½ cup blanched almond
slivers
6 dried Chinese mushrooms

¼ cup bamboo shoots, sliced
2 tablespoons oil

Soak the mushrooms in warm water for 30 minutes. Discard tough stems and slice. Heat oil in cleaned wok or heavy skillet until it smokes. Add dark meat cubes and Dark Sauce and cook over high heat 3 to 5 minutes, stirring constantly. Add Dark Ingredients and cook about 2 minutes more. Remove all ingredients and place on the other side of the heated platter in a warm oven.

1 lb. fresh spinach	1 tablespoon salt
2 tablespoons oil	1 teaspoon sugar

Heat oil in cleaned wok or skillet until it smokes. Add washed and thoroughly dried spinach, salt and sugar. Toss and cook vigorously, about 1 minute or until the spinach loses its crispness, but no longer. Place in the center of the heated platter to form a fence separating Two Seasons Chicken. Serve immediately with rice or Chinese Steam Buns (see Index). Serves 4 to 6.

HARVEY BISKIN
Timpani, San Antonio Symphony

COQ AU VIN EXTRAORDINAIRE

2 to 3 chickens, cut in serving pieces or 12 to 18 selected parts
$\frac{1}{4}$ cup butter
salt to taste
$\frac{1}{2}$ cup diced salt pork
2 large carrots, sliced thin
4 scallions, cut and slivered
2 cloves garlic, crushed
1 (16 oz.) can small onions
$\frac{1}{4}$ cup brandy
$1\frac{1}{2}$ tablespoons flour
$1\frac{1}{2}$ cups red wine
$\frac{1}{2}$ teaspoon sugar
$\frac{1}{2}$ lb. fresh mushrooms, sliced

Brown chicken parts in 3 tablespoons of butter over medium heat. Salt lightly and remove to a large casserole dish. Separately brown the salt pork over medium heat until crisp. Set aside. Add remaining butter and gently saute the scallions, carrots and garlic. Drain the canned onions and add to the other vegetable mixture. Add the pork crisps. Add brandy, ignite, gently shaking pan until flame burns out. Sprinkle with flour and cook over medium heat for 2 or 3 minutes, stirring constantly. Add wine, sugar, and mushrooms. Stir until smooth. Add salt to taste. Pour sauce over the chicken and bake, covered for 30 minutes at 375°. Just before serving, raise the heat to 450° for 5 minutes. Serves 6.

This recipe was given to Mr. Glaze by "one of my most distinguished fans," Lillian Bueno McCue, the author of mystery stories under the name of Lillian de la Torre. Miss McCue is also the author of *The 60 Minute Chef*.

The story of the origin of this particular Coq au Vin is, "Lillian McCue first had this dish in the home of Alice B. Toklas in the Rue Christine on the Left Bank in Paris. Lillian says that Alice made it with white wine, but she prefers the darker color and stronger savor of red, as I do myself".

GARY GLAZE
Tenor, "Die Meistersinger" - 1974

PAPRIKASCSIRKE - Hungarian Chicken Paprika

3 lb. chicken fryer, cut in serving pieces
3 onions, chopped fine
2 tablespoons oil
salt and pepper to taste
1 cup sour cream
1 tablespoon Hungarian paprika, or more to taste

Wash and dry chicken. Brown onions lightly in oil and add chicken. Sprinkle chicken with salt and pepper and add paprika. Cover and cook slowly until tender over very low heat about 1 hour. When chicken is done add sour cream and heat gently for 1 minute. Serve with cooked, wide noodles. Serves 4 to 6.

"Being of Hungarian heritage I thought it would be quite fitting for a Hungarian recipe to be our contribution to the San Antonio Cookbook II."

YOLANDA ANTOINE
Soprano, "Elixir of Love" - 1973
ANTHONY STIVANELLO
Stage Director, "Turandot" - 1969; "Aida" - 1970
           "Madame Butterfly" - 1970

CHICKEN IRENE

1 cut up stewing chicken
2 tablespoons oil
2 medium cans tomatoes, mashed
5 canned jalapeños, chopped
5 garlic cloves
1 small box raisins
½ tablespoon cinnamon
salt and pepper to taste
6 large onions, cut in 8ths.

"Brown chicken in shallow oil in covered large pot - salted and peppered. Then dump everything in the pot together and cook over medium flame until a good smell starts issuing from the kitchen (should be about 1½ to 2 hours). You may want to cook it even longer over a lower flame."

Mr. Brewer tells us this is a recipe from his mother, Irene Brewer, who lives in San Antonio. Mrs. Brewer's directions might be a bit more precise than those given to us by her son, but the results are the same.

BRUCE BREWER
Tenor, "Don Giovanni" - 1970; "Elixir of Love" - 1973
        "Creation" - 1975

SPECIAL BRANDY CHICKEN

¼ cup cooking oil
2½ lbs. chicken breasts
1 envelope onion soup mix
1½ cups water

¼ cup flour
¾ teaspoon marjoram
1 cup whipping cream
¼ cup brandy

In a large skillet, heat oil and slowly brown chicken, a few pieces at a time. Add onion soup mix, blended with water and marjoram. Simmer, covered for 40 minutes or until the chicken is tender. Remove chicken to a serving platter and keep warm. Blend flour with cream and brandy and add to the pan. Simmer gently, stirring constantly until the sauce is thickened. Serve with rice. Serves 6 to 8.

"I do hope that many will like this approach to an old chicken and rice combination dish."

JON ENLOE
Bass, "Boris Godunoff" - 1972; "Rigoletto" - 1973

VEAL A LA MARSALA

1 lb. veal
flour
2 or 3 tablespoons oil
1 teaspoon sage
½ cup Marsala or Sweet
  Vermouth

1 cup clear chicken broth
½ lb. mushrooms, sliced
1 tablespoon parsley, chopped
salt and pepper to taste

Cut veal in slices about 3 inches by 5 inches. (Beef may be substituted). Dip each piece lightly in flour. Brown quickly on each side in hot oil. Add sage. Remove meat and set aside. Add Marsala or Vermouth and chicken broth to the oil. Return the meat to the skillet and cook about 5 or 10 minutes. In another skillet, saute mushrooms and parsley in a little oil. Add salt and pepper. Mix with the meat and heat a few minutes. If sauce is too thick add a little more chicken broth. Serves 4.

MRS. ALDO DEL MISSIER
Aldo Del Missier
Violin, San Antonio Symphony

VIENNESE VEAL RAGOUT

2½ lb. lean leg of veal, cubed
6 medium onions, thin sliced
¼ cup lard or margarine
3 large tomatoes, peeled, chopped and seeded
3 green peppers, sliced thin
1 lb. fresh mushrooms, sliced, or 2 (1 lb.) cans sliced mushrooms

1½ tablespoons paprika
salt and pepper, to taste
¼ cup caraway seeds
1 cup sour cream or 1 cup yogurt
½ cup hot water

Brown the onions in lard or margarine. Stir in the paprika and blend well. Add veal, salt, pepper and hot water. Cover and simmer for about 30 minutes, shaking pan occasionally to prevent scorching. At this time, the meat will be only half done. Add tomatoes, green peppers, mushrooms and caraway seeds. Cover tightly and simmer for 30 minutes or until vegetables are tender. Taste for seasonings. Just before serving bring to a rapid boil and quickly add sour cream or yogurt, but do not allow to boil. Serves 4.

"This dish is delightful, light and equally successful on a dinner menu or on a buffet table. The recipe is my grandmother's who was a superb cook."

HILDE SOMER
Pianist, "Music With Lights" - 1971

SALMON MOUSSE SUPREME

1 envelope plain gelatin
2 tablespoons lemon juice
1 small slice of onion
½ cup boiling water
½ cup mayonaise

1 (1 lb.) can salmon, drained
1 cup heavy cream
paprika to taste
dill weed to taste

Empty the envelope of gelatin into the container of a blender. Add lemon juice, onion and boiling water. Cover and blend on high speed for 40 seconds. Turn off motor. Add mayonnaise, salmon, paprika and dill weed. Cover and turn on high speed. Remove cover and gradually pour in heavy cream. Blend for 30 seconds. Turn off motor immediately. Pour into a 4 cup ring mold and chill until firm.

Mr. Zukerman suggests the following sauce:
1 cup sour cream, 2 tablespoons mayonnaise, a little mustard, salt, pepper, curry powder; some brine from capers and a few mashed capers. Blend all ingredients. May be served warm with other fish dishes.

PINCHAS ZUKERMAN
Violinist - 1974

SALMON LOAF CANADIAN

1 (1 lb.) can salmon
2 cups soft bread crumbs
1 egg, beaten
½ cup milk
2 tablespoons parsley, minced
2 tablespoons onion, chopped

1 teaspoon salt
pepper to taste
2 tablespoons butter
2 tablespoons lemon juice
green pepper, chopped
celery, chopped

Drain salmon and reserve liquid. Flake the salmon and add bread crumbs and the remaining ingredients. Mix well. Turn into a lightly greased loaf pan, 7½ x 3½ x 3 inches. Smooth the top of the loaf and bake for 40 minutes in a 375° oven or until it is firm to the touch in the center.

Mr. Turini serves the salmon loaf with a cream sauce made from the reserved salmon liquid. Serves 4.

RONALD TURINI
Pianist - 1971

SEAFOOD JAMBALAYA A LA WENTWORTH

¾ lb. whole grain rice, cooked
1 lb. smoked bacon
2 large cans whole tomatoes
2 (8 oz.) cans tomato sauce
5 medium onions, chopped
1 small bunch parsley, chopped
3 bay leaves
1 cup celery, chopped
salt to taste

3 large tomatoes, peeled
½ lb. sharp cheddar cheese
1 large green pepper chopped
1 teaspoon Tabasco sauce
2 dozen large oysters
3 medium lobster tails
1 lb. fresh crabmeat
2 lbs. medium to large shrimp
paprika

Fry bacon semi-crisp in a very large skillet. Remove bacon and allow to drain. Boil lobster tails for 20 minutes and remove shells. Cut lobster meat into ¼ inch slices and brown, slightly, in bacon drippings. Remove lobster meat and set aside. Peel and devein shrimp and saute in the same bacon drippings and set aside. Do the same with the crabmeat. Saute the oysters in the same pan, only until they begin to curl and set aside.

To the bacon drippings remaining in the pan add canned tomatoes, tomato sauce, onions, ¼ of the parsley, bay leaves, green pepper, Tabasco sauce, celery and salt. Bring to a boil, reduce heat and simmer, covered, for 2 hours.

Combine the cooked rice with the tomato sauce mixture and place in a 12 x 15 x 3 inch baking dish. With a spatula, mark off 6 to 8 serving sections on the top of the rice mixture. Place 3 or 4 shrimp, 3 or 4 pieces of lobster meat, 1 tablespoon of crabmeat, and 3 or 4 oysters on each marked off section. Press the seafood down gently into each section. Cover the marked off serving cuts with the bacon slices.

Cut cheese into pencil size fingers, about 3 inches long. Insert a piece into the center of each serving section. Press a fresh tomato half gently into the center of each section. Cut a slit in the top of each tomato and insert another piece of cheese. Grate the remaining cheese and sprinkle it and the remaining parsley evenly over the top of the casserole. Top it all with paprika. Bake the Jambalaya for 1½ hours in a 350° oven. It may be made in advance of cooking time if covered in the refrigerator. Allow it to come to room temperature before placing in the oven.

Mr. Wentworth sends this super seafood dish from the heart of the Florida Gulf Coast.

RICHARD WENTWORTH
Bass Baritone, "Elixir of Love" - 1973

COASTAL STUFFED TROUT OR RED SNAPPER

4 to 6 lbs. trout or snapper,
  dressed for stuffing
½ cup butter
¼ cup onion, finely chopped
¼ cup diced celery
¼ cup green pepper, chopped
½ lb. mushrooms, sliced

1 teaspoon salt
¼ teaspoon pepper
1½ cups cooked rice
½ teaspoon dried basil leaves
1 tablespoon chopped parsley
¼ teaspoon paprika

Grease shallow roasting pan. Melt ¼ cup butter in large skillet; saute onion, celery, green pepper 5 minutes. Add mushrooms, saute 5 minutes more,stirring lightly. Season with salt and pepper. Remove from heat, stir in rice, basil, parsley, paprika. Melt remaining butter. Sprinkle inside of fish with salt and fill cavity with stuffing. Tie with kitchen twine 4 times. Place in pan and brush with melted butter. Bake in pre-heated 400° oven for 1 hour or until fish flakes easily, 10 to 15 minutes per lb. Baste frequently with last of butter during cooking. Arrange fish on serving dish; remove twine, garnish with lemon and watercress. Serves 6 to 8.

BARBARA FAUGHT
Viola, San Antonio Symphony

STUFFED CABBAGE A LA QUELER

1 large, leafy, white cabbage
½ cup uncooked rice
2½ lbs. ground lean beef
2 eggs
4 to 5 onions, sliced

2 small cans tomato sauce
sour salt, to taste
paprika, to taste
2 tablespoons brown sugar
salt and pepper to taste

Cook rice according to directions and combine with meat and eggs.

Add a little water and salt and pepper to taste. Make a sauce of the tomato sauce, onions, sour salt, paprika, brown sugar and salt and pepper. Soak whole cabbage in boiling water to soften leaves. Separate leaves. Make meat patties, oval in shape like small cakes of soap. Wrap a cabbage leaf around each patty. Slice leftover cabbage and add to sauce. Place stuffed cabbage rolls in the tomato sauce in a large heavy pot with a cover. Cook 1½ hours, covered, over low heat and brown for ½ hour uncovered in a 350° oven. Serves 6.

Miss Queler recommends this dish be made the day before serving.

EVE QUELER
Guest Conductor - 1975

ZUCCHINI EVELYNA

3 slices Provolone cheese
2 cups shredded zucchini
3 tablespoons finely chopped
   onion

½ cup seasoned bread crumbs
½ teaspoon salt
2 eggs
1 teaspoon vegetable oil

Grate the cheese in an electric blender and combine all ingredients except oil. Stir with a fork until well blended. Heat oil in the cups of a muffin tin and spoon batter carefully into cups. Bake for 20 minutes in 375° oven or until puffed and golden brown. Makes 12 large or 24 small muffins.

Miss Lear and Mr. Stewart share the cooking chores in their household and this is one of their original recipes.

EVELYN LEAR
Lyric Soprano - 1972
THOMAS STEWART
Baritone, "Die Meistersinger Excerpts" - 1973

ZUCCHINI ITALIANO

10 small zucchini
1 medium onion, sliced
1 (1 lb.) can tomatoes
garlic salt to taste
black pepper to taste
salt to taste

oregano to taste
3 or 4 eggs, well beaten
1 jar Kraft Romano Cheese
   grated
3 tablespoons oil

Slice zucchini about ¼ inch thick and allow to stand in a colander, sprinkled with salt for about 30 minutes. Heat oil in a sauce pan and saute onion. Add tomatoes, garlic salt, black pepper, salt and oregano. Simmer 30 minutes. Add zucchini and cook until tender. Combine egg and cheese and mix well. Bring zucchini and tomato mixture to a boil, add egg mixture and stir gently. Cover and simmer until slightly thickened. This may be served as a main dish with a tossed salad or as a side dish vegetable. Serves 4.

MRS. ADOLPH ABBENANTE
ADOLPH ABBENANTE, Cello, San Antonio Symphony

BORSCHT — LIGHT AND FIZZY

1 bottle commercial Borscht   1 egg
1½ cups yogurt   fresh chives

Beat all ingredients in a blender at high speed exactly ½ minute. Float chives on top. Serve with brown bread and cheese.

Miss Somer enjoys cooking, but also appreciates the modern "convenience" foods. She sends us this delicious, low calorie soup.

HILDE SOMER
Pianist - "Music With Lights" - 1971

MICHAEL DEVLIN'S GLYNDEBOURNE PICNIC VICHYSSOISE

4 cups potatoes, chopped   pepper to taste
5 cups leeks, sliced thin   1½ cups heavy cream
   (include 2 inches green) or   red or black caviar to taste
   3 cups onions   horseradish to taste
2 quarts chicken stock   chopped parsley or chives
1 teaspoon salt

In a heavy, large pan simmer the potatoes, leeks or onions, and salt in the chicken stock, partially covered, for 40 to 50 minutes or until tender. Force through a sieve or foodmill into a mixing bowl. Return mixture to the pan and stir in the cream. Heat gently, but do not boil, if you wish to serve it warm. For cold soup, chill and stir in horseradish and caviar before serving. Garnish with parsley or chives. Serves 6 to 8.

Mr. Devlin suggests "It's marvelous for taking on picnics in a thermos!"

MICHAEL DEVLIN
Bass Baritone, "Madame Butterfly" - 1970

VEGETABLE CHEESE SOUP

¼ cup barley	2 potatoes
1 can tomatoes	4 bouillon cubes
2 onions	1 stalk celery
1 bunch carrots	Parmesan cheese to taste
1 quart salted, boiling water	salt and pepper to taste

Add barley to water and boil for 20 minutes. Add tomatoes, onions, carrots, potatoes, celery and bouillon cubes. Cook for 1 hour. "Add several tablespoons of cheese, don't be stingy." Cook for another ½ hour.

EVE QUELER
Guest Conductor - 1975

SALAD FLORENTINE

1 lb. fresh spinach leaves	½ teaspoon dried summer
1 medium red onion	savory or 1 teaspoon fresh
6 large brown mushroom caps	¼ cup olive oil
1½ teaspoons Jane's Krazy	2 tablespoons Tarragon vinegar
Mixed-up Salt	3 hard cooked eggs finely chopped

Wash spinach leaves well and remove all stems. Tear into medium pieces. Slice onion thin and separate into rings. Wash and slice mushroom caps. Combine leaves, onion rings and sliced mushrooms in a large salad bowl mixing with seasoned salt and summer savory. Sprinkle oil over all; then add tarragon vinegar. (More or less vinegar may be used according to taste.) Toss lightly and top each serving generously with chopped egg. Serves 6.

BARBARA FAUGHT
Viola, San Antonio Symphony

NEAPOLITAN ORANGE SALAD

4 navel oranges   2 tablespoons olive oil
1 garlic clove   salt and pepper to taste

Peel and cut oranges, across the sections, into bite size pieces. Do not lose the juices! Chop garlic as finely as possible and sprinkle on the oranges. Add oil, salt and pepper and mix slightly, pressing orange slices with fork so oil and juice mix well.

Mr. de Gaetano says, "This is an old family recipe and is ideal as a luncheon plate with French or Italian bread and, also, is delicious with pork."

ROBERT DE GAETANO
Pianist - 1971

BLENDER MAYONNAISE

1½ cups salad oil   2 tablespoons lemon juice
1 teaspoon sugar   1 teaspoon salt
1 teaspoon prepared mustard   1 egg

Put ¼ cup of salad oil and the remainder of the ingredients in a blender. Turn motor to "beat" and immediately add the remaining oil in a slow steady stream. Use a spatula to keep mixture turning into the blender blades. Makes approximately 2 cups.

BARBARA FAUGHT
Viola, San Antonio Symphony

CHINESE STEAM BUNS

1 package dry yeast   1 cup lukewarm milk
¼ cup lukewarm water   4 cups sifted flour
1 tablespoon sugar

Dissolve yeast in water and add sugar. Allow to stand until it becomes bubbly and doubles in volume. Gradually pour yeast mixture and milk into a bowl with the flour. Work together, by hand until a firm dough is formed. Place dough on lightly floured surface and knead 5 minutes or until dough loses stickiness, add more flour if necessary. Place the dough in a large greased bowl and cover. Allow to rise until doubled in volume. Punch down dough, cover, and allow to rise again - 20 to 30 minutes. Turn dough onto a floured board and knead 5 minutes. Roll the dough by hand into a long tube, 2 inches in diameter. Cut into 1½ inch rounds with a sharp knife. Roll each round into a ball and set, covered, on steamer rack for another 30 minutes. Place buns in a steamer with boiling water and steam 8 to 10 minutes. Transfer to a heated platter and serve immediately. Makes 16.

HARVEY BISKIN
Timpani, San Antonio Symphony

ELLIE'S BRAN MUFFINS

4 oz. butter
1 cup sugar
2 eggs
1 cup Kellog's All Bran
1 cup buttermilk
2 cups flour
1 cup raisins
2 tablespoons corn oil

grated orange and/or
    lemon rind to taste
1½ teaspoons baking powder
1 scant teaspoon baking soda
½ cup uncooked oatmeal
pinch of nutmeg
pinch of ginger
sugar and cinnamon mixture

Combine bran and buttermilk in a bowl and set aside. Cream sugar, butter and corn oil. Add eggs, one at a time, and blend well. Sift flour, baking powder and baking soda together. Add this flour mixture and bran-buttermilk mixture alternately to sugar and butter mixture. Blend very well. Add raisins, oatmeal, grated rind, nutmeg and ginger. Fill greased muffin tins half full and sprinkle sugar and cinnamon mixture on top. Bake at 325° for about 30 minutes. Makes 1½ dozen.

NANCY LIBOWITZ
Cello, San Antonio Symphony

FINNISH HEALTH CAKE

¾ cup safflower oil
¾ cup soybean oil
3 eggs
2 cups sugar
1 teaspoon vanilla
3 cups graham pastry flour

1 teaspoon soda
2 teaspoons cinnamon
½ teaspoon salt
3 cups diced apples
1 cup nuts, chopped large

Beat safflower oil, soybean oil, eggs, sugar and vanilla together. Sift graham pastry flour, soda, cinnamon and salt together and gradually beat into the egg mixture. Add diced apples and nuts. Pour into a large, flat buttered pan or an angel food cake pan and bake 45 minutes at 350°.

RICHARD T. ANDREWS
Bass, San Antonio Symphony

CHOCOLATE MALT CAKE

½ cup shortening
1 cup sugar
¼ cup malted milk powder
½ cup cocoa
¼ cup powdered sugar
3 eggs, well beaten

1¾ cups flour, sifted before
  measuring
2½ teaspoons baking powder
1 teaspoon salt
¾ cup milk

Cream shortening well and gradually add sugar, malted milk and cocoa. Add eggs. Sift flour again with baking powder, salt and sugar. Add to creamed mixture alternating with the milk. Pour into well greased and floured cake pans and bake for 30 minutes at 350°. Use 2 (8 inch) layer cake pans. Remove from pans and cover with Chocolate Malt Icing, (see Index).

BERNARD F. BIRNBAUM
Flute, San Antonio Symphony

CHOCOLATE MALT ICING

4 tablespoons shortening
1½ tablespoons butter
½ teaspoon salt
1½ tablespoons malted milk
  powder

1 teaspoon vanilla
⅔ cup cocoa
½ cup cream
3 cups powdered sugar

Cream shortening and butter together. Add salt, malted milk powder and cream well. Add vanilla and cocoa and cream until smooth. Add cream and powdered sugar. Beat until smooth. Use as frosting for Chocolate Malt Cake, (see Index).

BERNARD F. BIRNBAUM
Flute, San Antonio Symphony

VIENNESE CHOCOLATE-ALMOND TORTE

¼ lb. sweet butter
4 oz. semi-sweet chocolate
½ cup confectioners sugar
½ cup almonds, grated

¼ cup graham cracker crumbs
4 eggs, separated
1 tablespoon cocoa

Melt chocolate in the top of a double boiler and allow to cool. Cream the butter until fluffy and add sugar and egg yolks, one at a time. Fold in the cooled chocolate, almonds and ½ the cracker crumbs. Beat egg whites until firm and add to mixture. Butter an 8 inch spring-form pan and sprinkle with the remaining crumbs. Pour the batter into the pan and bake at 400° for 30 to 40 minutes, or until a knife inserted in the center comes out clean. Bake the cake the day before serving.

¼ lb. sweet butter
¼ cup confectioners sugar
4 oz. semi-sweet chocolate
1 tablespoon instant Expresso
  coffee

1 egg yolk
1 tablespoon cocoa
¼ lb. candied cherries
12 blanched almonds

Melt chocolate in the top of a double boiler. Cream butter until fluffy and add sugar, egg yolks, coffee, cocoa and cooled, melted chocolate. Blend until smooth. Carefully cut the cake in half, horizontally with a sharp knife. Fill the center and cover the top with frosting. Decorate with almonds and cherries, alternating, around the edge of the cake. Refrigerate until 1 hour before serving time.

Miss Somer says "This cake is my pianist-mother's recipe, very elegant and serves 6 to 8. Light textured delicacy, equally effective for dessert course or for afternoon tea or coffee."

HILDE SOMER
Pianist, "Music With Light" - 1971

VIENNA CHESTNUT TORTE

2 (1 lb.) cans pureed chestnuts
  (Puree de Marrons)
2 cups mixed candied fruits
1 cup walnuts, diced
¼ cup confectionary sugar

2 jiggers brandy or rum
2 cups whipping cream
6 oz. coffee-flavored
  chocolate, grated
10 large brandied cherries

Mix pureed chestnuts with diced fruits and walnuts. Add sugar and brandy or rum. Fold into a 9x10 inch spring form pan which has been lined with wax paper. Chill for at least 12 hours. Whip the cream and remove sides of the spring pan. Cover the Torte with whipped cream and sprinkle the entire cake with grated chocolate. Decorate with brandied cherries. Serves 8 to 10.

"This dessert, which comes from my great-grandmother, took six hours to make in her day when chestnuts had to be boiled, shelled, skimmed, mashed and steamed. I made it yesterday afternoon with pureed chestnuts from a tin. It took 10 minutes."

HILDE SOMER
Pianist, "Music With Lights" - 1971

POST CONCERT CHEESE CAKE

5 (8 oz) packages cream
  cheese
1¾ cups sugar
3 tablespoons flour
¾ teaspoon grated
  lemon rind
¼ teaspoon salt

¾ teaspoon grated
  orange rind
¼ teaspoon vanilla
5 eggs, room temperature
2 egg yolks
¼ cup cream, whipped
graham cracker crumbs

Grease a 10 inch spring-form pan and dust sides and bottom with crushed graham cracker crumbs. Set aside. Beat cream cheese, one package at a time, with electric mixer until light and fluffy. Combine sugar, lemon rind, orange rind, salt, vanilla and flour and gradually add to cheese, beating constantly. Add eggs and egg yolks, one at a time, beating well after each addition. Gently stir in whipped cream. Pour mixture into spring-form pan and very gently make a few cuts in the top to eliminate any air bubbles. Bake in 475° oven for 12 minutes and then turn oven to 250° and bake 1½ hours. Turn off oven and allow cheesecake to sit in the oven for 1½ hours. Remove cake and allow it to sit on a rack for a few minutes before removing sides of the spring-form. Invert the cake on a serving platter and gently remove the bottom of the pan. Cover and refrigerate until serving time.

"IMPORTANT: Do not open the oven door once the cake has been placed in the oven until it is finally ready to be removed. The top may crack during baking but, because it is inverted on the serving plate, it doesn't matter and does not impair the flavor."

Mr. Bar-Illan says, "I am afraid that in the cooking department my talents are rather limited. After years of arduous practice I can just about fry water, with varying results. But I am famous in New York as the husband of Beverly B-I, who makes the greatest cheese-cake extant."

DAVID BAR-ILLAN
Pianist, 1962 - 1964 - 1972

GORGEOUS CHEESE CAKE

20 graham crackers, crumbed
$\frac{1}{2}$ stick butter, softened
7 tablespoons sugar
$\frac{1}{2}$ cup sugar

3 (3 oz.) packages cream cheese
3 teaspoons vanilla
2 eggs, well beaten
2 cups sour cream

Combine cracker crumbs, butter, 2 tablespoons of sugar and press into the bottom of an 8x8x2 inch pan. Bake for 5 minutes in a 375° oven. Cream the cheese, $\frac{1}{2}$ cup of sugar and 1 teaspoon of vanilla. Add to eggs and pour into the crust. Bake for 20 minutes at 250°. Combine sour cream, 5 tablespoons of sugar and 2 teaspoons of vanilla. Spread carefully on the top of the cake and bake for 5 minutes at 250°. When cool, place in the refrigerator and chill. Will keep for 2 or 3 days.

LOUISE RUSSELL
Coloratura Soprano, "Creation" - 1975;
                    "Beethoven Ninth Symphony" - 1976

JUSSI JALAS' FAVORITE RECIPE
A Cheesecake Made Without Sugar

$\frac{1}{2}$ inch thick slice of round sponge cake
2 large containers creamed cottage cheese
1 large container Sour Dressing (This is a substitute for sour cream, but if not available, use sour cream)
$\frac{1}{4}$ lb. yellow raisins
6 drops vanilla
4 small packets of Sweet n' Low powdered saccharine, or dissolve

regular saccharine in a little milk.

Place the slice of sponge cake in a round cake mold. In a mixing bowl, combine cottage cheese and Sour Dressing. Add raisins, vanilla and saccharine. Blend all ingredients in a blender or stir thoroughly by hand until it is a creamy consistency that can be cut with a knife. It should have the texture of a regular cheese cake. If it is too thick, add a little Sour Dressing. If too thin, add a little cottage cheese. Spread the mixture on the cake and refrigerate for a minimum of 6 hours. Remove the cake from the mold and "enjoy it with your friends".

JUSSI JALAS, Conductor Finland National Opera
Guest Conductor, 1966 - 1969 - 1974

A VERY DIFFERENT CHEESECAKE

1 box Zwieback, crushed   4 tablespoons sugar
4 tablespoons melted butter

Mix all ingredients well and line a greased 9 or 10 inch spring-form pan with the mixture. Reserve 1/2 cup to sprinkle on top of the cake.

1 (8 oz.) package cream cheese   1½ cups, plus 3
3 tablespoons flour   tablespoons sugar
6 egg yolks   pinch salt
6 egg whites   2 cups sour cream
                     1 tablespoon vanilla

Place cream cheese, flour, egg yolks, 1½ cups sugar, salt, sour cream and vanilla in a large bowl. Beat until smooth. In another large bowl beat egg whites until stiff, gradually adding 3 tablespoons of sugar. Fold egg whites into cheese mixture and pour into the Zwieback lined spring-form pan. Sprinkle the remaining crumbs over the top and bake at 325° for 1 hour. *Do not open oven while baking or for at least 3 hours after the oven has been turned off.*

Miss Cruz-Romo offers a different cheesecake. The crust is made with Zwieback instead of the expected graham crackers.

GILDA CRUZ-ROMO
Soprano, "Madame Butterfly" - 1974

Beverages

Tequila, a harmless-looking white or pale yellow liquid, comes to us from the city in Mexico which bears its name. It is made from the juice of the *pina* (pineapple) of the agave, known in the United States as the century plant. The agave is not a cactus, as is commonly believed, but is more closely related to the yucca and amaryllis.

The custom of drinking Tequila requires practice. The back of the left hand is politely moistened with one good lick of the tongue and sprinkled with salt. A quartered lemon is magically produced from the palm of the same hand and quickly sucked. The Tequila is then swallowed in one gulp and the ritual is finished by licking the salt.

Sangria, another drink widely enjoyed in San Antonio, was originally imported into Mexico from Spain. It is made with dry Spanish red wine, oranges, lemons, limes, sugar, soda water, and brandy. Add tinkling ice in a tall pitcher on a sizzling hot summer day, and it's a taste treat to be savored.

MARGARITA

1 part Tequila
1 part lime or lemon juice

¾ part Licor de Naranjas or
   Cointreau

Combine all ingredients in a blender with ice. Blend until smooth. Serve in a salt-rimmed wine glass.

TEQUILA SOUR

1 jigger Tequila
1 teaspoon sugar

juice of 1 lime

Shake well with crushed ice and serve in a cocktail glass.

SOUTHWEST CRAFT CENTER — Benjamin K. Wyatt

TEQUILA PARTY PUNCH

juice of 6 limes
3 bottles of ginger ale
3 bottles soda water

2 bottles Tequila
1 cup sugar or to taste
juice of 6 oranges

Combine all ingredients. Mix well. Serve over ice and garnish with pineapple rings, strawberries and orange slices.

SANGRIA DE SAN ANTONIO

1 lemon, sliced
1 lime, sliced
1 orange, sliced
4 oz. brandy

$\frac{1}{4}$ cup sugar or to taste
1 bottle Spanish red wine
2 tablespoons lemon juice
soda water, to taste

Put lemon, lime and orange slices into a glass pitcher. Mix the brandy with sugar and add to fruit slices. Allow to stand 1 hour. Add wine, lemon juice and stir well. Refrigerate until ready to serve. At serving time, add soda water. Pour over ice and garnish with fruit.

To make SANGRIA BLANCA, combine 1 bottle chilled White Burgundy or Chablis and 1 split Champagne in a glass pitcher. Add 1 thin sliced lemon, seedless grapes and strawberries. Pour over ice and garnish with fruit.

MRS. C. W. ROBINSON, JR. (JOAN)

KAHLUA

2 cups water
4 cups sugar
2 oz. instant coffee

1 split vanilla bean
20 oz. brandy

Put water into pan, add sugar, bring to slight boil and add coffee. Stir until dissolved. Cool slightly, pour into a $\frac{1}{2}$ gallon bottle. Add vanilla bean and brandy. Place bottle in a paper bag and put in dark place for 30 days or more before serving.

JOHN HERWECK

BOB'S KUHLIEU—QUICK KAHLUA

10 tablespoons coffee
4 cups water
$2\frac{1}{2}$ cups sugar

3 tablespoons vanilla extract
2 cups bourbon

Tie coffee in cloth sack and boil for 20 minutes in 4 cups water. Remove sack, and replace any lost liquid. Add sugar to liquid and simmer slowly, partially covered, for 1 hour. Add vanilla. Allow to cool, and add bourbon. Serve in cordial glasses or over ice cream. Especially good with coffee ice cream. Makes 24 (2 oz.) servings.

MRS. JOHN R. BURKHART

MEXICAN HOT CHOCOLATE

2 squares bitter chocolate
1/2 cup boiling water
1 cup condensed milk
2 cups water
3 tablespoons sugar
pinch of salt

pinch of allspice
1/4 teaspoon nutmeg
1 teaspoon cinnamon
1 egg, beaten
1 teaspoon vanilla

Grate chocolate into top of double boiler with 1/2 cup boiling water. Stir until blended over low heat. Add condensed milk, 2 cups water, sugar, salt, allspice, nutmeg and cinnamon. Cook for 1 hour beating about 6 different times with a rotary beater. Add egg and vanilla. Serves 4.

MRS. JACK PITLUK, JR.

POOR MAN'S CHAMPAGNE

3 bottles very dry Champagne, chilled
3 bottles Sauterne, chilled
2 bottles gingerale, chilled

1 bottle club soda, chilled
1/2 cup lemon juice, chilled
sugar to taste

Combine all ingredients in a punch bowl. Add ice form which has been frozen in a plastic bag. This punch may be made with inexpensive Champagne. Makes 1 punch bowl.

RAINBOW CHAMPAGNE CUP

1 1/2 cups brandy
1 cup Benedictine

3 qts. sparkling water
3 bottles Taylor pink champagne

Chill all ingredients including punch bowl. Over large block of ice pour ingredients into punch bowl. Ladle over ice to blend well.

To make ice block — use mold appropriate for your punch bowl, freeze in layers, using cherries and thin slices of oranges, lemons and limes. Also, the water may be tinted pink. Serves 24.

GAY EASTWOOD

Appetizers

Whatever the occasion, appetizers should whet rather than dull the appetite. Here's a place to let your imagination run free.

We offer a variety of tempting treats — hot and cold. Some are ideal "finger food", while others are more formal and should be the first course of an elegant dinner. Serve them with cocktails, at buffets, receptions, or perhaps after the Symphony. They are a tasty addition to any gathering of friends.

MELBA TOAST

Remove the crust from thin sliced bread. Butter slices if a more golden color is desired. Flatten each slice as thin as possible and cut into desired shapes. Lay flat on a cookie sheet and bake in a very slow oven, 200° to 225°, for about 35 minutes or until bread dries and turns golden brown. The flattened slices may be pressed into muffin tins for baking, if desired, to use as cups for moist hors d' oeuvres.

MRS. ALEXANDER J. OPPENHEIMER

GOLDEN CHEESE STRAWS

½ lb. Wisconsin Cracker Barrel sharp cheese, grated
¼ lb. butter
¼ teaspoon salt
pinch cayenne pepper
1½ cups sifted flour

Cream butter, cheese, salt and cayenne together. Add flour. Form into a long roll, wrap in wax paper and refrigerate. Slice as needed. If you prefer, after the dough has been chilled, roll out and slice into strips. Bake in 375° oven until light golden brown. For variety, pecans or olives may be added to rolled dough.

MRS. LOUIS BISHOP

TRINITY UNIVERSITY — Bill Bristow

GOLDEN CHEESE FLAKES

2 sticks margarine or butter
$1\frac{1}{2}$ lbs. sharp cheese, grated
2 cups flour

$\frac{1}{2}$ teaspoon cayenne
1 teaspoon salt
4 cups corn flakes

Allow cheese to come to room temperature and cream together with the butter or margarine. Add flour, cayenne, salt and mix well by hand. Add corn flakes and mix. Form into small balls and place on greased cookie sheet. Bake about 25 minutes in 325° oven until brown. This may be assembled in advance and baked at serving time.

MRS. HERBERT C. BROOKE

EASY CHEESE PUFFS

1 (8 oz.) package cream cheese
8 to 10 oz. sharp Cheddar cheese
$\frac{1}{4}$ cup margarine

4 large egg whites,
    stiffly beaten
1 small loaf bread, unsliced
    (1 day old or more)

Melt cheeses and margarine in a double boiler. Allow to cool slightly. Fold egg whites into the cheese mixture. Remove the crust from the bread and cut into 1 inch cubes. With a fork, dip the bread cubes into the cheese mixture and place on a greased cookie sheet. Chill at least 4 hours or overnight. At serving time, place in a 400° oven for 5 minutes or until lightly browned. These freeze very well. Makes 4 to 6 dozen.

MRS. E. MORGAN SCHMIDT (SYBIL)

MUSHROOM CHEESE PUFFS

36 mushroom caps
36 bread rounds
6 oz. cream cheese

1 egg yolk, beaten
$\frac{1}{8}$ teaspoon grated onion
butter

Brown mushroom caps in butter. Mix cheese, egg yolk and onion. Cut bread rounds slightly larger than mushrooms, brush with melted butter and brown on the buttered side. Place a dab of cheese mixture on untoasted side of each round. Top with mushroom caps, round side down, and cover with cheese mixture. Broil until puffed and slightly brown. Serve hot.

MRS. WILLIAM McCRAE

PIMIENTO PERFECTO

3 tablespoons sugar
3 tablespoons vinegar
1/8 teaspoon salt
3 eggs

1 small package Velveeta Cheese, diced
1 small jar pimiento, chopped

In top of double boiler, combine sugar, vinegar, and salt. Add beaten eggs and cheese. Cook over boiling water, stirring often, until cheese is melted. Remove from heat, and add pimiento. Serve warm as a dip, or store in refrigerator in a pint jar, tightly covered. Spread on crackers, or sandwiches.

RUNELLE BAKER

CHUTNEY CHEESE PATE

1 (6 oz.) package cream cheese
1 cup grated Cheddar cheese
1/2 teaspoon curry powder
1/2 teaspoon garlic powder
1/4 teaspoon salt

4 teaspoons sherry
1 jar Major Grey's Chutney
1/2 bunch green onions, chopped
   (including tops)

Mix cream cheese, Cheddar cheese, curry powder, garlic powder, salt and sherry. Form into a flat-topped, round shape and cover with Chutney and chopped onions. Serves 6 to 8.

MRS. GEORGE C. VINEY (PEG)

SEAFOOD CHEESE ROLL

1 (8 oz.) package cream cheese
8 oz. well chopped, cooked
   shrimp or crab
2 garlic cloves, crushed or finely
   chopped

2 tablespoons green onions or
   chives, finely chopped
2 tablespoons lemon juice
1 1/4 cups walnuts, finely chopped

Combine cheese and seafood and beat until fairly smooth. Beat in lemon juice, onion, garlic, salt and pepper to taste. Stir in 1/2 cup of walnuts. Turn onto a sheet of foil, sprinkled with remaining walnuts. Roll in walnuts to desired shape. Wrap in foil and chill several hours.

POO-POOS

12 to 16 oz. sharp cheese grated   1 lb. raw hot sausage (Owens or
3 cups Bisquick   Jimmy Dean's)

Place all ingredients in a large bowl. Allow to stand at room temperature for 30 minutes. Mix together thoroughly by hand. Allow to rest 15 minutes. Form into 1 inch balls. Bake on a cookie sheet in 350° oven about 10 to 12 minutes or until slightly brown. These freeze very well. Makes 100 balls.

SHRIMP BISCUITS

1 package refrigerator $\frac{1}{2}$ cup mayonnaise
  biscuits (10) $\frac{1}{2}$ teaspoon onion, minced
40 shrimp, cooked   sesame seeds
$\frac{1}{4}$ cup Parmesan cheese

Bake biscuits according to directions. Cool and slice in half; then cut half-slices in half. Mix cheese, mayonnaise and onion. Place about a teaspoon of this mixture on the cut sides of the cooked biscuits. Top with shrimp and sesame seeds. Broil until brown and bubbly. The biscuits and shrimp may be cooked and the cheese mixed in advance, but the biscuits should be assembled and broiled at serving time. Makes 40 bite-sized appetizers.

MRS. HARRY C. BAYNE (MELBA)

PICKLED SHRIMP

$2\frac{1}{2}$ lbs. shrimp $\frac{3}{4}$ cup cider or wine vinegar
$\frac{1}{2}$ cup celery tops $1\frac{1}{2}$ teaspoons salt
1 small whole onion $2\frac{1}{2}$ teaspoons celery seed
$3\frac{1}{2}$ teaspoons salt $2\frac{1}{2}$ tablespoons capers and juice
$\frac{1}{2}$ cup mixed pickling spices dash of Tabasco sauce
2 cups sliced onions   7 or 8 bay leaves
$1\frac{1}{2}$ cups salad oil

Cover shrimp with boiling water and add the celery tops, whole onion, salt and pickling spices. Bring to a boil and cook for 10 to 12 minutes or until shrimps are pink. Drain and cool with cold water. Clean. In a shallow dish, alternate layers of shrimp with the sliced onions. Make a marinade of the bay leaves, salad oil, vinegar, salt, celery seed, capers and Tabasco. Pour over the shrimp and onions and refrigerate for at least 24 hours. Serves 8 to 10.

MRS. ERNST V. KUNZ

FLO'S CRABMEAT DELIGHTS

¼ cup minced onion	salt to taste
3 tablespoons butter	dash of Tabasco
2 tablespoons flour	1 lb. crabmeat, flaked
2 cups whipping cream	2 egg whites, beaten stiff
1 tablespoon parsley, chopped	½ cup mayonnaise
1 tablespoon chives, chopped	½ cup Parmesan cheese, grated
grated rind of 1 lemon	Pepperidge Farm thin sliced
½ teaspoon dry mustard	bread, cut into desired shapes

Saute onion in 1 tablespoon of butter for 1 minute. Add flour and cook 2 minutes. Add cream gradually and cook over medium heat until sauce is reduced by half, stirring constantly. Add parsley, chives, lemon rind, dry mustard, salt and Tabasco. Saute crabmeat in 2 tablespoons of butter until warmed through. Drain and add to the sauce. Saute bread shapes in a little butter to toast. (These may be done ahead and frozen, then allowed to thaw). Place a little of the crabmeat sauce on top of toasted bread. Fold egg whites, mayonnaise and Parmesan cheese together and place on top of crabmeat sauce. Broil for a very short time to brown the top. Serve hot.

MRS. WILLIAM MCCRAE

SPICED CRAB DIP

1 (8 oz.) package cream cheese	2 tablespoons Cavender's
2 tablespoons Durkee's Salad	Greek Seasoning
Dressing	dash Worcestershire
2 tablespoons hot horseradish	1 (6 oz.) can or frozen crabmeat
2 tablespoons onion juice	sour cream (optional)

Mix all ingredients thoroughly. Thin to dip consistency with sour cream.

GRAHAM B. MILBURN M.D.

VELVET CRAB

1 (10¾ oz.) can cream of shrimp
    soup
6 oz. cream cheese
¼ cup onion, minced
1 cup mayonnaise

2 envelopes unflavored gelatin
1 cup cold water
1 (7½ oz.) can crab meat
1 cup celery, minced

Combine soup, cheese and onion in a saucepan. Heat until cheese is melted, stirring constantly. Blend in mayonnaise. Dissolve gelatin in water, heat and stir into soup mixture. Add crab meat and celery. Pour into a 6 cup mold and refrigerate about 6 hours. Unmold, garnish with olives, pimiento strips, lemon wedges and salad greens. Serve as a spread on crackers. Fresh or frozen crab may be used.

MRS. WILLARD WOODRING (ALYNE)

CRAB RAVIGOTTE

2 cups lump crab meat
1 cup mayonnaise
2 tablespoons minced parsley
2 tablespoons chopped capers
1 tablespoon dry mustard

1 tablespoon horseradish
2 tablespoons chopped pimiento
1 hard boiled egg, chopped
½ teaspoon lemon juice

Thoroughly mix all ingredients except crab meat. Add crab meat and toss lightly. Mound into individual shells and garnish with slices of pimiento. May also be used as a dip with crackers.

MRS. CLIFFORD J. BUCKLEY (HELEN)

COLD FISH MOUSSE

2 envelopes unflavored gelatin
2½ cups water
1 small onion, sliced
2 teaspoons salt
½ teaspoon peppercorns
½ teaspoon basil
1 (16 oz.) package frozen
    flounder, sole or cod fillets

½ cup mayonnaise
1 tablespoon lemon juice
¼ teaspoon hot pepper sauce
½ cup cream, whipped
lettuce, lemon wedges, ripe
    pitted olives sliced, and
    pimientos

Sprinkle gelatin over the 2½ cups water in a pan and stir over low heat. When it comes to a boil, add the sliced onion, salt, peppercorns and basil. Reduce heat, cover and simmer 5 minutes. Add the flounder, sole or cod and bring to a boil. Cover and simmer 15 minutes until flaky. Remove fish and strain liquid, adding more water if necessary to make $2\frac{1}{4}$ cups. Add fish, cover and refrigerate until thickened. When thickened, put fish with gelatin into the blender with the mayonnaise, lemon juice, and hot pepper sauce. Blend at medium speed until smooth then pour into a large bowl. Fold in the whipped cream, pour into a mold and refrigerate 4 hours. Unmold on lettuce leaves and use the lemon wedges, olives and pimientos as garnish. Serves 8 for appetizers or 4 for main course.

CHEESE LIVER PATE

1 large package cream cheese
1 can bouillon soup
1 package unflavored gelatin

2 cans liver pate or spread
garlic salt

Mix cream cheese and liver pate. Dissolve gelatin with a small amount of soup in a saucepan. Add the rest of the soup and bring to a boil over low heat. Pour soup into an oiled mold and chill until firm. Add a generous amount of garlic salt to liver and cheese mixture and pack on top of the set bouillon. Chill again. Unmold and serve with melba toast or crackers.

BAKED CHICKEN LIVER PATE

1 lb. raw chicken livers
$\frac{1}{3}$ cup flour
2 tablespoons brandy
$\frac{1}{3}$ cup butter
1 small onion, chopped
1 cup heavy cream
1 teaspoon white pepper

$\frac{1}{2}$ teaspoon ground ginger
$\frac{1}{8}$ teaspoon allspice
1 whole egg
1 egg yolk
$\frac{1}{2}$ teaspoon MSG
$\frac{1}{2}$ teaspoon salt

Blend all ingredients in a blender. Place in a lightly oiled mold and bake in 1 inch of water at 350° for 45 minutes to 1 hour, or until set. Allow to cool, garnish with stuffed olives.

Mrs. Stanley Frank

CHICKEN LIVER PATE

1 lb. chicken livers cut into
small pieces
2 tablespoons minced green
onions
2 tablespoons butter
⅓ cup Cognac

¼ cup whipping cream
⅛ teaspoon pepper
½ teaspoon salt
pinch of thyme
⅛ teaspoon allspice
4 oz. melted butter

Remove membranes and any spots on chicken livers and saute with the onions in the butter. Remove from pan while they are still rosy inside and place in blender. Pour the Cognac into the pan and reduce it rapidly till you have 3 tablespoons. Scrape it into blender. Place the rest of the ingredients, except the butter, in the blender, cover and blend at top speed for about a minute until ingredients are smooth. Add melted butter and blend thoroughly for a few seconds. Pack into bowl and cover with wax paper or plastic wrap. Chill a few hours before serving on small party breads.

MRS. PETER V. WESTON (YVONNE)

CHIAO TZU

6 to 8 pork chops
3 large onions, minced
3 cups flour
½ teaspoon salt

soy sauce
wine vinegar
cooking oil

Cut pork chops into small pieces. Saute with onions, salt and a little soy sauce. A small amount of cooking oil may be used to prevent the pork pieces from sticking. Make a stiff dough of flour, salt and water. It is best to make 1 cup of flour at a time. Divide the dough in half and roll very thin. Cut into rounds with a 2½ inch cutter. Place 1 teaspoon of the pork mixture on the round and fold in half. Pinch edges together. Drop in boiling water for 3 minutes. Drain on a paper towel; not too long as the dough will stick. Fry to a golden brown. Serve with a mixture of ½ soy sauce and ½ wine vinegar for dipping. Chiao Tzus may be frozen in the steamed state and then fried either frozen or thawed. Serves 6 to 8.

MRS. H. RANDOLPH BROWN (CLARISSE)

MANY MANY MEATBALLS

10 lbs. lean ground beef
3 or 4 eggs, beaten
2 cups seasoned bread crumbs
2 cups milk or water
6 (15 oz.) cans tomato sauce
4 packages Spaghetti Sauce
Seasoning Mix

Combine meat, eggs, bread crumbs and milk or water as you would for meat loaf. Roll into 1 inch balls and place in a single layer in a baking dish. (There is no need to brown the meatballs.) Combine tomato sauce and spaghetti seasoning mix and pour over the meatballs until barely covering them. Bake about 45 minutes in 325° oven, turning carefully only once. The meatballs may be baked and then frozen. Reheat at serving time and transfer to a chafing dish. Makes 300 meatballs.

ANTOINETTE S. BURDETT (MRS. ALLEN M. JR.)

ORIENTAL BEEF OR CHICKEN STICKS

3 dozen bamboo skewers
1 lb. sirloin steak cut into
 3/4 inch cubes
1/2 cup dark soy sauce
1/4 cup brown sugar
1/4 teaspoon ground ginger
2 tablespoons sherry

Combine soy sauce, brown sugar, ginger and sherry. Allow meat to marinate in this sauce for 1 hour. Place 4 or 5 pieces of meat on each skewer and broil in the oven or over hot coals. Makes 3 dozen sticks.

To make Chicken Sticks, cut chicken meat into cubes. Marinate chicken pieces in 1/2 cup soy sauce, 1/4 cup brown sugar, 1/4 teaspoon ground ginger, and 2 tablespoons sherry. Place marinated chicken pieces on skewers with a few pieces of pineapple chunks and whole mushrooms. Cook in the same manner as the Beef Sticks.

DEVILED EGGS AUX FINES HERBES

6 hard cooked eggs
4 tablespoons Miracle Whip
1 teaspoon capers
2 teaspoons prepared mustard
1/2 teaspoon Lawry's Seasoned
 pepper
salt and pepper to taste
Spice Island Fines Herbes to taste

Split eggs lengthwise, remove yolks and reserve whites. Mash yolks. Add remaining ingredients to yolks and mix well. The mixture should be moist but not runny. Fill each half egg white with yolk mixture and garnish with parsley, stuffed green olives, pitted ripe olives, pimiento strips or paprika. For variation, add curry powder, chutney or a square of watermelon pickle in the center. Eggs may be boiled in advance if the yolks are kept in a covered bowl and the whites in a plastic bag.

SUE EASTWOOD

CURRIED OLIVE CANAPES

8 oz. Swiss cheese, grated
1 small can ripe olives, chopped
1 small onion, chopped fine
2 dashes Tabasco

1 teaspoon curry powder
  or to taste
mayonnaise
Triscuits or cocktail rye bread

Mix all ingredients with enough mayonnaise to spread easily. Spread on light or dark slices of cocktail rye bread or on Triscuits. Place under the broiler until bubbly. Serve immediately.

MRS. LAWRENCE A. STONE (MARNETTE)

FLORENTINE DIP

2 packages frozen chopped
  spinach
1 cup mayonnaise

¼ cup prepared mustard
garlic salt to taste
pepper to taste

Cook spinach according to package instructions. Drain very well. Combine with other ingredients. May be served warm or chilled. 24 hours in the refrigerator will improve the flavor. Serve with dip chips. Serves 20.

MRS. BOB S. CARTER (MARY)

CHAFING DISH BROCCOLI DIP

2 packages frozen chopped
  broccoli
1 small onion, chopped
2 stalks celery, chopped
1 can chopped mushrooms

1 stick butter
2 rolls garlic cheese
1 can cream of mushroom soup
Tabasco or red pepper sauce

Saute onion, celery and mushrooms in butter. Melt garlic cheese in top of double boiler with mushroom soup. Cook broccoli according to package directions and drain well. Combine all ingredients and season with dash of Tabasco and/or red pepper sauce. Serve from chafing dish with chips.

MRS. JAMES W. GRAHAM

SPANOKOPITA — SPINACH PIE

1 cup onions, chopped fine
8 scallions, including some of
   the green, chopped fine
1/4 cup butter
2 tablespoons olive oil
1 1/2 lbs. fresh spinach
1/4 cup fresh dill, finely chopped

1/4 cup parsley, finely chopped
4 eggs, lightly beaten
1/2 lb. Feta cheese, coarsely
   chopped
salt and pepper to taste
18 Phyllo Pastry leaves
1/2 stick melted butter

Wash, trim and thoroughly dry spinach. In a deep skillet, lightly brown onions and scallions in 1/4 cup of butter. Transfer to a large mixing bowl. In the same skillet, heat 2 tablespoons olive oil, add spinach and cook over medium heat for 3 minutes, or until it is wilted. Drain well, pressing out as much liquid as possible. Chop fine. Add spinach to onions and add dill, parsley, eggs, Feta cheese and salt and pepper.

Separate 9 Phyllo sheets, and following the directions for Phyllo (see Index) brush each one with a generous amount of melted butter. Line a 9 x 12 x 2 inch baking pan with the 9 sheets of pastry, leaving at least a 1 inch overhang of pastry all around the dish. Pour in the spinach mixture and spread evenly in the dish. Cover the spinach with the remaining 9 Phyllo sheets, each brushed with melted butter. Trim the pastry overhang to 1 inch and roll it to form an edging of crust just within the rim of the dish. Brush the edging with melted butter. Using a sharp knife with serrated edge, cut the pie into serving pieces. Cover the crust lightly with buttered foil and bake in a 350° oven for 1 hour or until the top is golden. Remove the foil during the last few minutes to allow it to brown evenly. Remove the pie from the oven; cool slightly. Slice the pie, following the original cuts. Transfer the slices to a serving dish. Serve as a first course or vegetable. Serves 4 to 6.

MRS. KENNETH GAARDER (MARIE)

OTIE'S ITALIAN CARROTS

1 lb. carrots, cut in strips   6 to 8 cloves of garlic, slivered
¼ cup wine vinegar   1 to 2 teaspoons sugar
½ cup oil   oregano

Cover carrots with salted water and bring to a boil. Drain immediately. Mix oil and vinegar with the sugar. Place a layer of carrots in a refrigerator dish with a cover. Sprinkle with oregano and garlic slices. Sprinkle with the oil mixture. Continue layering and pour remaining liquid over the top. Cover, shake a few times and refrigerate for several hours or overnight. Shake occasionally while marinating. This will keep in the refrigerator for weeks. Drain and serve as hors d'oeuvres or part of antipasto for Italian dinner.

The late Otie McNemry Rossi, San Antonio Symphony Orchestra member for many years, and wife of the former Personnel Manager, gave me this recipe when we first came to San Antonio to make for an Orchestra picnic. I have enjoyed it ever since.

BAYLA BISKIN

TOMATOES CAPPRICIO

6 large fresh tomatoes   1 clove garlic
2 cups cooked rice   1 teaspoon Tabasco
2 small cans minced clams   1 teaspoon oregano
1 teaspoon olive oil   6 anchovies
2 teaspoons tarragon vinegar   1 cup chopped mushrooms

Blanch tomatoes in boiling water 10 seconds and remove skins. Carefully hollow out, discarding seeds but preserve flesh. Do not remove too much of the flesh as tomatoes must retain enough shape to be stuffed. Set aside and while they cool, mix all the ingredients, except the anchovies, (including tomato flesh) and heat thoroughly. Coat the bottom of an ovenware casserole with ¼ cup water and ¼ cup olive oil. Place tomatoes in casserole, stuff and decorate tops with strips of anchovies. Bake 10 minutes at 400°. Cool, then refrigerate. Serves 6.

This dish is on the menu at Cappricio's which is a well-known Via Veneto restaurant in Rome. Their cold, elegant antipasto is the specialty of the house. They can be a tasty change from the cold soups and seafood cocktails which usually precede summer suppers. They may be prepared several days in advance as marinating improves their flavor.

MRS. LEO F. DUSARD, JR. (BETTY)

EGGPLANT CAVIAR

2 medium eggplants
½ cup parsley, chopped
½ cup onions, chopped
3 tablespoons lemon juice
2 garlic cloves, minced
3 tablespoons olive oil

1 cup fresh dill, chopped
   (optional)
2 small green peppers,
   chopped fine (optional)
1 ripe tomato, chopped fine
salt and pepper, to taste

Bake unpeeled eggplant in ¼ inch of water for 1¼ hours in 350° oven until soft. Scoop out pulp and combine in a blender with remaining ingredients except chopped tomato and green peppers. Blend at very low speed until just spreadable — not liquified. Add tomato, green peppers, salt, pepper and chill. Serve with crackers or cocktail bread.

MRS. LEO F. DUSARD, JR. (BETTY)

SHRIMP STUFFED ARTICHOKES

6 medium artichokes
1½ lbs. raw, small shrimp
8 tablespoons lemon juice
4¾ teaspoons salt

½ teaspoon tarragon
¼ teaspoon black pepper
1 cup good mayonnaise

To prepare artichokes, remove the stems so that the artichoke will sit upright. Cut one half inch off the tops and snip off the sharp tips of each leaf. Cook, tightly covered, in about 2 inches of water to which is added 2 tablespoons of lemon juice and 2 teaspoons salt, until the base can be pierced with a fork, (30 to 40 minutes). Drain well. When cool, very carefully pull apart the center leaves, removing the tender leaves on the inside of the artichoke. Use a grapefruit knife to gently cut around the choke, lifting it out very carefully. Cover and chill the artichokes until serving time.

To cook shrimp, bring 1 quart water to a boil, add 1 tablespoon lemon juice and 2 teaspoons salt. Add shrimp and bring the water to a boil. Reduce heat and simmer, covered, 3 to 5 minutes. Drain, peel and clean shrimp. Reserve 18 shrimp for garnish. Place remaining shrimp in a blender with the remaining 5 tablespoons lemon juice, seasonings, including the remaining ¾ teaspoon salt and 1 cup mayonnaise. Blend until the shrimp are broken up. Chill in refrigerator.

Place artichoke on salad plate or artichoke plate and fill with shrimp sauce. Garnish top with whole shrimp.

The artichokes and shrimp sauce may be prepared separately in advance and assembled just before serving. Serves 6.

MRS. CARLOS PERRY (JAN)

MARINATED MUSHROOMS AND ARTICHOKE HEARTS

2 packages frozen artichoke hearts
2 lbs. fresh mushrooms
1½ cups water
1 cup cider vinegar
½ cup salad oil

1 clove garlic, halved
1½ teaspoons salt
½ teaspoon pepper corns
½ teaspoon thyme
½ teaspoon oregano

Cook artichokes until tender. Drain. Slice mushrooms in half through stem. Add to artichokes. Combine water, vinegar, salad oil and seasonings. Toss lightly. Cover and marinate overnight in refrigerator. Drain before serving. Serves 16 to 20.

MRS. CAREY PAGE (MARILYN)

ARTFUL ARTICHOKES

4 medium artichokes
½ cup Wesson or sesame oil
⅓ cup cider vinegar
2 or 3 bay leaves
Lemon-Pepper Marinade

3 chicken bouillon cubes or
  dehydrated onion soup mix
1 garlic clove, chopped
generous amount of oregano

Remove stem from artichokes and snip the tip from each leaf. Cover artichokes with water, and about half the oil. Add bouillon cubes or soup mix and cook for about 45 minutes. Transfer to a suitable container and add remaining oil, vinegar, lemon-pepper, bay leaves, oregano and garlic. Use additional oil if you think necessary. Refrigerate for 24 hours. When ready to serve, drain artichokes and use marinade as dressing. Serves 4.

CLEO LUX DE ARREDONDO

SNAILS IN WHITE WINE

3 cups dry white wine   6 dozen snails with shells
1 teaspoon chopped shallot   snail butter

   Boil wine and shallots until reduced by half. Strain. Add a little
wine to each shell, insert a snail and cover the opening with snail
butter. Bake in a 450° oven 10 minutes.

Snail Butter:
½ cup butter   ¼ cup parsley, minced
2 cloves garlic, minced   salt and pepper to taste

   Cream butter and garlic. Add remaining ingredients and mix
well.

TEXAS DRIED BEEF DIP

1 jar dried beef, chopped   1 (8 oz.) package cream cheese
½ green pepper, chopped   1 tablespoon Green Goddess
½ onion, chopped   Dressing
½ cup Miracle Whip

   Combine all ingredients and refrigerate. Remove 2 hours prior to
serving.

MRS. MIKE CUMMINGS (SHERRY)

Caroline Shelton

Soup

To walk into a country kitchen, with the aroma of a hearty soup simmering on the stove, must have been one of the experiences that made the "good old days" so good. Today, soup still belongs at a party —whether an elaborate dinner or an informal get-together.

Good soup cannot be hurried. The secret of its delicious flavor is simple, but vital; long gentle cooking and careful seasoning. However, you'll find in these recipes that our judicious use of modern "convenience" products will enable you to serve soup that really tastes of hours of slow cooking on the back burner.

Many of our soups are intended to be served chilled, befitting our warm San Antonio climate where "the sunshine spends the winter and roses bloom at Christmastime."

GAZPACHO PICANTE

2 cans tomatoes or 3 large
  fresh tomatoes
1 large cucumber, peeled
  and diced
1/4 cup diced green pepper
1/4 cup diced onion
3 tablespoons vegetable oil
1 or 2 drops Tabasco

2 teaspoons tarragon wine
  vinegar
2 teaspoons cider vinegar
2 teaspoons salt
1/8 teaspoon pepper
1 tablespoon jalapeño juice
1 sliver of jalapeño, diced

If using fresh tomatoes, put them in blender first and blend quickly. Add all other ingredients and give it a turn or two depending on what consistency you prefer. If using canned tomatoes, put oil and vinegar in first and blend, then add all other ingredients and barely blend. Serves 5.

MRS. SAM MADDUX, JR. (BETTY)

MISSION CONCEPCION — Caroline Shelton

GAUCHO GAZPACHO

4 cups ripe tomatoes, peeled and diced

1½ cups green pepper, chopped

¾ cup onions, chopped

2 cups beef bouillon soup

½ cup lemon juice

¼ cup Bertolli Olive Oil

1 tablespoon paprika

½ cup cucumber, chopped

1 tablespoon salt

fresh ground pepper

1 garlic clove, minced fine

Combine all ingredients except cucumber. Allow to stand at room temperature for 1 to 2 hours, stirring frequently. Chill 2 hours. Add cucumber just before serving. (If ripe tomatoes are unavailable, use canned Italian Plum Tomatoes.) Serves 4 to 6.

MRS. GEOFFREY P. WIEDEMAN (CAROLYN)

GAZPACHO ESPANA

4 large ripe tomatoes

1 cucumber

1 green pepper, chopped

½ onion, chopped

1½ cups tomato juice

1 garlic clove, minced

3 tablespoons olive oil

2 tablespoons vinegar

¼ teaspoon paprika

salt and pepper

Peel, seed and chop cucumber and tomatoes. Combine all ingredients in a blender and blend until smooth. Serve chilled, garnished with extra finely chopped onion, peppers, cucumbers, tomatoes and croutons. Serves 6.

HELEN HOGAN

GAZPACHO BLANCO

2 cups chicken stock

1½ cups watercress leaves chopped

2 cucumbers, peeled and sliced

1 green pepper, sliced

3 tablespoons dill, chopped

2 tablespoons scallions, chopped

3 tablespoons mayonnaise

3 tablespoons sour cream

3 tablespoons white wine vinegar

2 tablespoons sugar

1 teaspoon salt

½ teaspoon pepper

hard-boiled eggs, finely chopped for garnish

Puree watercress, cucumbers, green pepper, dill, scallions and chicken stock in a blender. Add mayonnaise, sour cream, vinegar, sugar, salt and pepper. Blend well. Cover and chill overnight. At serving time, garnish with chopped eggs. Serves 6 to 8.

AVOCADO CREAM

3 avocados
2⅔ cups chicken broth
½ cup whipping cream
¼ cup dry white wine
juice of ½ lemon
1 tablespoon sour cream

pinch cayenne pepper
salt and black pepper
1 hard-boiled egg, chopped
croutons
1 clove garlic

Peel and slice avocados. Add garlic, chicken broth, whipping cream, and sour cream to avocados. Blend at low speed for 1 minute. Add wine and lemon juice, and blend at high speed for 30 seconds until smooth. Chill well. Garnish with hard-boiled egg and croutons which have been fried in olive oil and rubbed with onion. Serves 6.

MRS. TONY CHAUVEAUX (KATHRYN)

TOMATO AVOCADO

2 large avocados, peeled and
chopped
1 cup sour cream
4 small tomatoes, chopped
1 can beef bouillon
¼ cup onion, minced

1 teaspoon salt
fresh ground pepper to taste
2 tablespoons lemon juice
1 teaspoon Tabasco
minced chives or green onion tops

Set aside the chives or green onion tops and enough sour cream for garnish. Blend all other ingredients in blender. Serve ice cold in chilled mugs. Garnish with a dollop of sour cream sprinkled with chives or green onion tops. Serves 6.

MRS. WILLIAM J. PLEWES

PANAMANIAN AVOCADO

4 cups beef broth
5 avocados
1 bay leaf
garlic (optional)

salt and pepper to taste
¼ teaspoon marjoram
2 cups whipping cream
1 teaspoon salt

Prepare beef broth, using soup bone covered with 5 or 6 cups cold water. Boil until beef is tender. Skim off fat particles, and remove meat and bone. At least 4 cups of broth should remain. Add bay leaf, salt, pepper, garlic and marjoram. Broth may be prepared the day before.

1 hour before serving, mash 3 peeled avocados. Add to hot beef broth, and mix well. Cut 2 remaining avocados into cubes. Sprinkle

with lemon juice to prevent discoloration, and set aside. Beat cream until thick, adding 1 teaspoon salt. Cover and refrigerate until serving time. When ready to serve, bring broth to a boil. Add a portion of whipped cream, and stir well. Put soup in tureen. Top with whipped cream, and sprinkle with avocado cubes. May also be served in individual bowls. Serves 6.

MRS. ALEXIS SHELOKOV (PAULA)

GOLDEN VEGETABLE SOUP

¼ cup butter
3 carrots, chopped
2 onions, chopped
1 cup shredded cabbage or lettuce
1 (9 oz.) package frozen green
  beans
¼ cup parsley flakes

½ teaspoon salt
2 (13 oz.) cans chicken broth or
  equivalent using bouillon
½ teaspoon caraway or sesame
  seeds
American cheese, sliced

Saute carrots, onions, lettuce or cabbage, and parsley flakes in butter and salt for 20 minutes. Add broth, beans and caraway or sesame seeds. Heat to boiling. Simmer covered for 15 minutes, or as long as 4 hours—it makes no difference. When ready to serve, put a slice of prepackaged cheese in bottom of soup bowls and cover with hot soup. The soup and cheese will mix. Serves 2 for lunch or 4 for first course at dinner.

MRS. BETSY CLARK CASTLE

GARDEN BOUILLON

4 cups beef stock (Spice Island)
2 tablespoons celery leaves,
  minced
4 green onions with tops
4 radishes

2 celery stalks
1 medium carrot
lemon juice to taste
salt and fresh ground pepper

Slice green onions, radishes, celery stalks and carrot very thin. Bring beef stock to boil, lower heat and add vegetables. Simmer for 15 minutes. Add lemon juice and salt and pepper. Vegetables and beef stock may be prepared in advance, but cook just before serving. Serves 4.

MRS. GEOFFREY P. WIEDEMAN (CAROLYN)

CUCUMBER VICHYSSOISE

1 can cream potato soup
1 cup chicken broth
1/2 cup sour cream

1 cup cucumber, peeled, seeded
    and cut in small pieces
chopped chives

Combine all ingredients except chives in a blender and blend at puree setting. Add a few drops of green food coloring. Chill. Garnish with chives. Serves 3 or 4.

MRS. JAMES H. CALVERT

VICHYSQUASH

1 medium onion, chopped
2 tablespoons margarine
1 (13¾ oz.) can chicken broth

1½ lbs. yellow squash, sliced
1 cup half and half
salt and pepper

Saute onion in margarine. Add chicken broth and squash. Continue cooking until squash is tender. Cool. Blend small amounts at a time in a blender. Add cream, salt and pepper to taste. Chill. Serves 6.

MRS. WYNN D. MILLER

LES HALLES ONION SOUP
("Soupe A L'Oignon" from Les Halles Market, Paris, France)

4 large onions, minced
3 tablespoons bacon grease
2 tablespoons flour
1/2 teaspoon salt
1/8 teaspoon ground pepper
1 garlic clove, minced
sprig parsley

pinch thyme
1 quart good chicken stock
1 cup dry white wine
1 tablespoon Cognac
toasted French bread
Parmesan cheese, grated

In a deep, heavy saucepan saute onions in bacon grease until just soft. Add flour, salt, pepper and garlic. Cook until mixture is golden brown. Add parsley, thyme, chicken stock and white wine. Simmer, covered for 45 minutes. Add Cognac. (If you prefer a darker color, add a little Kitchen Bouquet.) Place a thin slice of French bread in individual ovenproof bowls. Sprinkle a layer of cheese on each. Pour soup into bowls and top with another thin slice of bread and a thick layer of grated cheese. Place under the broiler until cheese melts and forms a brown crust. Serve with extra grated cheese. Serves 6.

PUMPKIN SOUP

4 tablespoons butter
4 scallions, chopped
1 small onion, sliced
1½ lbs. pumpkin, peeled and
  diced (canned pumpkin may
  be substituted)
4 cups chicken stock

½ teaspoon salt
2 tablespoons flour
¾ cup light cream, hot
toasted croutons for garnish
whipped cream, salted lightly
  for garnish

Melt 2 tablespoons butter in a large saucepan. Add scallions, onions and saute lightly until they are almost soft, but not brown. Add pumpkin, chicken stock and salt. (If fresh pumpkin is used, cover and simmer until pumpkin is soft.) Mix 2 tablespoons flour with 1 tablespoon butter and add to the soup mixture. Bring the soup to a boil and cook for a few minutes. Put soup through a fine sieve or puree it in a blender. Correct seasoning and add hot cream and 1 tablespoon butter. Heat just to the boiling point and serve garnished with croutons and whipped cream. Serves 6 to 8.

MAJOR WILLIAM DEAN RASCO

ARTICHOKE CREAM SOUP

2 large artichokes
¼ cup celery, minced
¼ cup onion, minced
3 tablespoons flour
1½ tablespoons lemon juice
½ teaspoon salt
⅛ teaspoon thyme

3 tablespoons butter
3 cups clear chicken broth
1 small bay leaf
⅛ teaspoon pepper
1 egg yolk, beaten
1 cup half and half

Prepare artichokes and boil until tender, about 45 minutes or bake for 7 minutes in microwave oven. Scrape the pulp from the artichoke leaves, remove choke and chop bottoms. In a large saucepan, saute onion and celery until tender. Add flour and cook 1 minute, stirring constantly. Add stock, lemon juice and stir until well blended. Add artichoke scrapings, bottoms, salt, pepper and thyme. Cover and simmer about 15 minutes. Add egg yolk, half and half and correct seasonings. Serve chilled. Serves 6.

MRS. CLARENCE A. FEY (HELEN)

ARTICHOKE SHRIMP BISQUE

2 tablespoons butter
1/4 cup green onions, chopped
1/2 teaspoon thyme
2 cans Campbell's tomato rice
  soup

2 3/4 cups chicken broth
1 cup artichoke hearts, chopped
1 cup shrimp pieces
seasoned salt
lemon juice or sherry (optional)

Cook green onions and thyme in butter for 5 minutes over low heat; do not brown. Stir in tomato rice soup and chicken broth. Add artichoke hearts, shrimp pieces, and seasoned salt to taste. Heat to serving temperature, but do not boil. Add either 2 teaspoons lemon juice or sherry, if desired. Serves 4 to 6.

PRIS FLAWN

SUSANA'S LENTIL SOUP

1 lb. dried lentils
6 to 8 cups cold water, or
  chicken bouillon
1 clove garlic, minced
1 medium green pepper, minced

1/4 teaspoon comino powder
1 smoked turkey carcass or ham
  bone
margarine

Wash lentils well and place in heavy pot with other ingredients except margarine. Bring to boil, reduce heat, and simmer until lentils are tender and mushy, at least 2 hours. Remove bones, mince meat, and return meat to soup after lentils have been pureed. If desired, thin soup with water or broth. Add salt to taste and margarine as desired. Serve with chopped tomatoes and onions on the side and a dollop of sour cream and/or sherry

Less cooking time is required if lentils are soaked overnight. Susana likes to make broth from turkey carcass or ham bone in advance and freeze it for future use. Excellent for split pea, navy bean, and many other soups. Use bouillon mix if broth is not available. Whole soup may be made in advance and frozen. When ready to serve, thaw slowly, heat over low heat. Serves 6.

MRS. MARTIN F. CASEY

Salad & Salad Dressing

A meal needs a salad. It needs the crisp texture of chilled salad greens, the bright color of fresh fruits and vegetables, the piquant flavor of a well-seasoned dressing.

Salad can be a first course, a main course or an in-between course. And on a hot August afternoon in San Antonio, there is no better light summer lunch.

The job of the salad dressing is to enhance the flavor of the fruits or vegetables. Use only enough to coat each leaf or berry and leave it sparkling and shiny, with no excess dressing left in the bowl.

MORTON'S HERB MAYONNAISE

2 teaspoons Mayonnaise Mustard (available in small jars)
2 teaspoons salt
2 teaspoons paprika
1 teaspoon sugar
4 egg yolks
2 tablespoons boiling water
2 tablespoons lemon juice
2 tablespoons vinegar
1 teaspoon oregano
1 teaspoon dill
1 teaspoon basil
1 teaspoon onion powder
1/4 teaspoon garlic powder
Angostura Bitters (optional)
2 cups salad oil

In a small deep bowl, combine all dry ingredients and mix well. Add the egg yolks and mix well. THEN ADD BOILING WATER. (The dressing will never separate.) Mix and add oil, a little at a time first, then faster. Add the lemon juice and vinegar. This keeps well, covered in the refrigerator but do not freeze.

MORTON BROWN

GREEN MAYONNAISE

1 cup mayonnaise
1 tablespoon chopped chives
1 tablespoon chopped parsley
1 tablespoon chopped tarragon
1 tablespoon chopped spinach
1 tablespoon chopped capers

Mix well, or blend in blender, as desired. Makes 1 1/4 cups.

- 111 -

SUPER BLEU CHEESE DRESSING

1 lb. Bleu cheese, crumbled
1 large onion, minced
1 quart mayonnaise
2 hard-boiled eggs, chopped fine

½ (14½ oz.) can evaporated
  milk
2 jiggers Brandy
salt and pepper to taste

Combine all ingredients and refrigerate. For best results this should be made in advance and allowed to chill thoroughly before serving. If the dressing seems too thick at serving time, very carefully thin with a tiny bit of evaporated milk. May also be made with Roquefort cheese.

For many years, this dressing was a closely guarded secret at the Officers' Open Mess, Tachikawa Air Force Base in Japan. Its distinctive flavor is the addition of Brandy.

MRS. JOSEPH J. JOHN (CUPE)

LOW CALORIE YOGURT DRESSING

1 cup yogurt
juice of ½ lemon
2 teaspoons tarragon vinegar

1½ teaspoons Dijon mustard
1½ teaspoons Beau Monde
  seasoning salt

Mix all ingredients well and chill. Vary the amount of seasonings to suit your taste. This is an excellent dip for raw vegetables.

MRS. CARRIGAN FITZSIMONS

POPPY SEED DRESSING

1½ cups sugar
2 teaspoons dry mustard
2 teaspoons salt
⅔ cup vinegar

2 teaspoons onion juice
2 cups salad oil
1 tablespoon poppy seeds

Combine and beat sugar, dry mustard, salt and vinegar. Add onion juice. Add salad oil, slowly. When thick, add poppy seeds. Chill before serving. Makes 3 cups.

JOSKE'S OF TEXAS
SAN ANTONIO

BEAUTIFUL BEANS

1 can French cut green beans
1 can wax beans
1 large can kidney beans, rinsed
1 green pepper, chopped
1 carrot, chopped
1 onion, sliced (optional)
1 package Italian Good Seasons salad dressing
⅓ cup sugar
½ cup vinegar
⅔ cup salad oil

Toss all ingredients together. Let stand at least 24 hours. Turn several times to insure even distribution of vegetables. Serves 6.

MRS. WILLIAM L. STARNES (MARY DEE)

MARINATED MEDLEY

1 package frozen artichoke hearts
1 (4 oz.) can mushrooms
1 (1 lb.) can French green beans
1 cup cooked carrot strips
1 medium red onion, sliced
Italian Dressing
anchovy fillets
pimientos, sliced
8 lettuce cups

Cook artichoke hearts according to directions and drain well. Combine with mushrooms, beans, carrots and onion. Moisten with dressing. Chill and marinate for 2 hours. Arrange on lettuce cups and garnish with pimientos and anchovy. Serves 8.

MRS. GERALD W. MASSY III (DOROTHY)

VEGETABLE GARDEN RELISH

1 small cauliflower
2 cups carrots
2 cups celery
2 green peppers
1 (4 oz.) jar pimientos, drained
2 (3 oz.) jars green pitted olives, drained
¾ cup white vinegar
½ cup salad oil
1 teaspoon salt
½ teaspoon oregano
¼ teaspoon pepper
2 tablespoons sugar
½ cup water

Break cauliflower into flowerettes and slice. Cut carrots into 2 inch strips and celery into 1 inch strips until you have 2 cups of each. Cut green peppers and pimiento into strips. Combine all ingredients in a large skillet. Bring to a boil, stirring occasionally. Reduce heat, cover and simmer for 5 minutes. Allow to cool and refrigerate for at least

24 hours. Drain well before serving. Serves 8 to 10 for dinner or 25 for a buffet.

ROSE SPECTOR
Judge, Bexar County, State of Texas

COLORFUL CAULIFLOWER

4 cups cauliflower
1 cup coarsely chopped ripe
  olives
2/3 cup chopped green pepper
1/2 cup coarsely chopped
  pimiento

1 grated onion
1/2 cup salad or olive oil
3 tablespoons lemon juice
1 teaspoon seasoning salt
1/2 teaspoon sugar
1/4 teaspoon pepper

Break cauliflower into flowerettes and slice, fan-shaped, until you have 4 cups. Combine all ingredients and mix well. Serves 4 to 6.

MRS. JOHNSON LEWENTHAL (PAT)

CAULIFLOWER SLAW

3 cups cauliflower, coarsely
  shredded
1 cup radishes, coarsely shredded
1/3 cup mayonnaise
1/4 cup milk

1 tablespoon fresh lemon juice
1/4 teaspoon dried dill weed
1/4 teaspoon salt
dash white pepper
Lawry's seasoned salt

Combine cauliflower and radishes and season with Lawry's salt. Combine mayonnaise, milk, lemon juice, dill, salt, and pepper. Pour over vegetable mixture, toss, and chill. Garnish with thin slices of radish, and sprinkle with dill weed. Serves 6.

GAY EASTWOOD

VEGETABLES VERONA

1 cup celery, chopped
1 cup French-style green beans
1 cup Leseur peas
1 small can Leseur "Shoepeg"
  white corn

1 cup onions, chopped
1 cup green peppers, chopped
1 (8 oz.) bottle Wishbone
  Italian dressing

Drain beans, corn, and peas. Mix with onions, celery, and green pepper. Add dressing. Marinate for 3 days. Drain. Serve in glass bowl, and garnish with slices of pimiento. Serves 8.

ELIZABETH HAMILTON O'NEILL (MRS. LARRY)

DOLORES SALAD

2 to 3 yellow summer squash,
  cubed
2 to 3 zucchini, cubed
1 can baby whole carrots

1 box cherry tomatoes, halved
1 bottle Italian Salad Dressing
salt to taste

Drop squash into boiling salted water and boil for 2 minutes so the vegetables will retain crispness without tasting raw. Drain and cool. When cool add the baby carrots, cherry tomatoes and marinate in the Italian Dressing for at least 4 hours or better still, overnight. Serves 4.

MRS. MARGARET A. WRIGHT

CABBAGE APPLE SALAD

1 medium green cabbage
½ can Diamond Hickory Smoked
  Almonds, chopped
3 celery stalks, chopped
2 unpeeled apples, cubed

lemon juice
sour cream
mayonnaise
Kraft Coleslaw Dressing
1 small red cabbage

Chop the cabbages and combine with almonds and celery. Moisten the apples with lemon juice and mix with equal parts mayonnaise, sour cream and Coleslaw Dressing. Serves 6 to 8.

MRS. EUGENE E. MASSY

TWENTY FOUR HOUR SALAD

1 lb. fresh spinach
4 hard-boiled eggs, sliced
1 lb. bacon, broiled crisp
1 small head lettuce, shredded
2 Bermuda onions, sliced thin
1 large bag frozen peas, regular
  size

½ cup mayonnaise
½ cup Miracle Whip Salad
  Dressing
salt and pepper
sugar to taste
12 oz. Baby Swiss cheese,
  shredded

Place spinach, washed, dried well and torn in pieces into a large glass salad bowl so the layers may be seen. Sprinkle with salt, pepper and sugar. Add a layer of eggs, crumbled bacon, lettuce and again sprinkle with salt, pepper and sugar. Add a layer of onions and uncooked frozen peas. Repeat this process until the bowl is filled. Cover and refrigerate overnight. Early in the morning of the day the salad is to be used, mix mayonnaise and Miracle Whip and spoon on top of the salad. (This serves as a topping and will penetrate through the salad.) Add cheese and refrigerate until serving time. Serves 12.

MRS. WILLIAM GLASSER (MARLENE)

DRESSED SPINACH SALAD

2 lbs. fresh spinach	1 tablespoon sugar
6 slices bacon	1 tablespoon vinegar
3 tablespoons flour	1/4 teaspoon salt
1 1/3 cups water	2 hard-boiled eggs, sliced

Clean spinach, drain well and tear, uncooked, into bowl. Cut bacon in fine pieces and fry crisp. Remove and drain. Add flour to bacon fat and cook until bubbly. Add water and stir into a sauce. Add sugar, vinegar, and salt. Pour piping hot sauce over spinach and bacon mixture and toss. Transfer to a hot dish for serving. Garnish with sliced egg. Serves 8.

MRS. VICTOR VAN NUFFELEN

SESAME SNOWPEA SALAD

1 (7 oz.) package frozen snowpeas	1/3 cup salad oil
	1 tablespoon lemon juice
1/2 head cauliflower	1 tablespoon vinegar
1 (5 oz.) can water chestnuts, drained and sliced	1 tablespoon sugar
	1/2 clove garlic, minced
1 tablespoon pimiento, chopped	1/2 teaspoon salt
2 tablespoons sesame seeds	

The day before serving, bake sesame seeds in shallow pan at 350° 5 to 8 minutes, or until golden brown; cool. In covered jar, combine salad oil, lemon juice, vinegar, sugar, garlic, salt, and sesame seeds. Chill overnight. Cook peas in small amount of boiling salted water until barely tender, about 1 minute and drain. Separate cauliflower into bite-size clusters to make 2 cups. Cook 3 minutes in boiling salted water until tender, but still crisp. Combine peas and cauliflower with chestnuts and pimiento; cover and chill. Shortly before serving, combine vegetable mixture with 3 tablespoons sesame seed dressing. Serve on lettuce. Serves 4 to 6.

VIVIAN M. GERSEMA

CUCUMBER SOUR CREAM SALAD

1 medium cucumber
1 teaspoon salt
1/2 cup sour cream
1 tablespoon vinegar

1 or 2 drops Tabasco sauce
2 tablespoons chopped chives
1 teaspoon dill seeds
dash pepper

Slice cucumber thin and sprinkle with salt. Let stand 30 minutes. Drain. Combine other ingredients. Stir and pour over cucumber slices. Chill 30 minutes. Serve as relish or salad. Serves 4 to 6.

CUCUMBER CHEESE RING

2 cucumbers, peeled, seeded and
  diced
1 lb. Cottage cheese
1/2 cup milk
1 cup mayonnaise

1 cup sour cream
2 envelopes plain gelatin
2 tablespoons onion, grated
salt and pepper to taste

Mix sieved cottage cheese with sour cream, mayonnaise and onion. Add gelatin which has been softened in milk and dissolved over hot water. Stir cucumbers into mixture. Pour into mold after seasoning with salt and pepper. Chill well. To serve, unmold on lettuce and garnish with tomato and onion slices. Serves 6 to 8.

MRS. MADISON NEILSON

TOMATO ASPIC

2 lbs. canned tomatoes
3/4 cup cold water
1 teaspoon salt
2 teaspoons sugar
1/2 teaspoon Worcestershire
1/2 teaspoon pepper
1 tablespoon onion, chopped
2 tablespoons celery, chopped
2 cloves

1 bay leaf
generous dash Tabasco
2 tablespoons gelatin
1/2 cup cold water
1 can tomato soup
1 tablespoon lemon juice
small can imported caviar
5 eggs, hard-boiled
mayonnaise

For 30 minutes, slowly cook tomatoes, water, salt, sugar, Worcestershire sauce, pepper, onion, celery, cloves, bay leaf, and Tabasco. Soak gelatin in 1/2 cup cold water for 15 minutes. Add tomato soup to tomato mixture, and stir while still over fire. Add gelatin. Puree in food mill. Add lemon juice. Pour small amount of aspic into molds that have been rinsed or sprayed with Pam. Chill until firm. Split eggs lengthwise. Remove yolks and mash with enough mayonnaise to make a smooth paste. Add caviar to paste, mixing gently. Stuff eggs with mixture. Place an egg half, stuffed side down, on top of set aspic. Fill molds with remaining aspic and chill until firm. Serve unmolded on lettuce, topped with mayonnaise. Makes 8 to 10 molds. For variety, replace eggs with seafood, asparagus tips, or mixed vegetables, such as peas and celery.

MRS. HARRIS OPPENHEIMER

ASHVILLE MOLDED SALAD

2 tablespoons unflavored gelatin
1/2 cup cold water
1 can tomato soup, undiluted
1 large package cream cheese
1 1/2 cups celery, chopped
1 cup Hellmans mayonnaise

2 tablespoons green pepper, chopped
1/4 cup green or ripe olives, chopped
1/4 to 1/2 cup nuts, chopped

Soak gelatin in cold water for 5 minutes. Heat soup to boiling, remove from heat and add gelatin. Stir until dissolved. Add cream cheese, stirring until smooth. When almost cool, fold in mayonnaise and vegetables and turn into a large mold or 10 or 12 individual molds. Chill. Serve on lettuce leaves and garnish with mayonnaise or French dressing. Serves 6 as a main dish salad or 10 to 12 as a side dish salad.

MRS. LYMAN R. FINK (FRANCES)

ARTICHOKE SURPRISE

artichoke hearts
1 can tomato soup
1/2 can water
1 (8 oz.) package cream cheese
1 envelope gelatin

1 cup mayonnaise
1/2 cup celery, chopped
olives, chopped
salt and pepper to taste
Worcestershire to taste

Heat soup, water and cream cheese. Dissolve gelatin in 1/4 cup cold water and add to mixture with other ingredients except artichokes. Pour into individual molds, place 1 artichoke heart in center of each mold. Serves 12.

MRS. JOHN KEFAUVER (LISA)

AVOCADO MOUSSE

2 envelopes unflavored gelatin
1/4 cup cold water
1 cup chicken broth
1 1/2 teaspoons Worcestershire
1 1/2 tablespoons lemon juice
2 to 3 tablespoons green onion

1/2 teaspoon sugar
1 teaspoon salt
3/4 cup sour cream
3/4 cup mayonnaise
2 large or 3 small avocados

Dissolve gelatin in cold water; heat broth, and add gelatin. Add Worcestershire, lemon juice, sugar and salt. Chill. Puree avocado, green onions, mayonnaise, and sour cream in blender. Mix well. Add to gelatin mixture, and place in oiled ring mold or 8 individual 1/2 cup molds. Serves 8.

MRS. E. MORGAN SCHMIDT (SYBIL)

BROCCOLI MOUSSE

1 (10 oz.) package frozen
chopped broccoli
1 can beef consomme
1 1/2 envelopes unflavored gelatin
1/4 cup cold water

2 tablespoons lemon juice
1 tablespoon garlic flavored
vinegar
2/3 cup mayonnaise

Cook broccoli according to package directions until almost done and drain well. Heat consomme. Soften gelatin in cold water. Combine consomme, gelatin, lemon juice and vinegar. Stir until gelatin is dissolved. Chill until syrupy. Beat the mixture with a rotary beater, add mayonnaise and beat again. Fold in broccoli and pour into a lightly oiled 3-cup mold. Chill until firm. Serves 6.

MRS. GEORGE V. SHAW

BORSCHT FRUIT MOLD

1 (16 oz.) can shoestring beets
1 (8 3/4 oz.) can crushed pineapple
2 (3 oz.) packages lemon Jello

2 cups boiling water
2 tablespoons lemon juice
dash salt

Drain beets and pineapple, reserving 1 1/2 cups of combined liquid. Dissolve gelatin in boiling water. Stir in reserved beet-pineapple liquid, lemon juice, and salt. Chill until partially set. Fold in beets and pineapple. Pour gelatin mixture into a 6 1/2 cup mold or 8 to 10 (1/2 cup) molds. Chill until firm. Serves 8.

MRS. W. M. IVES (MAUDE)

MOLDED RAINBOW FRUIT SALAD

2 (3 oz.) packages lemon Jello
¼ cup sugar
1½ cups boiling water
1 (8 oz.) package cream cheese
½ cup fresh orange juice
½ teaspoon lemon peel, grated
2 tablespoons lemon juice
1 cup carrots, shredded
1 cup pared or unpared apples, chopped

Dissolve gelatin and sugar in boiling water. Add cream cheese and beat well. Stir in orange juice, lemon peel and lemon juice. Chill until partially set. Add carrots and apples. Spoon into ring mold and chill until set. Unmold. Fill center and around the ring with a variety of fresh fruit such as blueberries, strawberries, melon balls, fresh pineapple, etc. Serves 8.

MRS. J. HOWARD FREDERICK

MAMA'S HOLIDAY SALAD

1½ packages lemon Jello
1 cup boiling water
1 cup cabbage, shredded
1 package miniature marshmallows
1 (15¼ oz.) can crushed pineapple, drained
3 cartons whipping cream
2 teaspoons sugar

Make Jello with the boiling water. When it cools add cabbage, marshmallows and pineapple. Whip cream, adding sugar and fold into the Jello. Pour into a shallow pyrex dish and chill. To serve, cut into squares and place on lettuce leaves. Serves 8.

MRS. JOHN THOMAS STEEN (NELL)

FRESH FRUIT COTTAGE CHEESE RING

½ cup pineapple juice
1 envelope unflavored gelatin
2 full cups Cottage cheese
1 cup fresh orange sections
1 cup fresh grapefruit sections
1 cup ripe bananas, cut in large cubes
1 cup apples, cut in small cubes
mayonnaise
lemon juice

Dissolve gelatin in pineapple juice in a double boiler. Heat gently. Add sieved Cottage cheese. Pour cheese mixture into a lightly buttered ring mold and chill until firm. Rub apples and bananas with a little lemon juice. Marinate apples, bananas, orange sections and grapefruit sections with a little mayonnaise. Unmold cheese mixture on a serving platter. Surround with crisp lettuce leaves and fill the center of the ring to overflowing with fruit. Serves 6 to 8.

MRS. LUTCHER BROWN

WALDORF CHICKEN SALAD

1 chicken
2 Delicious or Golden Delicious
  apples, peeled and chopped
1/2 cup celery, chopped
3/4 cup pecans or walnuts,
  chopped

3 heaping tablespoons homemade
  or safflower mayonnaise
1/2 cup jicama chopped
  (optional)

Boil chicken in salted water with a small amount of onion and celery for flavor. When tender, cool, remove meat from bones, and cut in small pieces. Combine apples, celery, nuts, and jicama with mayonnaise. Add chicken, and mix thoroughly. Additional mayonnaise may be required. Serve on large lettuce leaf with asparagus or broccoli and hot rolls for luncheon plate. Serves 6.

MRS. RICHARD D. SMALL, JR. (MARGE)

HAWAIIAN CHICKEN VELVET SALAD

1 cup cooked chicken, diced
1/2 cup drained pineapple tidbits
1 envelope unflavored gelatin
1/4 cup cold water
1 (10 1/2 oz.) can cream chicken
  soup
1 (3 oz.) package cream cheese

2 tablespoons lemon juice
dash ground ginger
1/4 cup celery, chopped
1/4 cup green pepper, chopped
toasted, slivered almonds
salad greens

Sprinkle gelatin in water to soften. Place over low heat, stir until dissolved. Gradually blend soup with cream cheese; stir in gelatin, lemon juice, ginger. Add chicken, pineapple, celery, green pepper. Pour into 1 qt. mold and chill until firm. Unmold on greens. Garnish with almonds. Serves 4.

DOSIE MYERS

CHINESE CHICKEN SALAD

2 chicken breasts, cooked
1 lettuce head
8 cocktail onions, sliced
1 small dill pickle, chopped
4 or 5 green onions, sliced
2 tablespoons sesame seed, toasted
1 tablespoon ginger root, grated
1/2 cup salted peanuts
1/2 bottle Italian Dressing
1 oz. Mei Fun (rice sticks or bean threads)
sliced cucumber

Tear chicken into small pieces and lettuce into bite-size pieces. Combine with the remaining ingredients, except Mei Fun. Break Mei Fun and fry, a small amount at a time, in deep fat. (Mei Fun puffs up to twice the original size.) Use as garnish for the salad. Serves 8.

LUCY S. GREER (MRS. RICHARD P.)

CHICKEN SALAD VERONIQUE

4 to 5 cups cooked chicken, cut in large chunks
2 teaspoons grated onion
1 cup chopped celery
1/2 cup minced green pepper
2 cups halved, seedless green grapes
1/4 cup light cream
2/3 cup mayonnaise
1 teaspoon salt
1/8 teaspoon pepper
2 tablespoons vinegar
2/3 cup slivered toasted almonds

Combine chicken, onion, celery, green peppers, almonds and grapes. Mix cream with mayonnaise, salt, pepper and vinegar. Toss with chicken mixture. Refrigerate. To serve, arrange salad on greens. Circle with asparagus tips and sliced hard cooked eggs. Serves 6 to 8.

JANE COOPER

ROCK LOBSTER NICOISE

3 (7 oz.) frozen lobster tails
1 cup celery, diced
1/2 cup almonds, slivered
1 tablespoon onion, minced
3/4 cup Hellman's mayonnaise
2 tablespoons cream
2 tablespoons lemon juice
1/4 teaspoon sugar
1/4 teaspoon salt
1/4 teaspoon tarragon
1/8 teaspoon white pepper

Boil lobster tails 1 minute longer than individual weight (plus 2 minutes, if frozen). Remove meat from shells, and cut in bite-size pieces. Add celery, almonds, and onion. Combine mayonnaise, cream, lemon juice, sugar, seasonings and add to other ingredients. Toss lightly. Serve on crisp greens. Garnish with almonds and ripe olives. Serves 3 to 4.

MRS. CLIFFORD J. BUCKLEY (HELEN)

AVOCADO SHRIMP SALAD

2 lbs. cocktail shrimp
4 large avocados, mashed
3 stalks celery, chopped fine
3 large tomatoes, peeled and
   chopped

canned milk, (optional)
salt and pepper, to taste
Tabasco (optional)

Cook, peel and devein shrimp. Combine all ingredients. Serve on lettuce cups. Serves 4 to 6.

MRS. ABE SAN MIGUEL

SAVOY SHRIMP SALAD

4 lbs. shrimp, cooked
12 hard boiled eggs
1 bunch celery
1 can pitted ripe olives, drained
2 cans bamboo shoots or
   artichoke hearts, sliced and
   drained

1 small onion, minced
1/2 cup lemon juice
1 cup real mayonnaise
salt and pepper
dash Tabasco (optional)
1/2 cup parsley, minced
   (optional)

Peel and devein shrimp. Coarsely chop hard boiled eggs and diagonally slice celery very thin. Combine all ingredients, adding more mayonnaise and lemon juice, if necessary. Serves 20 to 24.

ALTHEA D. ELEY

cocke

Meat

From the days of the pioneers, Texans have been cattlemen and ranchers. The great cattle drives, before the advent of the railroad, began in South Texas and San Antonio.

Today, the legendary Texas Longhorn of the Old West has given way to more modern breeds of cattle. Among them is the Santa Gertrudis which was developed on the famous King Ranch. This ranch was founded by Captain Richard King in 1853 and is still the largest ranch in the country today.

Texans will always love meat in any form — from hamburgers to sauerbraten — but a thick, tender sirloin sizzling over hot coals is a favorite with everyone, everywhere.

SUPERB PRIME RIB

Remove the roast from the refrigerator 2 to 4 hours before cooking time. Preheat oven to 500°. Place the roast in a shallow roasting pan, fat side up. Sprinkle with a little flour and rub the flour lightly into the fat. Season with salt and pepper. Place the roast in the very hot oven and bake according to weight, about 5 minutes per pound.

4½ to 5 lbs.	25 to 30 minutes
8 to 9 lbs.	40 to 45 minutes
11 to 12 lbs.	55 to 60 minutes

When cooking time is finished, turn off the oven. Do not open the door at any time. Allow the roast to remain in the oven until the oven is lukewarm, about 2 hours.

This method of cooking a Prime Rib will insure a crunchy brown outside and the internal heat will be suitable for serving juicy, medium rare beef for as long as 4 hours.

MRS. GILBERT L. CURTIS (LORRIE)

THE ARGYLE — Mildred Cocke

SOY SPICE MARINATED TENDERLOIN

1 cup soy sauce
2 teaspoons ground ginger
2 tablespoons molasses
4 cloves garlic, chopped

½ cup oil
2 teaspoons dry mustard
2 tablespoons brown sugar
dash ground pepper

Combine all ingredients. Marinate tenderloin for 24 hours at room temperature, or 36 hours in refrigerator. Broil over charcoal for 15 to 30 minutes, depending on size of tenderloin. May be baked at high temperature in oven. Double marinade recipe for two tenderloins.

MRS. LEO F. DUSARD, JR. (BETTY)

BEEF BOURGUIGNON

½ cup salt pork diced
1 tablespoon olive oil
3 lbs. lean top round of
   rump roast cut in 2 inch pieces
1 yellow onion, sliced
4 tablespoons brandy
3¼ cups good dry red wine
2 cups beef broth
1 large clove garlic pressed
1 pinch of thyme
1 pinch of sugar

1 carrot, sliced
salt and pepper to taste
2½ tablespoons flour
1 tablespoon tomato paste
1 bay leaf crumbled
24 pearl onions
4 tablespoons butter
12 mushroom caps
1 tablespoon minced parsley
lemon juice

Saute pork in olive oil in oven proof casserole until lightly browned and remove to a side dish. Cook beef quickly in hot oil and salt pork fat until browned on all sides. Season to taste with salt and pepper. Heat brandy and pour over meat in casserole, ignite and let flame burn away. Remove beef and set aside. Brown carrots and onion in same fat. Pour off excess. Return beef and pork to casserole. Sprinkle flour on meat to coat lightly. Place in covered casserole in center rack of preheated 450° oven for 4 minutes. Remove casserole from oven and toss meat with a fork. Return casserole to oven and roast 4 minutes longer to form a crust on meat. Reduce temperature to 325° and add 3 cups wine and enough beef broth to barely cover meat. Add tomato paste, garlic and herbs. Stir to blend, cover and return to oven. Cook about 3 hours or until meat is fork tender. Meanwhile, brown pearl onions in 2 tablespoons butter in a saucepan with a little sugar. Add remaining wine. Cover and cook over low heat until onions are tender. Keep warm. Saute mushrooms in remaining 2 tablespoons butter and a few drops of lemon juice. Keep warm. When meat is tender pour contents of casserole into colander, reserving liquid. Wash casserole. Arrange meat, vegetables, onions and mushrooms in casserole. Skim fat off sauce. Cook sauce to reduce volume to about 2½ cups. If sauce is too thin, cook longer to thicken, until it will lightly coat a spoon. Taste to correct seasonings. Pour sauce over meat. Garnish with parsley. Serve with small boiled potatoes, buttered noodles or rice. Can be made in advance, refrigerated overnight. Remove and discard congealed layer of fat. Heat thoroughly to serve. Serves 4 to 6.

MRS. LEO F. DUSARD, JR. (BETTY)

BURGUNDY BEEF

2 tablespoons shortening
5 medium onions, sliced
½ lb. mushrooms
2 lbs. boneless beef, chuck
  trimmed and sliced
  or round, cut in cubes
  1 inch thick
1 teaspoon salt
¼ teaspoon marjoram

¼ teaspoon thyme
⅛ teaspoon pepper
1½ tablespoons flour
¾ cup beef broth, 1 beef
  bouillon cube or 1 teaspoon
  instant beef bouillon dissolved
  in ¾ cup boiling water
1½ cups red Burgundy

Melt shortening in large skillet. Saute onions until tender and remove. In same skillet brown meat. Add mushrooms. Mix flour and broth. Stir into skillet. Heat to boiling, stirring constantly for one minute. Stir in wine then cover and simmer 1½ to 2 hours or until meat is tender. Liquid should always cover meat. If necessary, add more broth and wine, 1 part broth to 2 parts wine. Gently stir in onions and mushrooms. Cook 15 minutes or until heated through. Serves 4 to 6.

BEVERLY CARSON

BEEF TIPS NAPOLI

3 lbs. boneless chuck, rump
  or lean stew meat
1 teaspoon salt
1 teaspoon pepper
3 tablespoons vegetable oil
1½ cups water
1 cup dry red wine
2 (6 oz.) cans tomato paste
3 tablespoons lemon juice
½ teaspoon sugar

1 teaspoon marjoram or
  oregano
1 small carrot thinly sliced
1 clove garlic crushed or ⅛
  teaspoon garlic powder
1 pound sea shell or elbow
  macaroni, cooked
1 cup grated parmesan cheese
2 tablespoons chopped parsley
  or chives

Cut beef into 1½ inch cubes. Sprinkle with salt and pepper. In a large skillet brown meat in oil. Mix tomato paste with water, wine, lemon juice, sugar, marjoram, carrot and garlic. Pour over meat. Cover and simmer for 1½ to 2 hours or until beef is tender. Add more water and a little wine if sauce thickens too fast. Serve with boiled and drained macaroni blended with parmesan cheese and parsley. May be assembled in advance of cooking, and may be cooked in advance of serving time and reheated. Serves 6 to 8.

MRS. F. DANIEL FOLEY (CARROLL)

STROGANOFF SPECIALITE

3½ lbs. beef tenderloin
½ cup flour
1 teaspoon salt
¼ teaspoon pepper
1½ sticks butter, clarified
½ cup dry Sherry
1 lb. fresh mushrooms or
  2 to 4 cans

1 or 2 additional tablespoons
  butter
2 cups beef consomme
dash of monosodium glutamate
½ teaspoon paprika
½ cup sour cream
2 tablespoons chopped parsley

Remove all excess fat from beef and cut into pieces about 2 inches x ½ inch in size. Dredge beef in flour seasoned with 1 teaspoon salt and 1 teaspoon freshly ground pepper. Brown the meat quickly in clarified butter. Add sherry. Scrape skillet well so as to use all the residue and pour over meat which has been put into a larger pot. Wash and stem 1 lb. fresh mushrooms, slice fine. Cook a few minutes with 1 or 2 tablespoons of butter, just long enough to extract liquid. Add liquid to beef, reserving mushrooms. If using canned mushrooms, cook quickly in butter and add liquid during cooking if necessary. Add to the meat 2 cups hot beef consomme, a dash of monosodium glutamate and 1/2 teaspoon paprika. Simmer meat over a low heat for 20 minutes (this is a good point for freezing or refrigeration). Add the mushrooms and simmer for another 10 minutes. Allow to cool, remove fat from surface. (Strips of paper toweling laid for a second in the gravy will absorb the last bits of fat.) Before serving, reheat in top part of large double boiler over boiling water. Put into a serving casserole and hold in a low oven. When the meat is very hot, stir in sour cream to taste, about 1/2 cup, and garnish with chopped parsley. Serves 8.

MRS. GERALD W. MASSY III (DOROTHY)

BEEF STROGANOFF

1/4 cup butter
1 cup minced onion
2 lbs. tenderloin sliced thin
1 clove garlic, minced
2 tablespoons flour
2 teaspoons salt
1/4 teaspoon Accent

1/4 teaspoon pepper
1/4 teaspoon paprika
2 small cans sliced mushrooms
1 can undiluted cream of
  chicken soup
1 cup sour cream
snipped parsley

Saute onions in butter until golden. Add garlic and meat. Blend dry ingredients and sprinkle over meat mixture. Add undrained mushrooms and saute 10 minutes. Add soup and simmer uncovered 15 minutes. Add sour cream. Simmer 3 minutes. Sprinkle with parsley. Serve on rice. Serves 6.

MRS. CLIFFORD J. BUCKLEY (HELEN)

ROUND STEAK ITALIENNE

round steak cut approximately
  1/2 inch thick
1/4 cup flour
1 teaspoon salt
1/4 teaspoon pepper
3 tablespoons shortening
2 cups canned tomatoes

1/2 teaspoon oregano
1/2 teaspoon dry mustard
1 clove garlic, minced
1/2 teaspoon chopped parsley
1/4 cup dry red wine
1 cup mozzarella cheese, grated

Cut steak into serving pieces. Mix together flour, salt and pepper, and dredge meat in seasoned flour. Brown meat in shortening and remove to shallow casserole. Add tomatoes, oregano, mustard, garlic, parsley and wine to skillet in which meat was browned and bring to a boil. Pour sauce over meat, cover the casserole and bake in 350° oven for 1 hour. Uncover, top with cheese and bake about 5 minutes longer or until cheese melts. Serves 4.

MRS. RICHARD EDDLEMAN (CAROL)

POT ROAST INDIENNE

4 to 5 lbs. beef roast
1 teaspoon salt
2 tablespoons lemon juice
3 slices bacon
1 clove garlic
⅔ cup chopped onion

¼ cup chopped parsley
4 whole cloves
½ teaspoon cinnamon
½ bay leaf
1 cup canned tomatoes
1 cup orange juice

Season meat with salt and lemon juice. Cook bacon, remove from pan. Brown meat in bacon drippings. Combine all remaining ingredients except orange juice. Pour over meat and simmer 10 minutes. Add orange juice and simmer 3 hours. Add water if necessary. Delicious served with Curried Fruit (see Index). Serves 6 to 8.

MRS. ARTHUR E. GRANT

NO PEEK STEW

2 lbs. lean beef cut in bite
  size pieces
1 can mushroom soup
1 package dry onion soup
1 teaspoon beef concentrate or
  1 bouillon cube

¾ cup red wine
dash of herbs—thyme,
  marjoram, paprika, parsley,
  etc. to taste

Put beef cubes in large bowl. Add soups and herbs. Mix well with hands. Add wine and mix again. Put into closely covered casserole. Bake for 3 hours at 300°. Do not lift cover during cooking. NO PEEK! Serves 4 to 6.

MRS. JAMES M. TODD

BAKED COMPANY STEW

3 lbs. stew meat (sirloin tips or any good cut)

3 large carrots, diced or small chunks

10 to 12 small white boiling onions

1 (No. 2) can tomatoes

1 (No. 2) can tiny peas, drained

pepper, to taste

1 (No. 2) can small green beans, drained

½ can beef consomme

½ cup white wine

½ cup dry bread crumbs

4 tablespoons minute tapioca

1 bay leaf

1 tablespoon brown sugar

1½ teaspoons salt, to taste

Mix ingredients and put in large, heavy roaster. Cover and cook in 250° oven for 6 or 7 hours. Stir occasionally. Serve by itself or with tiny whole potatoes or wild rice. Serves 6.

SALLY KLENDSHOJ

HONG KONG BEEF

1 lb. stewing beef, cut into 1 inch cubes

3 tablespoons cooking oil

1 cup red wine

¼ cup soy sauce

1 (4 oz.) can mushrooms

1 tablespoon cornstarch

⅓ cup beef broth

1 cup onions, sliced

1 cup celery, sliced

fried noodles, packaged or canned, heated

rice, cooked

Brown beef cubes quickly in 2 tablespoons hot oil. Add wine and soy sauce. Simmer, covered about 1 hour. (Add more liquid during this time, if needed). Drain mushrooms, saving liquid. Combine mushroom liquid, cornstarch and beef broth and add to meat, stirring until mixture boils and thickens, then add mushrooms. Heat 1 tablespoon oil and cook onions and celery, stirring for about 5 minutes, or until vegetables are translucent. Do not let vegetables brown. Spoon beef and gravy, then vegetables over rice. Top with crisp fried noodles. Serves 4.

CYNTHIA SAROSDY

MEATBALLS MARIANNA

2 lbs. ground meat
1 can cream mushroom soup
½ cup sour cream
¼ cup white wine or sherry
¼ tablespoon summer savory
½ cup chopped onion

½ tablespoon salt
¼ tablespoon cracked pepper
6 large, fresh mushrooms, sliced
1 whole egg
2 tablespoons Worcestershire
2 tablespoons flour

Mix meat, onions, eggs, savory, Worcestershire, salt and pepper. Form into balls. Roll balls lightly in flour. Saute and brown meatballs in bacon grease for 15 minutes. Add soup, sour cream, sherry or white wine, fresh mushrooms, and simmer 10 minutes. Add crumpled bacon to the sauce. Serves 2 to 4.

MRS. JOE H. FROST

VERDURA MEAT LOAF

3 lbs. of ground chuck or
 ground round
2 (16 oz.) cans of mixed
 vegetables
1 large onion minced

2 eggs
1 tablespoon garlic powder or
 to taste
2 tablespoons sweet basil
salt and pepper to taste

Combine all ingredients and mix well. Form into an oblong mold and place in greased baking dish. Bake 1 hour about 375°. Remove from oven and pour off excess grease and continue baking another 15 minutes. Serves 6 to 8.

DON WACHTEL

KOFTA — MEAT CURRY

1 round steak, cut in small
 strips
1 teaspoon ground coriander
1 teaspoon ground ginger
¼ teaspoon ground cloves
¼ teaspoon ground cinnamon
1 tablespoon butter

2 tablespoons cooking oil
1 tablespoon tomato puree
1½ to 2 cups beef stock
2 to 3 tablespoons curry powder
1 medium onion
1 to 2 cloves garlic

Lightly salt and pepper beef, adding coriander, ginger, cloves, cinnamon and 1 tablespoon curry powder. Brown meat in a little butter.

Chop onion and garlic very fine. Heat oil and butter in skillet, cook onion till transparent. Add meat to onion mixture. Add tomato puree and more curry powder. Slowly add stock and stir gently. Cover skillet and simmer about 20 minutes or until meat is tender. For more sauce add more stock. Thicken with flour if too thin. Serve over white rice with side dishes of Major Grey's chutney, raisins, almonds, coconut, etc. Serves 4.

MARTHA BUCHANAN LUCERO

LEFTOVER BEEF CURRY

1 large onion,
  coarsely chopped
1 cup celery,
  coarsely chopped
2 tablespoons cooking oil
leftover cooked beef, cubed,
  (up to 3 cups)
1 small can drained mushrooms

$\frac{1}{4}$ teaspoon salt
1 tablespoon curry powder,
  or to taste
$\frac{1}{2}$ teaspoon Worcestershire
  sauce
2 cups brown gravy
1 small box raisins

Brown onions and celery in hot oil. Add meat, mushrooms, seasonings, and gravy. Cover and simmer for 1 hour. Serve over cooked noodles or rice with condiments of your choice. Serves 4.

MEAT—ZA PIE

1 lb. ground meat
$\frac{2}{3}$ cup canned milk
$\frac{1}{2}$ cup bread crumbs
$\frac{1}{2}$ teaspoon garlic salt
1 small can tomato paste

1 small can mushrooms
1 cup grated American cheese
3 tablespoons Parmesan cheese
1 teaspoon oregano

Mix together the meat, milk, bread crumbs and garlic salt and line a 9 inch pie pan with mixture. On top of the meat "crust" put a layer of tomato paste, then the mushrooms, oregano and last the cheese. Place in 350° oven for 30 minutes. Serve with green salad and garlic toast. Serves 4 to 5.

MRS. THOMAS N. PAYNE (BARBARA)

APPLE STUFFED PORK CHOPS

4 double thick pork chops (have
   butcher slash a pocket in each)
2 fresh apples, skin removed
   and thinly sliced
1 cup flour

⅛ teaspoon each thyme, marjoram,
   paprika, and pepper
¾ cup cream
¼ teaspoon salt

Place 5 or 6 slices of apple in each pocket of the pork chops. Dredge chops in flour seasoned with thyme, marjoram, paprika, salt and pepper. Brown lightly in 2 to 3 tablespoons shortening. Place in baking dish. Add cream. Cover and bake in 350° oven for 45 minutes. Serves 4.

MRS. J. ROBERT BURKHART

CREOLE PORK CHOPS

6 pork chops
6 slices lemon, thin
6 slices onion, thin

6 teaspoons dark brown sugar
½ cup catsup
½ cup water

Brown pork chops on both sides. On each chop place a lemon slice, an onion slice, and one teaspoon brown sugar. Separately mix together catsup and water, pour over chops. Cook covered 1 hour, or longer, over low heat. Serves 6.

CYNTHIA SAROSDY

PORK CHOPS A LA NOILLY

4 large, lean pork chops
1 teaspoon sage
salt and pepper
4 tablespoons catsup
4 large slices onion

4 thick slices tomato
Worcestershire sauce
paprika
5 oz. dry vermouth
dry mustard

Place chops in oven proof casserole. Sprinkle each liberally with sage, salt, pepper. Spoon generous tablespoon of catsup over each. Top with a slice of onion and then a slice of tomato. Sprinkle Worcestershire sauce over each. Season with dry mustard and paprika. Pour vermouth into the dish at the side to avoid washing off seasonings. Cover and bake at 350° for 1 hour. Remove lid. Bake additional ½ hour, basting. If desired, sauce can be slightly thickened with flour in a little water. Serves 4.

MRS. RICHARD H. ECKHARDT

MARGO'S BOURBON BARBECUED PORK

¼ cup soy sauce
2 tablespoons brown sugar
2 oz. bourbon

2 pork tenderloins or
pork chops

Combine soy sauce, sugar and bourbon; pour over meat. Marinate for 1 hour. Remove meat from sauce; and barbecue over low heat or bake in oven at 325°, basting every 10 minutes with marinade for 1 hour or until tender.

MRS. KENNETH GAARDER (MARIE)

PEKING SWEET AND SOUR PORK
(Benedictine Sisters of Peking Cooking School, Tokyo, Japan)

2 lbs. pork shoulder, cut into 1
    to 1½ inch cubes
3 tablespoons Kikkoman Soy
    Sauce
3 tablespoons cornstarch
1 medium onion, quartered

1 medium cucumber, unpeeled
    and coarsely cubed
1 green pepper, coarsely chopped
2 carrots, thick sliced
oil for deep frying
Sweet and Sour Sauce (see Index)

Boil pork in a large kettle of water for 20 minutes. Drain and allow to cool. Mix soy sauce and cornstarch. Heat deep oil very hot. Mix pork cubes, 2 or 3 at a time, in soy sauce mixture and drop into deep hot oil. Fry until crisp and brown. Drain on paper towels. This may be done in advance.

In a heavy skillet with a little oil, saute carrots for 10 minutes; onions for 7 or 8 minutes; cucumber and green peppers for 3 or 4 minutes. Chinese vegetables must be still crisp when served.

Mix pork, vegetables and Sweet and Sour Sauce (see Index) together and serve with white rice. If sauce seems a little too thick, add more water. Serves 4 to 6.

These proportions may be increased, and you may also serve just the pork in the Sweet and Sour Sauce in a buffet chafing dish. Serve with long oriental toothpicks over warm water. Keep fire very low and add water to sauce if it becomes too thick and sticky.

Two Americans, Sister M. Francetta and Sister M. Regia, fled the mainland of China when the Communists came to power. They established a cooking school in Tokyo, specializing in Chinese foods available in the United States. The Americans, fortunate enough to have known these ladies in their joy of cooking, will remember them with fond memories.

MRS. GEOFFREY P. WIEDEMAN (CAROLYN)

PORK AND SAUERKRAUT

1 tablespoon shortening
1 large onion, chopped
½ teaspoon paprika
1 small piece green pepper, chopped
2 to 3 tablespoons tomato sauce mixed into ¼ cup water

1¼ lbs. ground pork shoulder, lean
1 teaspoon salt
½ cup rice
1 large can sauerkraut
sour cream to taste

Saute onion in shortening, add paprika, green pepper, tomato sauce, ground pork and salt. Cook covered for 40 to 45 minutes on low heat. Cook rice according to directions and add to cooked meat. Rinse sauerkraut in a colander with cold water. Allow water to drain completely. Put one layer of sauerkraut in the dish then a layer of half of the meat and rice mixture. Continue to top of casserole with another layer of sauerkraut and meat and rice mixture. Bake for 40 minutes in 325° oven. Top with sour cream and serve. Casserole can be made up anytime, covered with foil and frozen. The day it is to be served place casserole in refrigerator early in the morning. Allow to come to room temperature and bake for 1 hour in 325° oven. Serves 4 to 6.

CORNEL SAROSDY

SAUCY SPICED HAM

1 baked ham
½ cup vinegar
1 cup brown sugar

¼ cup mustard
whole cloves

Combine vinegar, sugar and mustard and boil for 5 minutes. Remove the rind from the baked ham, score all over and insert cloves Pour sauce over the ham and bake for 30 minutes in 300° oven.

LILA COCKRELL
Mayor, City of San Antonio

HAM TETRAZZINI

2 to 3 lbs. ham (bite-size pieces)
1 package vermicelli
1 can mushroom soup
1 cup or more coffee cream
4 cans button mushrooms, drained

2 cups grated sharp Cheddar
    cheese
1 small grated onion
¼ teaspoon pepper
½ cup crushed potato chips

Cook vermicelli and drain as directed on package. Mix rest of ingredients with vermicelli and place in shallow greased casserole. Top with crushed potato chips and bake in 300° oven about 30 minutes until bubbly. Add more cream if necessary. Serves 8 to 10.

MRS. ROBERT F. McDERMOTT

HILL COUNTRY HAM LOAVES

1½ lbs. fresh pork, ground
1½ lbs. smoked ham, ground
3 eggs
1½ cups cracker crumbs
1½ cups tomato juice

pepper to taste
1 cup vinegar
1 cup brown sugar
1 cup water

Combine pork, ham, eggs, cracker crumbs, tomato juice and pepper. Form into 12 individual loaves. Place in shallow baking dish.

Combine vinegar, brown sugar and water and cook until sugar is dissolved. Pour sauce over the loaves and bake at 350° for 1 hour and 30 minutes to 1 hour and 45 minutes, basting every 15 or 20 minutes. This may be made the day ahead and reheated at serving time. Serves 12.

MRS. J. ROBERT BURKHART

SAVANNAH HAM SLICE

2 slices tenderized ham, 1½ inch thick
2 cups fruit juice (apricot, pineapple or orange)
1 cup sherry

½ cup honey
apricot halves or pitted cherries
mustard
peanut butter

Spread ham slices with prepared mustard and peanut butter. Place one slice on top of the other in a casserole. Pour fruit juice over the ham, bake at 325° for ½ hour. Add sherry and bake another hour. Place apricot halves or cherries on top and pour on ½ cup of honey and bake 20 minutes longer. Serves 10.

MRS. JOHN HIETT IVES

COMPANY HAM IN SOUR CREAM

1 cup cooked ham, julienne
¼ cup onion, chopped
2 tablespoons butter or margarine

2 teaspoons flour
1 cup dairy sour cream
1 (6 oz.) can broiled sliced mushrooms, drained

Saute ham and onion in butter, until onion is tender but not brown. Sprinkle with flour; gradually stir in sour cream. Add mushrooms. Cook over low heat, stirring constantly, just until mixture thickens. Serve over hot fluffy rice, and garnish with parsley. Serves 3 to 4.

MRS. ROBERT N. CAMPBELL, JR.

BUTTERFLY LEG OF LAMB

1 leg of lamb
lemon juice
butter
salt
dry mint flakes

rosemary
orange peel
pineapple slices
brown sugar
cinnamon

Have butcher bone lamb and slit it lengthwise so it will spread flat like a thick steak. Prepare a marinade of the lemon juice and butter and pour over the lamb in a shallow pan. Sprinkle generously with salt, mint flakes, rosemary and orange peel. Allow it to marinate for 1 hour or more. Place marinated lamb, fat side up, over hot coals. Broil, basting with marinade and turning to brown both sides for 45 minutes to 1 hour and 15 minutes. When lamb is done to your taste, place pineapple slices on squares of foil and heat for 5 minutes. Remove lamb and cut across the grain into thick slices. Sprinkle pineapple slices with brown sugar and cinnamon and serve as a garnish.

BOB KRUEGER
United States Representative, State of Texas

BOILED LEG OF LAMB AND CAPER SAUCE

1 leg of lamb
salt and pepper
boiling water
3 tablespoons flour

3 tablespoons butter
2 cups milk or 1 cup milk and 1
    cup defatted stock from lamb
4 tablespoons chopped capers

Place leg of lamb in a large deep saucepan. Cover with boiling water. When water comes to the boiling point again, draw saucepan off heat and remove scum. Add salt and pepper and allow to simmer gently until done, allowing 20 to 25 minutes to the pound. Remove and drain. To make the caper sauce, heat milk or milk and stock in a double boiler. Mix flour and melted butter to a smooth paste. Stir into the hot milk and allow to cook for 15 minutes over boiling water. Add capers, salt and pepper and serve over leg of lamb. Instead of capers, 1/2 cup chopped cucumber, pickles or mixed pickles may be used. Serves 6 to 8.

MRS. PETER V. WESTON (YVONNE)

BAKED LAMB AND POTATOES

1 leg of lamb
3 to 4 potatoes
salt and pepper

7 cloves garlic
parsley, minced
1 to 2 cups chicken broth

Grease large shallow baking dish with butter or margarine. Peel and slice potatoes 1 inch thick. Arrange slices in bottom of casserole. Sprinkle heavily with salt and pepper. Mash 6 cloves garlic, and spread on potatoes; sprinkle with parsley. Rub leg of lamb with clove of garlic, and place it on top of potatoes. Pour chicken broth over lamb, until potatoes are almost covered. Bake at 325° for 45 to 50 minutes per pound. Serves 6.

MRS. JOHN T. DYER (NANCY)

APPLE GLAZED LAMB CHOPS

6 rib lamb chops, about
    ¾ inch thick
⅓ cup light brown sugar
⅛ teaspoon ground cloves

⅛ teaspoon dry mustard
⅓ cup apple juice
salt and pepper to taste

In a small saucepan, combine sugar, apple juice, cloves and mustard. Heat until sugar dissolves. Season chops with salt and pepper and broil 3 to 4 inches from heat 5 to 7 minutes on each side. Brush frequently with apple glaze sauce. Serves 6.

MRS. CONRAD SALINAS

VEAL PEPPER STEAK

1½ lbs. veal steak
¼ cup salad oil
¼ cup lemon juice
1 teaspoon salt
1 teaspoon paprika
1 clove garlic, mashed or minced
1 teaspoon prepared mustard

¼ teaspoon nutmeg
¼ cup flour
3 tablespoons butter
1 can (10½ oz.) chicken bouillon
1 green pepper cut in strips
¼ pound fresh mushrooms
1 medium onion, thinly sliced

Marinate meat for at least 15 minutes in a mixture of oil, lemon juice, salt, paprika, garlic, mustard and nutmeg. Remove meat from

marinade, dredge in flour and brown on all sides in butter. Mix together remaining marinade, bouillon, green pepper and mushrooms.
Pour over browned meat. Cover and bake in moderate oven, 350°
for 30 minutes. Remove cover and top with onion rings and bake 15
minutes longer or until tender. Serves 8.

MRS. ROBERT DAWSON (JEANNIE)

SUISSE VEAL

1 pound veal cut in small pieces
1 clove garlic
2 tablespoons salad oil
salt and pepper
2 (3 oz.) cans mushrooms
1 medium can tomatoes

1 cup dry white wine
1 cup grated Parmesan cheese
1 package wide egg noodles
1 cup sour cream
¼ pound sliced Swiss cheese

Brown garlic and veal in oil. Add salt and pepper. Add mush-
rooms, tomatoes, wine and Parmesan cheese. Simmer for 20 minutes.
Cook noodles 5 minutes and toss with sour cream. Arrange noodles,
Swiss cheese, veal, mushrooms and part of the sauce in alternate
layers. Top with Swiss cheese and sauce. Bake 350° for 45 minutes.
Serves 4 to 5.

MRS. WILLIAM L. STARNES (MARY DEE)

Joyce Ward

Poultry

However you serve it, poultry of any kind has always meant a special meal. Smoked turkeys from the German ovens of the Texas Hill Country are close by in San Antonio, and all enjoy the traditional stuffed bird for the holidays.

Perhaps your taste is haute cuisine — Coq au Vin or Duck a l'Orange. Maybe Mexican chicken with chocolate sauce, *mole,* or a tangy Chicken Cacciatore is your choice.

But, let's remember the old fashioned favorites. Tender, crispy, fried chicken or roasted with fluffy mashed potatoes and country style creamed gravy is still a mouth-watering delight.

CHICKEN CACCIATORE

In an old cookbook, a recipe for "Chicken Alla Cacciatora," (meaning Hunter Style), is listed as the real Italian way of preparing this classic dish. It is totally different from the tomato sauce dish we think of today as "Chicken Cacciatore". The recipe says, "Cut up a chicken into eight or ten pieces and fry them in a little boiling olive oil. When they are nice and brown (about 20 minutes), salt and pepper them, and after a few minutes more cooking, squeeze the juice of a lemon over them".

We have not tried the "real Italian way", but this one is delicious.

2 fryers, cut in serving pieces	1 cup dry red wine
½ cup flour	1 teaspoon salt
6 tablespoons olive oil	½ teaspoon black pepper
1 cup onion, chopped	½ teaspoon allspice, ground
¾ cup green pepper, chopped	½ teaspoon oregano
2 garlic cloves, chopped fine	3 bay leaves
1 large can tomatoes	½ teaspoon thyme
1 (8 oz.) can tomato paste	¼ teaspoon cayenne pepper

- 143 -

Dust chicken pieces lightly with flour. Saute in a large skillet in olive oil until brown on all sides. Remove chicken from the skillet and set aside. Lower the heat and saute onions, green pepper and garlic until soft and lightly brown. Add all other ingredients, except chicken, and cook over low heat until the mixture bubbles. Add chicken, cover, and simmer for about 45 minutes, or until chicken is tender. Remove chicken and if the sauce is too thin add a little Beurre Manie (see Index) for thickening. Serves 6.

LEMON CHICKEN AARON

8 chicken breasts, split and boned
flour
1¼ cups butter
5 onions, chopped
8 tablespoons flour

5 teaspoons dry mustard
1¼ teaspoons sweet basil
1¼ cups fresh lemon juice
2½ cups chicken broth

Brown the floured chicken and place in a baking dish. Saute onions until yellow. Stir in flour, mustard, basil, lemon juice, salt, pepper and chicken broth. Pour over the chicken and bake at 350° for 45 minutes to an hour. Serve over buttered rice. Serves 6 to 8.

MRS. CHARLES F. SHIELD III (KITTY)

CHICKEN PIQUANT

4 to 5 lbs. chicken pieces
1½ cups orange juice
cayenne pepper to taste
¼ cup blanched almonds
½ cup pineapple chunks
⅓ cup raisins

⅛ teaspoon cloves
⅛ teaspoon cinnamon
2 tablespoons flour
¼ cup water
¼ cup oil

Rub chicken pieces with cayenne pepper. Heat oil in a large skillet and brown the chicken. Remove chicken and add flour. Cook a few minutes and add orange juice, water and chicken. Add remaining ingredients, cover and simmer until chicken is done, about 40 minutes. Serves 10.

MRS. J. ROBERT BURKHART

CHICKEN KIEV

4 large half chicken breasts
⅓ cup real butter
2 tablespoons chives, chopped
½ teaspoon salt
pepper
⅔ cup Progresso Italian
  bread crumbs

oil for deep frying
1 egg
1 tablespoon milk
flour
sour cream sauce (optional)

Bone and remove skin from breasts. Place each one between sheets of waxed paper and pound very thin with a smooth surfaced meat mallet or rolling pin Remove waxed paper. Place 1½ tablespoons of butter in the center of each breast. Combine chives, salt and pepper and sprinkle over the butter. Roll each breast, overlapping and tucking in the sides so the butter is completely enclosed. The meat should adhere to itself without picks. Beat the egg and milk together. Roll chicken in a little flour, then in the egg mixture, then in bread crumbs, again in egg and once more in the crumbs to coat evenly. Refrigerate at least 2 hours.

Preheat oven for 30 minutes at 200°. Line a shallow pan with paper towels and place in the oven. Heat oil to 375° and fry chicken until crisp and brown, about 5 minutes. Drain on towels in the oven. They may remain in the oven about 15 minutes. You may serve them with a sour cream sauce. Serves 4.

This is a delicious dinner party dish and is easy to do if you prepare them properly. Take the time to make sure the butter is well enclosed and the crumbs and egg mixture completely cover the chicken.

MRS. GEORGE C. VINEY (PEG)

CHICKEN CREPES SUISSE

1 large chicken, cut in
  serving pieces
¼ cup white wine or vermouth
2 green onions, chopped
3 tablespoons flour

1 cup whipping cream
½ cup Swiss cheese, grated
10 crepes (see Index)
mushroom caps for garnish

Stew chicken pieces in water to cover for 1½ to 2 hours. Remove the chicken from the broth, bone and chop . Set aside. Add wine and green onions to the broth and boil down quickly to about 2 to 2½ cups. Mix flour with cream and add slowly to the broth. Strain and add the Swiss cheese. Mix ¾ cup of sauce with the chopped chicken and fill crepes with chicken mixture. Repeat until all crepes and chicken mixture have been used. Place rolled crepes in a buttered shallow baking dish. Pour the remaining sauce over the rolled crepes and bake at 350° until bubbly. Garnish with mushroom caps sauteed in butter. Serves 5.

MRS. LAWRENCE MARTIN, JR. (DOLORES)

CHICKEN CRUNCH

½ cup canned chicken broth
3 cups cooked chicken, diced
1 (9 oz.) can tuna, drained
1 cup celery, diced
2 cans mushroom soup

1 (5 oz.) can water chestnuts, sliced thin
1 (3 oz.) can Chinese Chow Mein Noodles
⅓ cup toasted almond slivers

Combine chicken broth and mushroom soup. Add other ingredients, except noodles. Mix well. In a 2 quart baking dish, alternate layers of noodles and chicken mixture, ending with the chicken mixture. Bake about 35 or 40 minutes in a 325° oven. Sprinkle with toasted almonds. Serves 8.

MRS. WILLIAM K. DOUGLAS (MARIWADE)

PARTY CHICKEN

8 large chicken breasts
8 slices bacon
1 jar chipped beef

1 can mushroom soup
½ pint sour cream
Parmesan cheese

Bone and skin chicken breasts; pound each breast; sprinkle with Parmesan cheese and roll up. Wrap in bacon and secure with toothpicks. Grease an 8 x 2 x 2 dish, arrange circles of chipped beef, and top with rolled chicken breasts. Mix soup and sour cream, pour over rolled breasts. Sprinkle with Parmesan cheese. Refrigerate until time to put in the oven. Bake 1 to 1½ hours at 300°, uncovered. Serve with curry rice. Serves 8.

MRS. H. RANDOLPH BROWN

COUNTRY CAPTAIN

12 chicken pieces, breasts
  and thighs
3 medium onions, chopped
2 garlic cloves, chopped
1 tablespoon parsley, chopped
1 green pepper, chopped
2 large cans tomatoes
¼ teaspoon pepper
¼ teaspoon curry powder
½ teaspoon thyme
1 teaspoon salt
⅔ cup currants
1 lb. blanched almonds
1 large tomato can water
1 tablespoon butter
flour
paprika

Remove skin and sprinkle chicken pieces with salt and pepper. Roll in flour and season with paprika. Fry in deep fat until golden brown. Set aside. In a skillet large enough to hold chicken pieces melt the butter. Add onions, garlic, parsley, green pepper, curry powder, thyme, salt and pepper. Allow to cook 15 minutes over very low heat. Add water and cook for a few minutes. Add tomatoes and cook slowly until smooth. Add browned chicken pieces, cover, and cook gently for 45 minutes. 15 minutes before the chicken is done, add the currants. At serving time, add the almonds. Serves 8.

MRS. GILBERT L. CURTIS (LORRIE)

CHICKEN CHIPINQUE

30 to 40 chicken pieces
olive oil
flour
salt and pepper to taste
¾ cup chopped onions
½ cup chopped green pepper
1 clove minced garlic
3 cups chopped celery
3 cups chopped carrots
4½ cups tomato juice
1 can chicken broth
2 to 3 cups sauteed mushrooms
1 cup stuffed green olives

Sprinkle chicken pieces with salt and pepper and dredge in flour. Heat olive oil in a skillet and brown the chicken. Place in a baking dish. Saute onion, pepper and garlic. Add carrots, celery and tomato juice and stir well to absorb all the flavors in the skillet. Pour these ingredients over the chicken, cover and bake in 325° oven for about 1 hour or until tender. (Do not overcook or the meat will fall off the bone.) Add chicken broth as necessary during the baking. When done, remove chicken and thicken drippings with flour. If serving immediately, add olives and mushrooms to the thickened gravy. If freezing, add mushrooms and olives after thawing and reheating. Serve with rice. Serves 20 to 25.

MRS. GERALD W. MASSY III (DOROTHY)

CHICKEN BREASTS CHABLIS

4 chicken breasts, boned,
  skinned and halved
2 tablespoons butter

2 teaspoons cornstarch
½ cup whipping cream
½ cup dry white wine

In a wide frying pan, over medium heat, brown lightly salted chicken breasts on both sides. Add wine and simmer in a covered pan for about 20 minutes, or until breasts are white through. Remove breasts and place on a warm serving dish. Blend the cornstarch with a little water. Add whipping cream to the pan juices and bring to a rolling boil. Remove from the fire, add the cornstarch mixture and return to the boil, stirring constantly. When the sauce thickens, pour over the chicken. Serves 4.

MRS. MADISON NEILSON

CHICKEN DIVAN

1 fresh bunch or 2 (10 oz.)
  packages of frozen broccoli
2½ cups sliced cooked
  chicken breasts
2 cans cream of chicken soup
1 cup mayonnaise

1 tablespoon lemon juice
½ teaspoon curry powder
½ cup shredded Cheddar cheese
½ cup bread crumbs
1 tablespoon melted butter

Cook broccoli, drain and arrange in greased 11½ x 7½ x 2½ baking dish. Place chicken on top. Combine soup, mayonnaise, lemon juice and curry powder; pour over chicken. Sprinkle with cheese. Combine bread crumbs and butter and sprinkle over the top. Bake at 350° for 25 to 30 minutes or until thoroughly heated. Serves 6.

MRS. FRED J. SILVEY

POULET CHASSEUR

2 chickens, cut in pieces
½ cup olive oil
½ cup margarine
3 slices bacon
½ lb. mushrooms, sliced
1 large onion, sliced
2 cups celery, chopped
1 (6 oz.) can tomato paste
1 (28 oz.) can tomatoes, drained
¼ teaspoon parsley

¼ teaspoon bay leaf
¼ teaspoon garlic
¼ teaspoon oregano
¼ teaspoon pepper
2 cups beef bouillon
3 tablespoons flour
1 cup red wine
1 eggplant, peeled and cubed
5 to 6 zucchini, cut in finger strips
Parmesan cheese

Brown unseasoned chicken in oil and margarine and place in baking dish. Fry bacon until crisp; remove and drain. Saute mushrooms, onion and celery in bacon grease. Add tomato paste and tomatoes. Make bouquet with parsley, bay leaf, garlic, oregano and pepper. Simmer bouquet in bouillon and add to tomato mixture. Thicken with flour, made into a paste. Add wine, eggplant, and zucchini. Cover chicken with mixture. Sprinkle with cheese and crumbled bacon, and bake at 350° for 20 to 30 minutes. Serves 6 to 8.

INA MAE KELLAM

CHICKEN CORDON BLEU

8 thin slices chicken breasts
  or veal
4 ham slices
4 slices Swiss or Gruyere cheese
3 eggs, beaten
flour
bread crumbs

salt and pepper to taste
oil
lemon, sliced
parsley
mushroom gravy, canned
  or package

Season chicken or veal and place a slice of ham and cheese in between 2 slices. Secure with skewers. Dip in flour and then in eggs and in bread crumbs. Cook slowly in oil on both sides until golden brown. If desired, allow the chicken to drain in a warm oven on paper towels to absorb extra oil. Place chicken on a serving dish and cover with mushroom gravy. Garnish with parsley and lemon slices. Serves 4.

MRS. RALPH ROWDEN (FRANCINE)

CHICKEN TETRAZZINI

1 (3 to 4 lb.) chicken
1 onion
1 bay leaf
2 stalks celery with leaves
salt and pepper
1/4 lb. butter
1 bunch scallions, minced
1/2 cup green pepper, minced
1/4 lb. mushrooms, minced
1/4 cup parsley, minced

1/2 cup celery, minced
1 garlic clove, crushed
1 cup whipping cream
1 cup chicken stock
2 tablespoons Vermouth
1 tablespoon lemon juice
2 tablespoons flour
2 tablespoons butter
1 (10 oz.) package vermicelli
3/4 cup Parmesan cheese

Boil the chicken with onion, bay leaf, celery, salt and pepper until done. Remove the chicken, strain the stock and save. Cut the chicken off the bone into bite size pieces. Saute the scallions, green pepper, mushrooms, parsley, celery and garlic in the butter until soft. Add whipping cream, chicken stock, Vermouth, lemon juice, salt and pepper to taste. Add the chicken and cook on low heat until heated. Make a paste of butter and flour (Beurre Manie, see Index) and add to the chicken mixture. Blend until smooth and thickened. Cook the vermicelli in chicken stock and drain. Combine in a buttered baking dish and top with Parmesan cheese. Bake 20 minutes in 350° until hot and bubbly. May be made in advance. Serves 8 to 10.

MRS. ROBERT F. MCDERMOTT

CHICKEN TETRAZZINI HOLLANDAISE

1/2 cup butter
2 cups mushrooms, sliced
6 cups cooked, diced chicken
1/2 cup sherry
2 cups Supreme Sauce
  (see Index)
1 cup half and half, heated
1/4 teaspoon white pepper

6 cups very thin spaghetti,
  linguine or fettuchini
  noodles, cooked
11/2 cups Hollandaise Sauce
  (use a package mix)
3/4 cup Parmesan cheese
salt
paprika and parsley

Melt butter in a large, heavy skillet. Add mushrooms and saute for 5 minutes. Add chicken and sherry. Stir well and cook 5 minutes more. Add Supreme Sauce (see Index) and half and half. Mix thoroughly and simmer gently for 5 minutes. Add pepper and salt to taste. Butter a very large, deep casserole and cover the bottom with pasta. Fill with chicken mixture and top with Hollandaise Sauce. Sprinkle Parmesan cheese evenly over the top and add paprika and parsley for color. Cover and refrigerate until ready to bake. When ready to bake, allow to come to room temperature and bake in 350° oven for 1 hour or until hot and bubbly. If it seems a little dry, add more heated half and half. This recipe may be cut in half and may be made the day before serving. Serves 12 to 15 for buffet.

MRS. GEOFFREY P. WIEDEMAN (CAROLYN)

EASY COQ AU VIN

1 chicken cut in pieces
4 tablespoons butter
⅓ cup brandy
2 cups red wine
1 bay leaf
⅛ teaspoon thyme
1 clove garlic

1 or 2 tablespoons Beurre Manie (see Index)
1 (8 oz.) can small white onions drained
1 (3 oz.) can whole mushrooms drained.

Heat butter in a skillet with garlic. Remove garlic. Add chicken and brown quickly. Pour the brandy over the chicken, allow it to warm slightly and then ignite. Lower the heat and add wine and herbs. Cover and cook for 30 to 40 minutes. Thicken the gravy with a little Beurre Manie (see Index), bit by bit. Add onions, mushrooms and heat gently. Serve immediately. Serves 4 to 6.

MRS. KENNETH GAARDER (MARIE)

CHICKEN AND RICE AMBASSADOR

1 cup uncooked rice
6 boned chicken breasts
1 cup cream of mushroom soup
1 cup cream of celery soup

1 cup cream of chicken soup
toasted slivered almonds
3 tablespoons melted butter
¾ cup dry sherry

In a shallow casserole place rice and cover with chicken breasts. Mix soups, butter and sherry; pour over chicken. Sprinkle with almonds. Bake at 350° for 1 hour. Cover with foil for first 30 minutes, but uncover for the last 30 minutes. Be sure rice is completely cooked. Serves 6.

MRS. HENRY E. CATTO (MAURINE)

CHICKEN SAUTE AU PARMESAN

1 chicken cut in serving pieces
salt and black pepper
4½ tablespoons butter
1½ tablespoons flour
¾ cup milk
¼ cup heavy cream

¼ teaspoon nutmeg
½ cup freshly grated Swiss or
  Gruyere cheese
½ cup freshly grated Parmesan
2 tablespoons fresh bread crumbs

Sprinkle chicken with salt and pepper and brown on all sides in 3 tablespoons of butter, about 20 minutes. Melt remaining butter in a sauce pan and stir in flour. Cook for a few minutes and gradually add milk and cream, stirring constantly. When mixture is thick and smooth, remove from heat and add nutmeg and Swiss cheese. Sprinkle a baking dish with half the Parmesan cheese and arrange the chicken pieces on the cheese. Spoon sauce over chicken and sprinkle with the remaining cheese and bread crumbs. Bake until golden brown and chicken is done, about 20 to 30 minutes. Serves 4.

CAROLYN H. SPEARS
Judge, Bexar County, State of Texas

ROLO ME KOTAPOULO — Greek Chicken Rolls

2 lbs. chicken breasts, cooked
  and boned
2 medium onions, chopped fine
1 large celery stalk, chopped fine
6 tablespoons butter
2 tablespoons parsley, chopped
1 cup chicken broth

1 tablespoon flour
¼ teaspoon grated nutmeg
salt and pepper to taste
4 eggs, well beaten
6 Phyllo leaves (see Index)
melted butter

Put chicken through the fine blades of a food chopper or chop in a blender. Saute onions and celery in butter until tender, but not brown. Add chicken, parsley and chicken broth and cook over moderate heat until all liquid is absorbed. Blend in flour, add salt, pepper and nutmeg and cool. After mixture has cooled completely, blend in the eggs. Following the directions for using whole Phyllo pastry sheets, (see Index), make 2 stacks of Phyllo leaves - 3 sheets in each stack. Spread ½ of the chicken mixture on each stack. Roll, jelly-roll fashion, and continue recipe instructions for baking whole Phyllo pastry.

MRS. KENNETH GAARDER (MARIE)

CHICKEN OKRA GUMBO

2 tablespoons butter
1 cup onions, chopped
1 garlic clove, minced
1 cup green pepper, diced
1/4 cup fresh parsley, chopped
1 chicken, cut in serving pieces
2 teaspoons salt
1 quart water

1/4 teaspoon cayenne pepper
1/2 teaspoon thyme
2 bay leaves
20 oz. sliced okra, cooked
1 (15 oz.) can tomato sauce
2 1/2 cups cooked rice
gumbo file (optional)

Melt butter in Dutch oven or heavy pot. Add onions and garlic and cook just until onion is transparent. Stir in green pepper and parsley. Add chicken, water, salt, pepper, thyme and bay leaves. Cover and bring to a boil over moderate heat. Reduce heat and simmer for 40 minutes or until chicken is tender. Remove chicken and when cool enough to handle, remove skin, bones and dice. Skim excess fat from broth. Add tomato sauce, okra and diced chicken and cook, uncovered, over moderate heat for 2 or 3 minutes or until mixture is well heated. Place 1/2 cup of cooked rice in each serving bowl and laddle gumbo over the rice. If desired, sprinkle gumbo file over rice before adding mixture. (Never cook file in the broth, add it after the mixture has been removed from the heat to prevent stringiness.) Serves 6.

SHARON MAGRUDER

CHICKEN CURRY

1 (3 1/2 lb.) chicken, cooked
3/4 cup onions, chopped fine
1 1/2 cups apples, chopped fine
1/2 cup butter or margarine
8 tablespoons flour
1 1/2 tablespoons curry powder

3 to 4 cups chicken stock
3 tablespoons lemon juice
3 tablespoons apple jelly
grated lemon rind
salt and pepper to taste

Cook apples and onions in butter until soft. Add flour and curry powder and blend well. Slowly add the chicken broth. Bring to a boil, reduce heat, and simmer gently, covered for 30 minutes. Remove from heat and strain. Add the lemon rind, lemon juice and apple jelly. Add salt and pepper. Cut chicken into bite-size pieces and add to the curry. Serve with curry condiments: chutney, chopped almonds, coconut, crumbled bacon, raisins. The sauce may be made early in the day or frozen and the chicken added at serving time. Serves 6 to 8.

MRS. THOMAS BERG (EVELYN)

ROYAL PALM CHICKEN BREASTS

8 half chicken breasts
8 hearts of palm
½ lb. butter

salt and white pepper
fresh parsley, chopped
Hollandaise Sauce (see Index)

Bone chicken breasts and pound very thin. Wrap the breasts around heart of palm. Spread with butter, using ¼ of a lb. for 4 breasts. Salt and pepper to taste. Place in a baking dish and bake for 30 to 40 minutes in a 350° oven. Serve with Hollandaise Sauce (see Index) and sprinkle with parsley. Serves 8.

VIVIAN M. GERSEMA

HOT CHICKEN SALAD

⅔ cup cream of chicken soup
⅔ cup mayonnaise
4 cups cooked chicken, chopped
2 cups celery, chopped
½ cup onion, chopped
pimiento, sliced

juice of 1 lemon
1 teaspoon salt
4 hard-boiled eggs, chopped
⅔ cup almonds, slivered
1 cup sharp Cheddar cheese, grated
1½ cups potato chips, crushed

Combine soup, mayonnaise, chicken, celery, onion, pimiento, lemon juice, salt, and eggs. Place in baking dish in the order given. Top with almonds, cheese, and potato chips. Bake at 350° for 20 to 25 minutes. Serves 8 to 10.

MRS. RICHARD H. ECKHARDT

HOT CHICKEN MOUSSE

1½ cups raw chicken breast
1 cup soft bread crumbs
1 cup cream
5 egg whites

salt and pepper
Worcestershire
chopped onion
chopped parsley

Put chicken breasts through a grinder or in a blender. Add seasonings, onion, and parsley. Combine bread crumbs and cream in a saucepan and bring to a boil. Add chicken and boil for 2 minutes. Remove from heat and add egg whites. Butter a ring mold and sprinkle with dry bread crumbs. Fill 2/3 full and bake 20 minutes in a pan of hot water. Unmold and serve with creamed mushrooms in the center. Serves 8.

MRS. JAMES W. NIXON

CHICKEN SUPREME

1/2 cup butter
1/2 cup flour
1 teaspoon salt
1/2 teaspoon pepper
2 cups chicken broth
2 cups whipping cream
1 box Rice-A-Roni
2 3/4 cups chicken stock
1 cup Parmesan cheese, grated

5 cups cooked chicken breasts or turkey, cubed
2 (3 oz.) cans sliced mushrooms
1 package frozen green peas
1 can cream of mushroom soup
1 soup can half 'n' half
1/2 teaspoon Worcestershire
5 drops Tabasco sauce

Cook Rice-A-Roni according to directions but use chicken stock instead of water. (omit "flavor packet"). (In place of stock, 2 3/4 cups water and 3 chicken bouillon cubes may be used.) Cook peas just enough to separate, drain. Slowly add to peas, cream of mushroom soup, stirring until smooth. Add half 'n' half, Worcestershire and Tabasco, stirring until smooth. Set mixture aside. Melt butter over low heat; blend in flour and seasonings. Cook, stirring until mixture is smooth and bubbly. Remove from heat. Stir in broth and cream. Heat to boiling, stirring constantly. Boil 1 minute. Add cubed chicken, drained mushrooms, Rice-A-Roni, and peas-mushroom soup mixture. Mix well and season to taste. Spoon into 13 1/2 x 8 3/4 x 1 3/4 inch casserole. Sprinkle with Parmesan cheese. Bake at 350° for 30 minutes or until bubbly in center. If desired, brown under broiler. Garnish with parsley and sliced stuffed green olives. May be frozen. Thaw, and increase baking time. Serves 10 to 12.

MRS. DONALD RATTAN

CRAB STUFFED CHICKEN

2 chickens, split in half
2 tablespoons margarine or butter
1 teaspoon salt
¼ teaspoon black pepper
paprika (optional)
¼ cup melted butter or margarine
parsley (optional)

½ cup sherry
½ cup ketchup
1 small can button or
  sliced mushrooms
½ teaspoon garlic salt
1 tomato, sliced (optional)
Crabmeat Stuffing

Rub chicken with soft butter, salt, pepper, and sprinkle with paprika. In a 13 x 9 x 2 inch baking dish, arrange side by side, with wings tucked back and under, and skin side up. Bake 35 minutes in 350° oven. In small saucepan, combine melted butter, sherry, ketchup, drained mushrooms, and garlic salt. Heat. Spoon 1 to 2 tablespoons of sauce over each chicken half. Bake 10 minutes longer, then remove from oven and cool in baking dish while preparing stuffing. After stuffing is prepared, turn chicken over, and generously fill each shell with stuffing. Baste each with 1 to 2 tablespoons of butter sauce. Bake 30 to 35 minutes, basting frequently with sauce. When chicken is fork-tender, remove from oven, garnish with bits of parsley and sliced tomato in center. Serve stuffing-side up. Serves 4.

Crabmeat Stuffing

3 slices white bread
5 tablespoons light cream or milk
2 (6 oz.) packages frozen
  crabmeat, thawed, drained, or
  2 (6½ oz.) cans king crabmeat,
  drained
¼ cup melted butter or
  margarine

¼ teaspoon cayenne
1 teaspoon prepared mustard
1 teaspoon salt
½ teaspoon dried thyme
½ teaspoon poultry seasoning
¼ teaspoon dried sage
  (optional)

Cut bread into small cubes. In medium bowl, toss cubes with cream until absorbed. Remove membrane from drained crabmeat, then toss with bread cubes. Into melted butter, stir seasonings and add to bread and crab mixture. Toss lightly with fork. Stuffing may be assembled in advance. Enough to fill 4 chicken halves.

MRS. F. DANIEL FOLEY (CARROLL)

PORTO CHICKEN SCAMPI

1 chicken, cut in serving pieces
1 tablespoon salt
1/2 teaspoon pepper
2 tablespoons butter or margarine
3 small onions finely diced
1 clove garlic, minced

3 tablespoons snipped parsley
1/2 cup Port wine
1 (8 oz.) can tomato sauce
1 teaspoon dried basil
1 lb. shrimp

Peel and devein shrimp. Rub chicken with salt and pepper. Saute chicken in hot butter or margarine, in a large skillet until golden on all sides. Add onion, garlic, snipped parsley, wine, tomato sauce and basil. Simmer 30 minutes or until chicken is tender. Push chicken pieces to one side and turn up heat so tomato mixture boils. Add shrimp. Cook uncovered 3 to 4 minutes or until they turn pink. Pile chicken on a serving dish. Top with shrimp and fresh snipped parsley. Skim fat from sauce, pour into serving boat and serve with chicken. May be made in advance up to adding the shrimp. Serves 4.

MRS. F. DANIEL FOLEY (CARROLL)

FIESTA FRIED CHICKEN

3 to 4 lb. fryer, cut up
1 cup sour cream
1 tablespoon lemon juice
2 cloves garlic, crushed
1/2 teaspoon salt

3/4 teaspoon white pepper
1/2 teaspoon paprika
1 teaspoon Worcestershire
1 cup flour
1/2 cup cooking oil

Place chicken in a casserole. Combine all ingredients, except flour and cooking oil, and pour mixture over chicken pieces. Marinate overnight in refrigerator. When ready to cook, remove chicken pieces and dust with flour. Fry chicken in oil, turning only once. Serves 4.

MRS. FELICIA VAN NUFFELEN

MY! OH MY! CHICKEN

3 chicken breasts, halved
2 tablespoons flour
3 tablespoons salad oil
1/2 cup dry white wine
1/4 cup bleu cheese, crumbled

1 cup cream of chicken soup
1/2 teaspoon salt
1/4 teaspoon pepper
fresh asparagus or 1
  package frozen

Coat chicken with flour, brown lightly in oil. In a 3 quart baking pan mix wine, bleu cheese and soup over low heat. Add chicken, baste with sauce and bake in a 325° oven for 30 minutes. Add asparagus, cover tightly and bake 30 minutes more. Serves 6.

MRS. JOEL W. WESTBROOK, III (ELAINE)

WILD RICE HENS

6 Cornish hens	1½ cups wild rice, cooked
½ cup onions minced	⅛ teaspoon marjoram
2 tablespoons butter or margarine	⅛ teaspoon thyme
½ cup ham diced	½ cup chicken broth
½ cup mushrooms, chopped	¼ cup sherry

Saute onion in butter until golden. Add ham and mushrooms and saute for 5 minutes. Remove from heat and stir in wild rice, marjoram and thyme. Sprinkle Cornish hens inside and out with salt and pepper. Fill cavities with stuffing. Truss birds loosely and arrange side by side in buttered shallow casserole. Spread soft butter over breast and thighs. Roast in 350° oven for 1 hour, or until slightly brown, basting occasionally with pan juices. Remove to heated platter and garnish. To casserole add chicken broth and sherry and bring to a boil on top of the stove, stirring all brown bits from edge of casserole. Strain over hens or serve separately. At the table you may pour ¼ cup warm brandy over hens and flame. Serves 6.

MRS. RICHARD EDDLEMAN (CAROL)

CRISPY CORNISH HENS

2 Cornish game hens	¼ teaspoon salt
¼ cup melted butter	fresh ground pepper
2 tablespoons lemon juice	

Split hens lengthwise through the breast and place, cut side up, on a foil lined broiler pan. Brush with a mixture of the butter, lemon juice, salt and pepper. Broil for 15 minutes, about 8 inches from heat, brushing frequently with butter mixture. Turn the hens over, brush with more butter mixture and broil for 15 more minutes. Serves 2 or 3.

MRS. GEOFFREY P. WIEDEMAN (CAROLYN)

DUCK A L'ORANGE

1 (4 to 6 lb.) duck
salt and pepper to season
⅛ teaspoon ginger

1 cup dry white wine
4 tablespoons orange marmalade
5 tablespoons orange juice

Rub duck inside and outside with salt and pepper. Sprinkle the ginger inside the cavity. Close the cavity opening with skewers and tie the legs together. Prick the fat with a fork. Place the duck on a rack, breast side down, in a hot oven 425° for 15 minutes. Reduce temperature to 350° and roast, allowing 25 minutes per lb. During the first hour, baste with white wine, pricking the fat skin occasionally with a fork. Pour off the drippings and skim off fat; save the juices. Combine the orange marmalade and orange juice and baste with mixture until it is all used. 30 minutes before the duck is done, return the saved juices to pan, scrape roasting pan well and stir. Continue cooking duck until done. Garnish with orange sections and serve with wild rice. Serves 4.

MRS. KENNETH GAARDER (MARIE)

CHINESE SOUP DINNER

1 (4 lb.) hen chicken
1 cup chopped celery
1 large green pepper, chopped
1 small package Chinese noodles
1 can Chinese vegetables
1 large can mushrooms

Worcestershire to taste
soy sauce to taste
toasted almonds
1 package frozen snowpeas
chicken broth

Cook chicken with an onion and a few stalks of celery, tops included, covered with water until tender. Reserve broth. Cut chicken off the bone into medium size pieces. In a large pan cook celery and 6 cups of chicken broth for 10 minutes. Add green pepper and noodles. When tender, add Chinese vegetables, mushrooms, Worcestershire sauce, soy sauce and thawed snow peas. Add chicken pieces, heat and serve in large soup bowls with toasted almonds sprinkled on top. Serves 8.

MRS. JOHN H. MCCORMICK

E. GORDON WEST

Seafood

There is a wealth of seafood in the waters along our Texas Gulf Coast. Redfish, flounder, crab, shrimp and oysters are just a few that find their way to Texas tables. The variety is endless.

Fresh water catfish and trout abound along the Guadalupe River and inspire local cooks to invent recipes which bring out their subtle flavors.

The preparation of seafood is equally varied. Fish may be filleted or left whole; poached, broiled, baked or fried. Tender, juicy shellfish become delicacies of elegance. We offer a collection we are certain you will enjoy.

SHRIMP CREOLE

Each Wednesday, Thursday and Friday during Lent, with the exception of Holy Week, Lenten luncheons are held at St. Mark's Episcopal Church. These luncheons were begun by The Women of St. Mark's in order to give the hungry business people of downtown San Antonio a pleasant noon meal after they had attended Lenten services.

All the food is prepared and served by The Women of St. Mark's and preparations begin in September, when meals are planned and menus readied. In January, shrimp is cooked, peeled, cleaned and frozen in huge containers. Chicken is prepared months in advance, to be ready for the tasty casseroles and salads to be served. The proceeds from these popular luncheons benefit various missions and other charitable organizations in San Antonio.

The following recipe for Shrimp Creole is one of the delicious home cooked items on the luncheon menu. According to Rose Peale, it's author, 8 to 10 lbs. of this marvelous concoction disappear at each luncheon!

ROSA'S WINDOW—SAN JOSE MISSION — E. Gordon West

SHRIMP CREOLE

1 lb. raw, cleaned shrimp
1 (1 lb.) can tomatoes
1 can (6 oz.) tomato paste
1 green pepper, chopped
1 large onion, diced
1/2 cup celery, chopped
2 cloves garlic, chopped
1/4 cup parsley, chopped

1 teaspoon chili powder
1 teaspoon sugar
1 tablespoon Worcestershire
1 bay leaf
1/2 teaspoon gumbo file
salt and pepper to taste
1 tablespoon bacon drippings

Fry onions, celery, garlic, green pepper and parsley in bacon drippings until soft. Add tomato paste, canned tomatoes and 1 cup of water to thin. Add other ingredients, except gumbo file, and cook slowly, about 1 hour. Add raw shrimp and cook 15 minutes. Then add gumbo file. Serve over cooked rice. Serves 6 to 8.

ROSE PEALE

CHARCOAL SHRIMP

1 lb. raw jumbo shrimp
1/2 cup Madeira
2 tablespoons soy sauce
black pepper, to taste
1 teaspoon Tabasco
1 teaspoon Worcestershire
1 stick butter, melted

1/2 teaspoon garlic powder
1/2 teaspoon onion powder
1/2 teaspoon black pepper
1 teaspoon fresh parsley,
  chopped
2 tablespoons Madeira
a bit of beer

Combine 1/2 cup Madeira, soy sauce, Tabasco, Worcestershire sauce, and black pepper, to taste. Peel and devein shrimp and marinate for not over 2 hours. Combine butter, garlic powder, onion powder, 1/2 teaspoon black pepper, parsley and 2 tablespoons Madeira. Place marinated shrimp on skewers and brush heavily with the butter sauce mixture. Let it congeal on the shrimp. Place shrimp skewers over a low fire on a grill. (As the butter sauce drips onto the fire it will flame — dampen it with beer.) Lower the top of the grill, if you have one, to hold the smoke. Cook the shrimp not more than 5 minutes, turning the skewers frequently. Remove shrimp from the skewers and pour the rest of the warmed butter sauce over the shrimp. Serves 4.

COLONEL JACK C. YOUNG

FANTAIL STUFFED SHRIMP

3 lbs. large shrimp
½ cup butter
½ cup green onions, minced
2 cloves garlic, chopped
1 cup flour
2 cups clam juice
3 egg yolks
salt and pepper
bread crumbs

Saute onions and garlic in butter. Blend in flour. Add clam juice, and slowly stir in egg yolks, one at a time. Season and cook slowly 5 to 10 minutes. Peel shrimp, leaving tail on. Partially split each shrimp and spread out. Arrange shrimp in buttered baking pan, with 1 teaspoon of stuffing mixture on each shrimp. Sprinkle with bread crumbs, dot liberally with butter, and bake at 350° for 25 minutes, or until shrimps are cooked. Serves 8.

MRS. CLIFFORD J. BUCKLEY (HELEN)

BAKED SHRIMP PARMESAN

8 jumbo shrimp
1 cup packaged bread crumbs
½ cup grated Parmesan cheese
1 tablespoon sherry
dash garlic powder, salt, pepper
2 teaspoons olive oil or melted butter

Mix all ingredients except shrimp. Shell shrimp and leave first joint attached. Place shrimp in buttered baking dish with tails up. Cover shrimp with stuffing and bake in 350° oven for 20 minutes. Serve with lemon wedges and melted butter. Serves 2.

MRS. RICHARD A. CUDWORTH

GARLIC SHRIMP

2 lbs. jumbo raw shrimp
½ cup olive oil and butter, mixed
½ cup dry white wine
¼ cup lemon juice
3 cloves garlic, chopped fine
1 teaspoon dried oregano
3 tablespoons parsley, chopped
salt and pepper to taste

Peel and devein shrimp and arrange in a large shallow baking dish. In a saucepan combine oil-butter mixture, wine, lemon juice, garlic, oregano, parsley, salt and pepper. Heat just to the boiling point and pour over shrimp. Bake in a 375° oven for 15 minutes or until shrimp turn pink. May be served as an appetizer or entree. Serves 4 as entree.

MRS. JAMES W. NIXON, JR.

SHRIMP IN BEER

24 jumbo shrimp
1 (12 oz.) bottle beer
1 teaspoon salt

1½ cups flour
oil for deep frying

Peel, devein and butterfly the shrimp. Mix salt, flour and beer until smooth. (Batter should be thick, but not pasty.) Dust shrimp with a little flour and dip in the beer batter. Deep fry at 350° for about 5 minutes until golden brown. Serve with Pungent Sauce. Serves 6.

KING ANTONIO LIII — PORTER LORING, JR.

Pungent Sauce

1 cup orange marmalade
1 teaspoon ginger

1 oz. lemon juice
1 tablespoon horseradish sauce

Puree all ingredients in a blender. Serve with Shrimp in Beer.

KING ANTONIO LIII — PORTER LORING, JR.

SAUCY SHRIMP

1 lb. shrimp, cooked
1 cup onions, minced
½ cup green onions, minced
2 to 4 cloves garlic, minced
½ cup margarine
2 tablespoons flour
2½ cups water
1 slice lemon

1 (8 oz.) can tomato sauce
2 bay leaves
1 tablespoon Worcestershire
¼ teaspoon pepper sauce
5 whole allspice
1 teaspoon salt
1 teaspoon sugar
½ teaspoon thyme

Saute onions, green onions, and garlic in butter until soft. Blend in flour. Add water, tomato sauce, and all other ingredients, except shrimp. Cover and simmer about 10 minutes, stirring occasionally. Uncover and continue cooking over low heat until mixture is reduced by about half. Add shrimp and serve over rice. Sauce is better made the day before. Add shrimp at serving time. Sauce may be frozen. Serves 4.

MRS. PAUL C. WENGER, JR.

SHRIMP FLAMBE JALAPENO

1½ lbs. medium to small raw
  shrimp, peeled and deveined
½ cup onion, chopped
½ cup jalapeño peppers with
  seeds, chopped

1 stick butter
flour
⅔ cup Brandy
1 tablespoon Green Chartreuse

Dust shrimp very lightly with flour. Saute onions and jalapeños in butter until onion is transparent. Add shrimp and saute until they just turn pink. Remove shrimp from the pan and with a slotted spoon, transfer to a flame pan or chafing dish. While still hot, add ⅔ cup of brandy. Fold in 1 tablespoon of flaming Green Chartreuse. (Chartreuse will ignite the brandy.) Allow to flame until it burns out. Serve immediately. Serves 4 to 6.

COLONEL JACK C. YOUNG

SHRIMP CACCIATORE

2 lbs. raw shrimp
4 small onions, quartered
1 cup canned tomatoes
5 tablespoons olive oil

1 cup mushrooms, sliced
1 large green pepper, sliced
1 clove garlic
salt and pepper to taste

Peel and devein shrimp. Heat oil and add onions, tomatoes, garlic, and green pepper. Cover and simmer slowly for 10 minutes. Add shrimp and mushrooms, and season to taste. Simmer an additional 10 minutes. Serve either plain, over hot rice or spaghetti. Serves 4 to 6.

MRS. JAMES W. PRESSLEY

SHRIMP SCAMPI

2 lbs. fresh jumbo shrimp
3 cloves garlic, minced
¼ teaspoon salt
2 tablespoons parsley

¼ cup olive oil
¼ cup melted butter
½ teaspoon green pepper
2 tablespoons lemon juice

Peel and devein shrimp, leaving tails on. Split each lengthwise, 1 inch from head. Combine all other ingredients and dip shrimp in mixture. Place shrimp in shallow pan in single layer. Pour remaining sauce over shrimp. Broil 6 to 8 minutes, 3 inches from heat. Serve on warm platter. Pour drippings on top. Serves 4.

MRS. JAMES W. GRAHAM

KARI INDIAN DINNER FOR 4 — Shrimp Curry

MENU	CONDIMENTS
Kari—Shrimp Curry	Chopped Fresh Bananas
Chatni—Fresh Mango Chutney	Fresh Grated Coconut
Salat—Tomato and Onion Salad	Chopped Scallions

Shrimp Curry — Kari

3 lbs. shrimp
2 cups whipping cream
1 cup light cream
1 teaspoon salt
½ lb. butter
2 cups onions, minced

1 garlic clove, minced
¾ green pepper, minced
⅓ cup curry powder
¼ cup flour
3 cups chicken stock

Peel and devein shrimp. Combine shrimp, light cream, whipping cream and salt in a covered bowl and chill. Saute onions, garlic and green pepper in butter until the onions are soft but not brown. Add curry powder and flour and cook for 2 or 3 minutes, stirring constantly. Gradually add chicken stock, bring to a boil stirring constantly. Reduce heat and simmer for about 15 minutes. Drain the cream from the shrimp and add it to the sauce. Simmer for another 30 minutes. Add the shrimp at serving time and cook 3 or 4 minutes or until they turn pink. Serve with curry rice, Pappadums (Indian Bread available at local gourmet shops) and the condiments listed above. Serves 4.

Mango Chutney — Chatni

1 lb. ripe mangoes
1 green chile, seeded
1 tablespoon salt
⅛ teaspoon hot, ground red
  pepper

1 tablespoon coriander
  (cilantro) chopped

Peel and remove center from mangoes. Cut into long, thin slices and place in a serving dish with the green chile, cut into rings. Add salt, red pepper and coriander. Toss lightly and chill for several hours before serving. Serves 4.

Tomato and Onion Salad — Salat

2 fresh ripe tomatoes
1/4 cup coriander, chopped
1 onion, chopped
lemon juice

1 teaspoon salt
1/4 teaspoon pepper
1/4 teaspoon ground red pepper
1 teaspoon cumin seed

Toast cumin seeds in an iron skillet for 2 or 3 minutes until they turn brown. Remove and crush with a mortar and pestle or rolling pin. Add coarsley chopped tomatoes and the remaining ingredients. Chill in a covered bowl until serving time. Serves 4.

MARGARET STANLEY

CRYSTAL SHRIMP WITH CASHEWS

1 cup raw shrimp
1/2 teaspoon salt
1/2 teaspoon MSG
1 egg white
2 1/4 teaspoons cornstarch
1/2 teaspoon sesame seed oil
dash white pepper
3/4 tablespoon water
1/4 teaspoon sugar

1 tablespoon sherry
3 oz. cashews, toasted or
    deep fried
1/2 cup bamboo shoots or water
    chestnuts, sliced
2 green onions, sliced diagonally
    (reserve green for garnish)
1/2 teaspoon ginger root, minced
2 cups frying oil

Peel and devein shrimp. Combine 1/4 teaspoon salt, 1/4 teaspoon MSG, egg white, 2 teaspoons cornstarch, 1/4 teaspoon sesame oil, and dash white pepper. Marinate shrimp in mixture for 20 to 30 minutes. Make sauce, using 3/4 tablespoon water, 1/4 teaspoon cornstarch, 1/4 teaspoon salt, 1/4 teaspoon MSG, 1/4 teaspoon sugar, 1/4 teaspoon sesame oil, and 1 tablespoon sherry. Set sauce aside. Deep-fry marinated shrimp briefly—until just turning in color. In separate skillet, stir-fry onion and ginger in 1 tablespoon oil, until just sizzling. Add fried shrimp, bamboo shoots, or water chestnuts; stir, then add sauce. Stir constantly until sauce turns shiny (almost immediately). Add cashews, and sprinkle with sherry. Garnish with raw onion greens just before serving. Serve immediately, but may be frozen and reheated. Serves 4 to 6.

MRS. P. M. KU (ANLIN)

SHRIMP STRUDEL

3 packages frozen patty shells
½ lb. mushrooms, sliced thin
3 tablespoons butter
1 small onion, chopped
1 lb. small shrimp

1 cup thick white sauce
2 tablespoons sherry
1 teaspoon dried dill weed
salt and pepper
1 egg white, beaten lightly

Cook shrimp in salted water, seasoned with sliced lemon, celery tops and onions. Peel and devein shrimp. Saute onion and mushrooms in butter and combine with shrimp seasonings and white sauce. Fit thawed patty shells together and roll into a flat dough. Spread with the shrimp mixture and roll, jelly-roll fashion. Pinch the ends together. Make 5 or 6 diagonal slits in the pastry and brush with beaten egg white. Bake at 425° for 25 minutes or longer. (Recipe may be made with chicken, veal or crabmeat.) Serves 6 to 8.

MRS. O. ELLIOTT URSIN (JERRY)

ACADIA SEAFOOD

8 oz. low calorie cream cheese
½ cup milk
½ cup sour cream
⅓ cup chopped green onions, including tops

3 cups cooked rice
2 lbs. crabmeat or shrimp
salt and pepper to taste
bread crumbs

Combine cream cheese, sour cream and milk. Whip until smooth. Fold in green onions, salt, pepper, rice and cooked seafood. Turn into a buttered 3 quart baking dish. Spread bread crumbs evenly over the top and bake at 350° about 20 minutes until bubbly and top is browned. Serves 10.

MRS. EDWARD CUYLER SULLIVAN

CREAMY CRAB ALASKAN

3 (6 oz.) packages Wakefield Alaskan King Crab
8 bread slices
½ cup mayonnaise
1 medium onion, chopped
¼ cup green pepper, chopped

½ cup celery, chopped
2 cups Half and Half
4 eggs
salt and pepper to taste
1 can cream of chicken soup
½ lb. Velveeta cheese, grated

Remove crust from bread slices and place in buttered 2½ quart baking dish. Combine crab, mayonnaise, onion, celery, green pepper and spread on top of bread. Mix Half and Half, eggs, salt, pepper and pour over the crab mixture. Cover and refrigerate overnight. Place the casserole in a 325° oven for 15 minutes. Remove from oven, cover with soup and bake for 55 to 75 minutes. After the first 30 minutes sprinkle with grated cheese. Serves 8 to 10.

NANCY S. PORTNOY

BAKED CRABMEAT RUSK

1 can crabmeat
1 package Holland Rusks
2 large tomatoes, sliced
1 (8 oz.) package cream cheese
8 slices Kraft Old English cheese

2 tablespoons Miracle Whip
2 tablespoons catsup
1 tablespoon Worcestershire
salt and pepper
butter or margarine

Butter rusks, and place on baking sheet or in baking dish. Place a tomato slice on each rusk. Soften cream cheese, and combine with Miracle Whip, catsup, Worcestershire, and seasonings. Add crabmeat. Spoon onto rusks, top with cheese slice, and bake 30 minutes at 350°. Allow 1 rusk per person. Excellent luncheon dish. Serves 8.

MRS. ROBERT DAWSON (JEANNIE)

MARYLAND CRAB CAKES

½ stick butter
½ tablespoon flour
¾ cup cream
2 lbs. lump crab meat
3 bread slices
1 tablespoon mayonnaise

1 tablespoon parsley, chopped
1 egg, beaten
bread crumbs
deep fat for frying
salt and cayenne to taste

Make a thin white sauce with butter, flour and cream. Combine crab meat, finely crumbled bread slices, mayonnaise, salt, cayenne, and parsley. Stir in white sauce. (If necessary, soften with a little more cream.) Shape into patties the size of a thick hamburger. Dip into the beaten eggs diluted with a little water. Roll in bread crumbs and fry in deep fat until golden brown. Serves 4 to 6.

MRS. HENRY COHEN (IRENE)

BAKED CRAB SHELLS

1 lb. lump crab meat
1 cup table cream
1 green pepper, chopped
1 cup onions, chopped
1 cup cracker crumbs
2 cups celery, chopped

Tabasco, to taste
Lea and Perrins sauce
lemon
paprika
parsley

Saute onions, celery and green pepper in a little butter. In a bowl mix cracker crumbs, cream, Tabasco and Lea and Perrins sauce. Add sauteed vegetables and crabmeat. Fill crab shells and top with parsley and paprika. Bake at 350° for 40 minutes. Garnish with lemon.

LLOYD BENTSEN
United States Senator, State of Texas

IMPERIAL CRAB CASSEROLE

1 cup crabmeat
1 cup mayonnaise
1 cup cream
1 cup soft bread crumbs
6 hard-cooked eggs, chopped

½ teaspoon salt
⅛ teaspoon pepper
dash cayenne
2 tablespoons onion, chopped
1 tablespoon parsley, chopped

Combine all ingredients. Pour into greased casserole or shells and sprinkle with bread crumbs. Bake at 350° for 30 minutes. May be frozen. Chicken may be substituted for crabmeat. Serves 4.

MRS. EDWARD C. HELD

LOBSTER CHICKEN MADEIRA

2 cups lobster,
  cooked and cut into chunks
2 cups chicken,
  cooked and cut into chunks
½ cup butter
1 tablespoon onion, chopped
1 tablespoon celery, chopped
½ cup flour
⅛ teaspoon thyme

⅛ teaspoon rosemary
1 small bay leaf
1 garlic clove, minced
1 tablespoon tomato puree
3 cups brown stock or
  consomme, heated
1 tablespoon orange juice
1 tablespoon sugar
2 oz. Madeira

Melt butter in a skillet, add onions and celery. Saute for 5 minutes. Blend in flour and cook a few minutes. Add spices and tomato puree and cook slowly for 5 minutes, stirring constantly. Add the stock, cover, bring to a boil and simmer very slowly for 1 hour. Strain, if desired. Place orange juice and sugar in another saucepan and cook mixture until it turns a light caramel color. Combine both mixtures, add Madeira, chicken and lobster and heat gently. The sauce may be made in advance. (Lump crab may be substituted for the lobster.) Serves 4 to 6.

MRS. KENNETH GAARDER (MARIE)

ARTICHOKE AND CRAB SUISSE

2 sticks butter
10 heaping tablespoons flour
3 cups milk
salt and pepper
Tabasco
1 onion minced

½ bunch green onions, chopped
parsley, minced
2 cans lump crabmeat
2 cans artichoke hearts
½ lb. Swiss cheese

Melt butter and stir in flour until smooth. Add milk and stir over low heat until mixture thickens. Season with salt, pepper, and Tabasco to taste. Add onion, green onions, and parsley. Set aside. Cut cheese in ⅓ inch cubes. Arrange crabmeat, artichoke hearts, and cheese in layers. Pour sauce over all. Sprinkle with bread crumbs and bake 30 minutes in 350° oven.

MRS. H. H. PHILLIPS, JR. (MARY ALICE)

SEAFOOD CASSEROLE

6 slices white bread
1 lb. scallops
1 can crab or lobster meat
3 eggs
2 cups milk

¼ cup butter or margarine
¼ teaspoon dry mustard
6 slices American cheese
salt to taste

Remove crust from bread and place in an oiled oblong casserole. Cut scallops in bite-size pieces and parboil in a small amount of water for 5 minutes. To casserole, add scallops, slivers of cheese, melted butter, and crab or lobster. Beat eggs and combine with milk. Add salt and mustard and pour mixture over the seafood. Refrigerate overnight. Bake at 350° for 1 hour. Serves 4.

JOE SALEK

WHOLE BAKED SALMON—ALASKAN STYLE

1 (6 to 10 lb.) headless salmon	onions
Miracle Whip Salad Dressing	cayenne pepper
garlic powder	Tabasco
onion powder	juice of 1 lemon
black pepper	¾ cup good cream sherry

Wash salmon thoroughly, particularly making sure to remove the large blood vein that runs along the underside of the backbone. Coat the inside cavity with a thin layer of Miracle Whip Salad Dressing. (Do not use mayonnaise.) Sprinkle the entire cavity with a generous amount of garlic powder, onion powder and black pepper. Fill the cavity with chunks of onion.

Place the salmon in a baking pan long enough to accomodate it without bending and deep enough so the side of the salmon does not extend above the rim of the pan. Coat the entire "up" side with a thin layer of Miracle Whip and sprinkle generously with garlic powder and onion powder. Sprinkle lightly with cayenne and a few dashes of Tabasco. Cut onion slices in half and lay them on top of the Miracle Whip, rib fashion, about ½ inch apart. Squeeze the juice of the lemon gently along the fish but do not disturb any of the coating. Pour sherry into the pan and cover it tightly with foil. Bake at 350° until done. (A 6 lb. salmon should take about 55 minutes and an 8 to 10 lb. salmon about 1 hour and 10 minutes.

To check for proper cooking time, stick a sharp fork deep into the back. If juices still flow from the hole, it's not ready. If the fork hole stays open and is dry, it's OK. DO NOT OVERCOOK.

When done, lift the skin off with a tableknife. Run a thin spatula along the backbone and lift the fillet off in two pieces. Pull out the backbone, clean away the fins and fin bones and scoop out the bottom fillet in 2 pieces. If this is done right, the cooked fillets can be served boneless.

This same treatment of coating with Miracle Whip will work for any similar sized "dry" meat fish. Don't use the salad dressing on "oily" or moist fish.

COLONEL JACK C. YOUNG

THE JUDGE'S OYSTERS BORRACHO

4 dozen oysters
onion powder, to taste
garlic powder, to taste
black pepper, to taste

Tabasco sauce
cayenne pepper (optional)
juice of 1/2 to 1 lemon
1/2 cup cream sherry

Lightly rinse the oysters and drain in a colander. Place the oysters in a shallow baking dish. Place them edge to edge or slightly overlapping. (No stacking or layering, please, it annoys the oysters). Sprinkle them lightly with onion powder, garlic powder, and black pepper. Drop a minimum of 1 drop of Tabasco sauce on each oyster or sprinkle it liberally if desired. Cayenne pepper may be used, also. Squeeze the lemon juice over the oysters. Sprinkle them with cream sherry. (Use good drinking sherry—pamper the oysters as you would any respected guest!) Cover the pan tightly with foil and place in a preheated 450° oven for 12 minutes or until the oysters begin to curl. Be careful not to overcook them. They should be firm. Serve with a "hot" seafood sauce (see Index). Serves 8.

COLONEL JACK C. YOUNG

OYSTERS ELEGANTE

5 to 7 artichokes, boiled
1 1/2 pints oysters (3 dozen)
2 cups water
2 sticks butter
1/2 cup flour
1 1/4 cups finely chopped onions
9 cloves garlic, minced
1 teaspoon thyme

2 teaspoons salt
1/2 teaspoon pepper
1 teaspoon lemon juice
1/4 cup chopped parsley
bread crumbs
8 thin slices lemon
finely chopped parsley

Remove leaves from artichokes saving nice firm leaves to use as decoration and dippers. Scrape remaining leaves and reserve scrapings. Cut artichoke bottoms into eighths and place in ramekins. Drain oysters, reserving liquor. Soak oysters in 2 cups water for at least 30 minutes; drain, reserving this liquid also. Make a dark brown roux with butter and flour. Add onions and garlic, and saute until tender, about 20 minutes. Add thyme, salt, pepper, artichoke scrapings and lemon juice. Slowly stir in oyster liquid (approximately 1 to 1 1/2 cups).

The gravy should be very thick. Simmer slowly for 45 minutes, stirring occasionally. Add oysters and parsley and cook 10 minutes. Remove from heat and spoon into ramekins. Best made ahead of time or the night before. When ready to reheat, sprinkle with bread crumbs; top with lemon slices and thoroughly heat in 350° oven. Garnish with chopped parsley and surround ramekins with artichoke leaves. Use ¾ cup ramekins. (This may be served in a casserole instead of ramekins. You may also use canned artichokes or canned artichoke bottoms, but this is not as good.) Serves 6.

MRS. H. H. PHILLIPS, JR. (MARY ALICE)

TEXAS BAKED FISH

2 to 3 lbs. fillets or whole fish   ¼ teaspoon lemon-pepper
1 cup buttermilk   ¼ cup parsley, chopped
¼ teaspoon hickory-smoked salt   juice of ½ lemon
¼ teaspoon celery salt   ¼ cup sherry
¼ teaspoon onion salt   1 can cream of shrimp soup

Soak fish in buttermilk 10 minutes, or overnight in refrigerator if using frozen fish. Arrange 1 layer of fish in foil-lined pan that has been sprayed with Pam or Cooking-Ease. Sprinkle fish with seasonings, reserving 1 teaspoon parsley. Squeeze lemon juice over fish. Pour sherry evenly over all. Spoon cream of shrimp soup onto each fillet in small dots. More soup may be used, if necessary. Sprinkle with remaining parsley. Bake at 350° in oven for 15 or 20 minutes, or until fish flakes easily when tested with fork. Serve with lemon wedges. Serves 4 to 6.

MRS. WILLIAM L. STARNES (MARY DEE)

FISH A LA LEFTOVER

2 cups cooked fish   ¼ cup capers
½ cup mayonnaise   salt and pepper to taste
1 large onion, chopped   lemon juice

Mix all ingredients together and place in individual baking dishes. Bake in 350° oven for 15 minutes. Brown under the broiler for a few minutes and sprinkle with lemon juice. Serves 4.

MRS. GILBERT L. CURTIS (LORRIE)

BAKED FLOUNDER DELIGHT

2 lbs. flounder fillets
1 tablespoon butter, melted
1 tablespoon flour
3 tablespoons cream
1 can cream of mushroom soup
  or cream of celery soup

juice of 1 lemon
dash of nutmeg
dash of paprika
1/4 cup grated Parmesan cheese
1/2 teaspoon salt
4 sprigs parsley

Wipe fillets with damp cloth and sprinkle with salt and lemon juice. Melt butter in saucepan, blend in flour, nutmeg and paprika. Cook 4 minutes stirring constantly. Add soup and simmer 3 minutes. Arrange fish fillets in shallow baking dish, pour in cream, then add mushroom sauce. Sprinkle with Parmesan cheese and bake in 350° oven for 25 minutes. Garnish with parsley. Serves 4.

MRS. GEOFFREY E. GORING

BAKED FISH FILLETS

1 lb. fish fillets
1/2 stick butter or margarine

juice of 1/2 lemon
salt and pepper to taste

Put butter or margarine in an 8x8 baking dish and place in a 375° oven until brown flecks begin to appear in the butter, about 5 minutes. Watch closely, do not let it burn. Place lightly floured fish fillets in the butter and return baking dish to the oven for 12 to 15 minutes, or until fish flakes easily with a fork. After baking add lemon juice, salt and pepper. Serves 2 or 3.

MRS. GILBERT L. CURTIS (LORRIE)

TROUT AMANDINE

1 (3 lb.) fillet of trout
1 stick butter
milk, flour, salt, pepper

4 tablespoons sliced almonds
juice of 1/2 lemon
1 teaspoon chopped parsley

Dip trout in cold milk, sprinkle with flour and season with salt and pepper. Saute trout in 1/2 stick butter until golden brown and cooked through. Set aside and keep hot. Brown almonds in remaining 1/2 stick butter and add lemon juice. Pour over trout and sprinkle with parsley. Serves 2.

KAY MUSGRAVE

STUFFED FISH FILLETS AND
WATERCRESS SAUCE

2 cups packaged herb stuffing
1 (16 oz.) package frozen
  flounder, turbot, or whiting
  fillets thawed, or 8 small
  flounder fillets (1 lb.)
½ teaspoon salt

salad oil
⅓ cup margarine
1 medium onion, thin sliced
1 small garlic clove
1 bunch chopped watercress
¼ cup white wine

Preheat oven to 350°. Prepare stuffing mix according to instructions on package and set aside. Sprinkle fillets with salt. Brush a 12x8 baking dish with salad oil. Cut fillets into 8 serving pieces. Arrange 4 pieces in the baking dish. Top with stuffing and cover with the remaining 4 fillets. Brush with salad oil and bake 15 to 20 minutes until flaky. In a quart saucepan over medium heat, cook garlic and onion in margarine until onion is tender, about 10 minutes. Discard garlic. Stir in watercress and wine. Cook until watercress is tender, about 3 minutes. With pancake turner, lift fish to warm platter and pour on the sauce. Serves 4.

PAPPY'S CATFISH WITH GRAVY

4 catfish fillets
salt
corn meal

flour (optional)
vegetable oil
1 cup boiling water

Salt fillets well and roll in corn meal. (Add a small amount of flour to the meal if it fails to stick to the fish.) Drop the fillets into deep hot oil over high heat, (the oil should bubble). Turn the fillets when golden brown and remove from oil when the second side is golden brown. Total frying time, 4 or 5 minutes. Lower the heat and pour off all but ¼ inch of oil. To the crumbs that have fallen from the fish and remain in the bottom of the skillet, add enough corn meal to absorb all the oil. Cook over low heat, stirring constantly until golden brown. Gradually pour in hot water, adding more if necessary. Cook slowly until it becomes mush. Slowly add more water until it becomes the consistency of gravy. Pour hot gravy over fillets and serve. Serves 4.

MRS. HAROLD L. TAYLOR

BUTTERY BROILED FISH

1 whole dressed fish or fillets,
  fresh or frozen
Court Bouillon (see Index)
3 tablespoons butter

2½ tablespoons lemon juice
3 tablespoons parsley, minced
salt and cayenne to taste
¼ teaspoon Worcestershire

Marinate fish in Court Bouillon (see Index) for 30 minutes to 1 hour. (If using frozen fish, allow to thaw in the Court Bouillon). Combine remaining ingredients and heat in a saucepan. Place fish on buttered, foil-lined broiler pan and brush generously with butter mixture. Broil only until fish flakes easily with a fork, basting often. Do not overcook. If using whole fish, broil on both sides; fillets only, one side. Serve with lemon wedges.

Vegetables

In the culinary arts, there is little more pleasing to the palate or to the eye than a colorful vegetable, seasoned and served to perfection.

Today fresh produce is available in the marketplace no matter where we live. But San Antonio is particularly blessed. Just to the south of us is the lush Rio Grande Valley where nature's rich, dark soil and warm sunshine combine to create growing things of taste, quality and beauty. Treat them gently!

STUFFED ARTICHOKE HEARTS

8 artichoke hearts, cooked
2 shallots, chopped
2 oz. cooked ham, diced
2 oz. Gruyere cheese, grated
1 stick butter
2 oz. mushrooms, chopped

½ cup milk
2 teaspoons flour
2 teaspoons parsley, chopped
salt and pepper to taste
½ cup tomato sauce (optional)

Saute the artichoke hearts in butter for about 2 minutes on each side. In a saucepan saute the chopped shallots, mushrooms and ham. Add the parsley. Stir in the flour and cook it over a low heat, stirring for 2 minutes. Remove from heat and add the milk. Return to heat, and cook the mixture, stirring until it is thickened and smooth. Fill the artichoke hearts with about 1 tablespoon of the mixture. If desired spread about 1 tablespoonful of tomato sauce on each artichoke, sprinkle with cheese and dot with butter. Put under broiler or in a 350° oven for about 10 or 15 minutes, or until cheese is melted and lightly browned. Serves 4.

MRS. RALPH ROWDEN (FRANCINE)

SUNKEN GARDENS — Bill Reily

ARTICHOKE HEARTS AU GRATIN

1 package frozen artichoke
 hearts
1 can mushrooms
1 cup chicken stock
1 cup water or milk
1/2 cup dry white wine
2 oz. Swiss cheese, grated

1 garlic clove, crushed
 salt and pepper to taste
2 tablespoons butter
2 tablespoons flour
 bread crumbs and
 Parmesan cheese

Parboil the artichokes half the directed time on the package. Make a white sauce with butter, flour, milk and chicken stock. If sauce is too thick, thin with water. Add wine, mushrooms, Swiss cheese, garlic, salt and pepper. Mix well. Place the artichokes in a baking dish and cover with the sauce. Top with bread crumbs and Parmesan cheese. Bake in 350° oven for 20 to 30 minutes or until brown. Serves 3 or 4.

MRS. WARREN K. HOEN

ARTICHOKE AND CELERY DELIGHT

2 cans or 2 packages frozen
 artichoke hearts
2 cans mushroom soup
1 bunch celery, thin sliced

2 tablespoons onion, grated
3 tablespoons Sauterne
2 slices buttered toast

Saute celery in butter until clear. Layer artichokes and celery in casserole. Combine soup, onion, and wine, and pour over artichokes and celery. Crush toast between waxed paper or in blender, and sprinkle on top. Bake 1 hour at 375°, or until light brown and bubbly. May be prepared ahead of time to point of crumb topping. Serves 6.

MRS. RICHARD ANDRASSY

BRAISED CELERY

4 cups sliced celery
salt and pepper
1 tablespoon grated onion
1 1/2 tablespoons flour
1/2 cup double chicken bouillon

4 teaspoons butter
1 cup sliced almonds
1 tablespoon chopped chives
1 cup light cream

Slice celery to make 4 cups. Put into a saucepan. Season lightly with the salt and pepper. Then add butter, cover tightly and cook very slowly until the celery is tender, shaking the pan frequently. Uncover pan once during cooking and sprinkle with the chives and the onion. When the celery is tender (about 15 minutes), add flour and stir well. Gradually add the cream and chicken bouillon and cook, stirring constantly, or cook over hot water for 5 minutes. Check seasoning and stir in the almonds. Serves 6 to 8.

MRS. CHARLES F. SHIELD (KITTY)

CAULIFLOWER PORT SALUD

1 large cauliflower
3 eggs
1 cup Half and Half
½ lb. Port Salud cheese, sliced thin
¼ lb. butter

1 tablespoon lemon juice
½ cup bread crumbs
1 heaping teaspoon nutmeg
1 tablespoon salt
1 teaspoon pepper

Place cauliflower in a 5 quart pan with enough water to cover. Add salt and boil, over high heat, for 15 minutes. Drain and set aside to cool. Put egg yolks, Half and Half, lemon juice, bread crumbs, nutmeg and pepper into a mixing bowl and combine well. Melt butter in a 7 inch skillet over high heat. Break the cooled cauliflower into large pieces. Dip the pieces in the mixing bowl, coating well. Fry the cauliflower until brown and crisp. Place on an oven proof serving dish, cover the cauliflower with the cheese and place under the broiler long enough for the cheese to begin to melt. Serves 10.

MAJOR WILLIAM DEAN RASCO

KING WILLIAM SAUERKRAUT

2 (No. 303) cans sauerkraut
3 to 4 celery stalks, minced
½ green pepper, minced
½ cup onion, minced

1 small can pimiento, minced
1½ cups sugar
¾ cup vinegar
¾ cup cooking oil

Combine sugar, vinegar, and cooking oil. Heat to boil and set aside to cool. Rinse sauerkraut thoroughly and drain well. Combine sauerkraut, celery, green pepper, onion, and pimiento. Pour dressing over these ingredients and let stand at least 24 hours before serving. Serves 6.

MRS. JOHN R. BURKHART

ROYAL WESTERN CORN

4 or 5 ears of fresh corn
½ cup butter
1 tablespoon prepared mustard
1 teaspoon prepared horseradish
1 teaspoon salt
dash fresh ground pepper
snipped parsley

Combine butter, mustard, horseradish, salt and pepper. Cream until light and fluffy. Husk corn and strip off silk. Spread each ear with a little of the butter mixture. Wrap loosely in foil and bake at 450° for 30 to 40 minutes. Serve with extra butter mixed with parsley. Serves 4 or 5.

KING ANTONIO LII — JAMES CAVENDER, III

HERB STUFFED MUSHROOMS

16 large fresh mushrooms
½ cup butter
3 tablespoons shallots or green
  onions, finely chopped
1 cup fresh bread crumbs
½ cup parsley, chopped
½ teaspoon salt
⅛ teaspoon pepper

Wipe mushrooms with a damp cloth, remove stems and chop fine. Melt ¼ cup of the butter in a skillet. Saute mushroom caps a short time on both sides until they begin to turn a beige color and are well coated with butter. Remove to a jelly roll or flat pan. Melt remaining butter in same skillet and saute mushroom stems and shallots very briefly. Remove from heat, add bread crumbs, parsley, salt and pepper. Spoon mixture into mushroom caps. Bake in 350° oven for 20 minutes. Mushrooms may be prepared early in the day, covered and refrigerated. Serves 8.

NANCY S. PORTNOY

BROCCOLI RUSSE

1 (10 oz.) package frozen
  broccoli or fresh broccoli
¼ cup mayonnaise
1 teaspoon minced onion
⅓ cup sour cream
⅛ teaspoon cayenne pepper

Prepare broccoli according to package directions. Drain. When using fresh broccoli, cook in salt water until tender, and drain. Combine remaining ingredients. Heat gently (do not boil) in saucepan. Pour over broccoli and serve. Serves 4.

MRS. W. C. SCHORLEMER

BROCCOLI IMPERIAL

2 packages frozen chopped
broccoli
1 can cream of mushroom soup
1 cup mayonnaise
1 cup grated sharp cheese
½ small onion grated, or 2
teaspoons dried minced onion

2 eggs beaten
¼ teaspoon salt
¼ teaspoon pepper
dash of Lawry's seasoned salt
½ cup crushed cheese-crackers
or grated cheese

Cook broccoli until barely done. Drain, add mushroom soup, mayonnaise, sharp cheese, onion, eggs, and seasonings. Place in a greased 9 by 13 inch baking dish. Top with cheese-cracker crumbs or grated cheese. Bake for 30 minutes at 350°. May be prepared ahead of time and baked at serving time. Serves 8.

MRS. ROBERT G. DAWSON (JEANNIE)

MARINATED CASHEW BROCCOLI

3 lbs. fresh broccoli
½ cup olive oil
¼ cup lemon juice
½ teaspoon salt

dash of lemon pepper
2 teaspoons chervil
½ cup salted cashews, broken

Cook broccoli until just tender. Drain. Place in serving dish. Combine oil, lemon juice, salt, pepper and chervil. Pour over broccoli and chill. Just before serving sprinkle with salted cashews. Prepare up to 8 hours ahead. May be served as vegetable or salad. Serves 8.

VIVIAN M. GERSEMA

BROCCOLI PARMESAN

2 (10 oz.) packages frozen
broccoli spears
3 tablespoons butter
2 tablespoons onion, minced
¾ teaspoon salt
⅛ teaspoon pepper
½ teaspoon dry mustard

3 tablespoons flour
⅛ teaspoon marjoram
1 chicken bouillon cube
2½ cups milk
½ cup Parmesan cheese, grated
paprika

Preheat oven to 350°. Cook broccoli according to directions on package. When tender, drain and arrange in shallow baking dish. Saute onion in butter until tender. Add flour, blend in spices and

- 183 -

bouillon cube dissolved in milk. Cook over medium heat, stirring constantly until mixture comes to a boil and thickens. Add Parmesan cheese and stir until cheese is melted. Pour over broccoli. Sprinkle with paprika and more Parmesan cheese. Place in 350° oven and bake for approximately 20 to 25 minutes or until casserole is browned. Serves 8.

SANDY LAWRENCE (MRS. LESLIE J.)

BROCCOLI AND TOMATO PARMESAN

2 packages frozen or fresh
   chopped broccoli
1/2 cup dairy sour cream
1 small can mushrooms
2 tablespoons butter or
   margarine

salt and pepper to taste
dash Tabasco
3 or 4 fresh tomatoes, sliced
grated Parmesan cheese

Cook and drain broccoli well. Brown mushrooms in butter and mix with sour cream and broccoli, seasoned with Tabasco, salt and pepper. Place in a buttered baking dish. Season tomato slices with salt and pepper and dust heavily with cheese on both sides. Arrange them in a layer on top of broccoli mixture. Sprinkle a heavy layer of cheese on top and bake at 400° for about 30 minutes until top is brown. This may be made in advance. Serves 6 to 8.

JEAN HEARD

ASPARAGUS CASSEROLE

8 (15 oz.) cans green asparagus
   spears
3 (10 1/2 oz.) cans cream of
   mushroom soup
6 oz. extra sharp Cheddar cheese,
   grated

4 hard boiled eggs, sliced
1/2 cup toasted almonds, sliced
   (optional)

Drain asparagus spears in a colander at least 1 hour. (This is important, otherwise, the results will be watery.) Combine soup and cheese in a saucepan. Heat, stirring constantly, until cheese is melted. In a 9x13 inch baking dish, arrange a layer of asparagus, sliced eggs and nuts. Cover with cheese sauce. Repeat layers and top with nuts. Bake 30 to 40 minutes in a 325° oven. Serves 12.

ANTOINETTE S. BURDETT (MRS. ALLEN M., JR.)

STUFFED TOMATOES

4 large tomatoes
1 cup cooked beef or ham, diced
1 small onion, chopped
1 garlic clove, minced
1 potato, boiled and mashed
1/2 teaspoon parsley, chopped
1/4 cup Gruyere or Parmesan
  cheese

1 egg, beaten
1 teaspoon olive oil
1/4 cup bread crumbs
2 tablespoons butter
salt and pepper to taste
sliced mushrooms, (optional)

Cut the tomatoes in half and scoop out the pulp. Discard juice and seeds. Combine pulp, meat, onion, garlic, potato, parsley, cheese, egg, salt and pepper. Place a drop of oil in each tomato half and fill with meat mixture. Arrange in a buttered baking dish, sprinkle with bread crumbs and top each with a bit of butter. Bake 20 minutes in a 300° oven. (1 cup of cooked rice may be used instead of the potato.) Serves 4.

MRS. RALPH ROWDEN (FRANCINE)

TOMATOES ELEGANTE

5 ripe tomatoes
1 box broccoli, frozen
1 cup Swiss or Cheddar cheese,
  grated

2 tablespoons butter
1 tablespoon flour
1 cup milk
salt and pepper to taste

Remove tops of tomatoes and scoop out the inside. Set the tomatoes in a baking dish, dot with butter and bake 20 minutes in 350° oven, or until they are slightly soft. Do not overcook or they will lose their shape. Fill each tomato shell with broccoli, which has been cooked and drained well. Melt butter in a saucepan and add flour, salt and pepper. Slowly add milk, stirring constantly, until smooth and well blended. Add cheese. Put tomatoes on a serving plate and pour the cheese sauce over the top, letting it run on all sides. Garnish with parsley and lemon slices. Serves 5.

MRS. RALPH ROWDEN (FRANCINE)

EASY SPINACH SOUFFLE

2 packages frozen chopped
  spinach
2 eggs, beaten

1 tablespoon bacon grease
1 tablespoon garlic powder
1 can mushroom soup

Cook spinach according to direction and drain thoroughly. In a soufflé dish, combine eggs, melted bacon grease, garlic powder, and soup. Whip with a fork until thoroughly blended. Refrigerate until ready to bake. Bake for 1 hour to 1¼ hours in 350° oven or until firm. Serves 4 to 6.

MRS. JOE H. FROST

SAGE BAKED SPINACH

2 packages frozen spinach
8 oz. cream cheese
¼ lb. butter, cut in half

salt and pepper
1 cup bread crumbs
¾ teaspoon sage

Cook spinach and drain well. Soften cream cheese and butter and combine half the butter, cheese, spinach and salt and pepper. Place in a baking dish. Mix bread crumbs, remaining butter and sage. Sprinkle evenly on top of the spinach mixture. Bake at 350° for 30 minutes. Serves 6.

MRS. WILLIAM MCCRAE

SPINACH MADELEINE

2 packages frozen chopped
  spinach
4 tablespoons butter
2 tablespoons flour
2 tablespoons onion, chopped
½ cup evaporated milk
½ cup spinach liquid

½ teaspoon pepper
¾ teaspoon celery salt
¾ teaspoon garlic salt
½ teaspoon salt
6 oz. roll Jalapeño cheese
1 teaspoon Worcestershire

Cook spinach as directed, drain well and reserve liquid. Melt butter, add flour and cook until smooth but not brown. Add onions and cook until soft. Slowly add spinach liquid and milk and cook until smooth. Add seasonings and cheese and stir until cheese melts. Stir in spinach. This may be served immediately or put in a casserole, topped with bread crumbs and served the next day, heated in 325° oven until heated through. Freezes well. Especially good with baked ham or chicken. Serves 6.

DILLED FLORENTINE POTATOES

3 cups hot mashed potatoes
1 teaspoon salt
1/4 teaspoon pepper
2 tablespoons snipped chives
2 1/2 teaspoons fresh dill or
  1/2 teaspoon dry dill weed

1 package frozen chopped
  spinach
1/2 cup sour cream
1/2 cup grated Cheddar cheese

Cook the spinach according to directions and drain very well. Mix all ingredients except the sour cream and cheese. Place in a baking dish and spread sour cream on top, then the grated cheese. Bake at 400° for 20 minutes. (This dish works well with instant mashed potaties.) Serves 6.

MRS. EDWARD DROSTE

GOLDEN POTATO PUFFS

3 to 4 lbs. Idaho or Maine
  potatoes

deep fat for frying
salt

Peel and cut potatoes into 1/8 inch thick, even, lengthwise slices with a sharp knife or slaw cutter. (Slices must be even for potatoes to puff). Dry slices thoroughly. Half fill 2 large kettles with fat or oil. Heat the first pan to 300°; the second to 375° or 400°. Drop the slices, one at a time, into the first pan. Put in only enough for a single layer, don't overcrowd them. Cook 4 to 6 minutes or until they begin to puff. Stir slowly with a slotted spoon, moving the potatoes constantly. Keep fat temperature between 275° and 300°. Remove the potatoes with slotted spoon and plunge into the fat in the second pan. They will puff at once and rise to the surface. Turn until golden brown. Remove, drain on paper towels and sprinkle with salt.

To prepare Potato Puffs in advance, follow the directions and cook in the second pan until puffed. Remove at once. Place on paper towels

—they will deflate. Cover with another towel. Refrigerate up to 2 days. Before serving, plunge into a pan of fat heated to 400° to repuff and brown. Serves 6 to 8.

MRS. CARLOS PERRY (JAN)

BANANA YAM BAKE

3 to 5 bananas	1 teaspoon ginger
juice of 2 lemons	1 teaspoon pepper
3 cups cooked yams, sliced	$\frac{1}{2}$ teaspoon salt
1 cup light brown sugar, packed	2 tablespoons chopped nuts
4 tablespoons melted butter	1 tablespoon sugar

Cut bananas into $\frac{1}{2}$ inch slices and cover with lemon juice. Arrange bananas and yams in buttered $1\frac{1}{2}$ quart baking dish. Sprinkle each layer with brown sugar, butter, ginger, salt and pepper. Cover and bake at 350° for 40 minutes or until bananas are soft. Uncover, sprinkle with nuts and sugar and return to the oven for 10 minutes. Serves 6 to 8.

MRS. LYMAN R. FINK (FRANCES)

ZUCCHINI AU GRATIN

2 to $2\frac{1}{2}$ lbs. zucchini, grated to make 2 cups	2 tablespoons flour
3 tablespoons onion, grated	$1\frac{1}{2}$ cups hot milk
2 teaspoons salt	$\frac{1}{4}$ cup Parmesan cheese, grated
1 tablespoon olive oil	$\frac{1}{4}$ cup Swiss cheese, grated
3 tablespoons butter	salt and pepper to taste

Put zucchini in a colander and sprinkle with salt. Allow to stand about 5 minutes and then squeeze as dry as possible. If it is too salty, rinse in cold water and squeeze again. Saute onion in oil for 1 minute, add zucchini, stir and cook for 4 or 5 minutes. Remove from skillet. Make a cream sauce with butter, flour and milk. Combine cheeses and add to the sauce. (Reserve a little for topping). Add the zucchini and onion mixture and pour into a greased baking dish. Sprinkle with reserved cheese and bake at 375° for 30 minutes. Serves 4 to 6.

MRS. McGREGOR SNODGRASS

BROILED ZUCCHINI

6 zucchini of like size
1/4 cup melted butter
freshly grated Parmesan cheese

seasoned salt (Lawry's, Beau
Monde or Spike's Greek
Seasoning)

Wash and cut squash in half lengthwise and steam until just done (underdone is better.) Drain on layered paper towels cut side down until all moisture is gone. Place squash on cookie sheet cut side up. Brush with melted butter, sprinkle with grated Parmesan and seasoned salt. Broil until browned and bubbly. May be prepared ahead of time and refrigerated until about 1 hour before serving. Allow to come to room temperature and then broil. Serves 6.

MARY BETH WILLIAMSON

STUFFED MEXICAN SQUASH

4 Mexican squash (Calabassa)
1/4 cup celery, chopped
1/4 teaspoon poultry seasoning
bread crumbs
butter

2 bacon strips, chopped
1/4 cup onion, chopped
salt and pepper
Parmesan cheese

Parboil squash for about 5 minutes. Cut in half, lengthwise and scoop out inside. Leave a little thickness to the squash shell. Saute bacon until done and add celery, onion and scooped out squash. Saute until onion is clear. Add poultry seasoning, salt and pepper. Stuff the squash lightly and sprinkle the tops with bread crumbs and Parmesan cheese. Dot with butter. Place in a baking dish and bake for 30 to 40 minutes in 350° oven. Serves 4 for luncheon or 8 as a dinner vegetable.

VIVIAN M. GERSEMA

CINNAMON CARROTS

9 small carrots, scraped
3 tablespoons butter or
  margarine, melted
1/4 cup sugar

1/2 teaspoon salt
1/4 teaspoon cinnamon
3 tablespoons boiling water

Place carrots in a 1 quart casserole. Combine butter or margarine, sugar, salt, cinnamon and water and pour over carrots. Cover and bake for 1 1/4 hours in 350° oven. Serves 4.

MRS. JACK C. YOUNG (GERRY)

GLAZED ONIONS

24 small white onions   1½ cups chicken or beef stock
2 tablespoons butter   pinch salt
1 tablespoon oil   pinch sugar

Heat butter and oil in heavy skillet just large enough to hold 24 onions in one layer. Peel onions and heat in skillet with salt and sugar over moderately high heat for 4 or 5 minutes, until slightly browned. Add chicken stock, cover, and cook over low heat for 30 to 40 minutes until tender. Remove cover and shake pan to coat with glaze. May be placed in casserole for serving and held. Serves 8 to 12, depending on onion size selected.

MRS. GERALD W. MASSY III (DOROTHY)

SPICED BAKED ONIONS

3 spanish onions, halved   ¼ teaspoon nutmeg
6 whole cloves   dash cayenne pepper
3 tablespoons butter   ¼ cup toasted slivered blanched
1 tablespoon brown sugar   almonds (optional)
1 teaspoon salt

Place onions in a large saucepan with 2 inches of boiling, salted water. Bring to a boil, cover and simmer 20 minutes or until almost tender. Drain well. Insert clove into each onion half. Place in a baking dish. Melt butter, add brown sugar, salt, nutmeg and cayenne pepper. Drizzle this over the onions. Cover and bake at 325° for 45 minutes or until tender, basting occasionally with the sugar glaze. At serving time, sprinkle with almonds. (Note — a toothpick or two placed through the onions will keep them from boiling apart.) Serves 6.

MRS. JACK C. YOUNG (GERRY)

MRS. LINDER'S ONION PIE

1¼ cups sifted flour   3 eggs
1½ teaspoons salt   1 cup sour cream
¼ cup butter   ⅛ teaspoon white pepper
¼ cup shortening   1½ teaspoons chives
2½ tablespoons milk   ½ teaspoon caraway seeds
8 slices bacon   few drops soy sauce
2 cups onions, thinly sliced

Preheat oven to 425°. Sift flour and ¾ teaspoon salt into bowl. Cut in butter and ½ the shortening until mixture is very fine; cut in remaining shortening until particles are the size of peas. Sprinkle milk in small amounts over mixture, stirring with fork until dough clings together. Shape dough into smooth ball. On lightly floured surface, roll dough into 12 inch circle; fit into 9 inch pie plate. Fold overhang under, making a stand-up rim flute edge; with fork prick pastry well. Bake 10 minutes or until golden. Remove from oven. Reduce oven to 300°. Saute bacon until crisp; crumble. Saute onions in 3 tablespoons bacon fat. Beat eggs slightly; stir in sour cream, remaining salt, pepper, chives, onions, bacon, and soy sauce. Mix well. Pour mixture into baked pie shell; sprinkle with caraway seeds. Bake 30 minutes. Serves 8.

ENGLISH PEA CASSEROLE

2 cans English peas, drained or
  2 frozen packages
1 onion
½ cup celery, chopped
½ green pepper

1 can mushrooms
1 can pimientos
1 can water chestnuts, sliced
1 can mushroom soup
¾ stick butter

Saute onion, pepper, celery in butter. Combine all ingredients. Place in casserole and top with buttered crumbs. Bake at 350° for 30 minutes. Serves 6.

DOSIE MYERS

GREEN BEANS ORIENTAL

3 packages frozen French cut
  beans
1 can water chestnuts, sliced
1 tablespoon soy sauce
salt and pepper to taste

Seasonall to taste
⅓ cup slivered blanched
  almonds
¼ cup Parmesan cheese, grated
2 cans mushroom soup

Cook beans for 3 minutes. Drain well. Add other ingredients, except almonds and cheese and pour into a buttered baking dish. Top with a mixture of cheese and almonds. (A can of fried onion rings may be substituted for this topping). Bake in 350° oven for 30 to 45 minutes or until bubbly. Serves 8 to 10.

MRS. ROBERT DAWSON (JEANNIE)

VEGETABLES A LA GRECQUE

¾ lb. green beans
1 cauliflower
1 can artichoke hearts
1 pint cherry tomatoes
1 cup mushrooms, sliced
1 cup black olives
¾ cup vinegar

¼ cup chopped parsley
1 tablespoon thyme
1 tablespoon oregano
3 teaspoons salt
2 teaspoons coarsely ground
   pepper
¼ cup olive oil

Cut cauliflower into flowerettes and cook until just tender. Cook the beans until just tender. They should still be crisp. Combine vinegar, parsley, thyme, oregano, salt, pepper and olive oil. Shake well. Put beans, cauliflower, tomatoes, mushrooms, hearts and olives in a dish and cover with dressing. Refrigerate overnight. Serves 6.

MRS. ARTHUR E. GRANT

BEETS N' BEANS

2 (No. 2) cans Blue Lake green
   beans, drained
1 (No. 2) can shoe string beets,
   drained
2 large white onions, sliced

5 garlic cloves
2 cups salad oil
1 cup vinegar
2 tablespoons sugar
salt and pepper

Mix vegetables in a flat pan. Combine remaining ingredients and pour over vegetables. Chill in refrigerator for 24 hours or longer. Serves 12.

MRS. HARRIS K. OPPENHEIMER

DRESSY VEGETABLES

2 cups sour cream
4 hard-boiled eggs, sieved
1 medium onion, grated
1 teaspoon prepared mustard
4 tablespoons olive oil
4 tablespoons vegetable oil
1 teaspoon Worcestershire

dash Tabasco
1 teaspoon salt
1 package frozen English peas
1 package frozen lima beans
1 (No. 2) can French-style green
beans

Combine sour cream, eggs, onion, mustard, oils, Worcestershire, Tabasco, and salt. Refrigerate overnight. Remove from refrigerator 1 or 2 hours before serving. Cook peas and limas according to directions on package. Heat green beans. Drain vegetables and combine. Place vegetables in serving dish, and pour marinade over the top. Sprinkle with paprika. Serves 10.

MRS. GEORGE C. VINEY (PEG)

VEGETABLE CASSEROLE VARIE— GREEK BRIANI

1½ lbs. zucchini, sliced ¼ inch thick
2 large carrots, sliced
1 lb. potatoes, peeled and sliced
2 onions, sliced
2 cloves garlic, minced
1 (28 oz.) can whole tomatoes
2 lbs. whole okra, fresh or frozen
½ cup parsley, chopped
1 tablespoon oregano
½ cup olive oil
salt and pepper to taste

Parboil carrots and potatoes in salted water for 10 minutes. Remove tomatoes from liquid and chop. Recombine tomatoes with liquid, garlic, salt, pepper, oregano, parsley, and oil. In oiled casserole, arrange layers of potatoes, carrots, zucchini, onion, and okra, sprinkling each layer with the tomato mixture. Top casserole with remaining tomato mixture. Bake covered at 350° for 1 hour. May be served cold. Variations may be made using eggplant, green beans, or other fresh vegetables in season. Serves 6.

JOE SALEK

STIR FRIED SNOW PEAS

1 package snow peas, frozen
1 tablespoon salad oil
1 tablespoon soy sauce
1 garlic clove, minced
1 tablespoon cornstarch
1 (5 oz.) can bamboo shoots or mushrooms
1 (5 oz.) can water chestnuts, sliced
1 chicken bouillon cube

Wash and remove strings from snow peas. In a wok, over high heat, saute garlic in oil and soy sauce until brown. Add peas, bamboo shoots, water chestnuts or mushrooms. Toss and cook over high heat for 1 minute. Dissolve bouillon cube in 1 cup boiling water and pour over peas. Cover and cook at medium heat for 2 minutes. Combine cornstarch and 1 tablespoon cold water. Stir into snow peas and cook until thickened. Serves 3 to 4.

MRS. JOE H. FROST

EGGPLANT ESPANA

1 medium eggplant
6 bacon strips
1 cup sharp cheese, grated
1 (14½ oz.) can Hunts Stewed
  Tomatoes
1 small green pepper, chopped
1 medium onion or 4 or 5
  green onions, chopped
¼ package Pepperidge Farm
  Cornbread Dressing
1 small package Fritos

Peel eggplant, cut in slices and soak in salt water for 30 minutes. Drain. Boil eggplant until tender and drain well. Fry bacon until crisp and crumble. Drain skillet except for about 1 tablespoon of fat. Saute onion and pepper in bacon fat. Add the stewed tomatoes and simmer. Add eggplant and then cornbread dressing and crumbled bacon. Heat this mixture slightly and add ½ of the cheese. Pour in a greased baking dish, sprinkle the top with the remaining cheese and decorate with the Fritos. Bake for 30 to 40 minutes in 350° oven. This freezes well or may be kept in the refrigerator for hours without the Fritos. If frozen, thaw slowly before baking. Serves 6.

MRS. EDWARD DROSTE

EGGPLANT PROVENCAL

1 large eggplant
1 garlic clove, minced
½ cup onion, chopped
½ lb. mushrooms, sliced
4 tablespoons olive oil
½ teaspoon marjoram
½ teaspoon dill weed
1 teaspoon salt
1 (No. 2½) can tomatoes
½ lb. Mozarella cheese, grated
½ cup Parmesan cheese, grated

Peel and cube eggplant. Saute with garlic, onion and mushrooms in oil for 5 minutes or until onions are soft but not brown. Add marjoram, dill, salt and tomatoes and simmer for 10 minutes. In a greased 2½ quart baking dish pour half the eggplant mixture and sprinkle a layer of half the Mozarella and Parmesan cheese. Pour in the remaining eggplant and top with the remaining cheese. Bake at 350° for 45 minutes. This is a rich buffet vegetable dish that goes well with a simple entree and green salad. The recipe may be doubled. Serves 6 to 8.

MRS. MICHAEL BELISLE

STUFFED EGGPLANT

1 large eggplant
1 tablespoon butter
2 onions, shredded
1 tablespoon flour
1 large green pepper, chopped
1 small clove garlic, minced
1 tablespoon chopped parsley
¼ teaspoon cayenne
½ teaspoon thyme

3 to 6 pepper corns
1 cup tomatoes, canned
1 cup lamb, pork, shrimp or
    crabmeat
1 egg beaten
1 cup bread crumbs
1 cup well-buttered bread
    crumbs

Parboil eggplant and cut in half, lengthwise. Scoop out pulp and save shells. Saute onions in butter until golden. Add flour, seasonings and mix well. Add tomatoes and eggplant pulp. Stir well. Add egg, bread crumbs, cooked meat or seafood. (Omit egg if shrimp or crabmeat is used). Stuff eggplant shells and sprinkle with buttered crumbs. Bake at 300° for 40 minutes.

MRS. EDGAR TOBIN

EGGPLANT AU GRATIN

1 medium eggplant
3 medium onions, chopped
boiling salted water
1 cup cracker crumbs

1 egg, beaten
½ cup Bleu cheese, crumbled
3 tablespoons melted butter

Peel and dice eggplant and cook with the onion in boiling water until tender, about 10 minutes. Drain well. Add ¾ cup cracker crumbs, eggs and cheese. Mix lightly, but thoroughly. Spoon into a greased 1½ quart baking dish. Combine remaining crumbs and butter and sprinkle over the top. Bake for 30 minutes in 350° oven. Serves 4 to 6.

MRS. EDWARD C. HELD

MOUSSAKA

1 large eggplant
olive oil
2 medium onions chopped
2 cloves garlic minced
2 tablespoons chopped parsley
1 cup canned tomatoes
2 egg whites

1 lb. ground lamb
½ teaspoon thyme
½ teaspoon oregano
¼ teaspoon nutmeg
½ cup white wine
1 teaspoon salt
½ cup bread crumbs

Pare eggplant; cut into ½ inch slices, sprinkle with salt and allow to drain ½ hour. Rinse and dry thoroughly. Brown meat with onion and garlic. Drain off fat. Add salt, seasonings, parsley, tomatoes and wine. Cover and cook slowly 30 minutes. Cool. Mix in unbeaten egg whites and ½ the crumbs. Brown the dry eggplant slices in olive oil. Sprinkle bottom of rectangular oven dish with remaining crumbs. Cover with layer of eggplant. Spoon on all the meat mix, pour Moussaka Sauce over all and top with Parmesan. Bake at 350° for 45 minutes.

Moussaka Sauce

3 tablespoons flour
3 tablespoon butter
1½ cups milk
½ teaspoon salt

2 egg yolks
4 tablespoons grated Parmesan
   cheese

Melt butter but do not brown. Add flour slowly, stirring constantly. Remove from heat and slowly mix in the milk. Return to heat and stir until sauce thickens. Beat egg yolks well and add with salt and pepper to sauce, stirring constantly until blended. Pour sauce over Moussaka, top with Parmesan and bake as directed. Serves 8.

MRS. LEO F. DUSARD, JR. (BETTY)

GREEK MOUSSAKA

3 medium size eggplants
salt
3 medium size ripe tomatoes
2 cups finely minced onions
¾ cup butter or corn oil
   margarine
2 lbs. ground lean lamb
1 clove garlic, finely minced
1 can (8 oz.) tomato sauce

¼ cup chopped parsley
1 tablespoon salt
½ teaspoon cinnamon
¼ cup flour
2 cups milk
1½ teaspoons salt
dash of nutmeg
1 cup Ricotta or Cottage cheese
3 eggs, beaten

Pare eggplant and cut lengthwise in ½ inch thick slices. Sprinkle with salt. Set aside to draw out excess liquid and bitterness. Remove skin from tomatoes and dice. Cook onion in 2 tablespoons butter or margarine over medium heat until soft. Add lamb and garlic and stir to crumble meat. Add tomatoes, tomato sauce, parsley, 1 tablespoon salt and cinnamon. Cook, stirring, until most of the moisture disappears. Dry eggplant. Brown on both sides in butter or margarine, using 2 tablespoons per batch. Blend flour into 2 tablespoons melted butter or margarine in sauce pan. Cook 1 minute, stirring constantly. Slowly add milk, then salt and nutmeg. Bring to boil; stir and boil 1 minute. Cool slightly. Stir in the cheese and eggs. Heat oven to 375°. Layer ½ the eggplant in 13x9x2 inch baking dish. Spoon ½ the meat mixture over eggplant. Repeat layers. Spoon on cheese sauce. Bake 30 minutes. Brown under broiler. Allow to stand 15 minutes. Serves 8 to 10.

MRS. CARLOS PERRY (JAN)

THE QUADRANGLE, FORT SAM HOUSTON

Grain & Pasta

San Antonio's melange of mixed ancestry prepares an array of authentic Mexican, German, Italian, Oriental and Middle Eastern foods. Each one has its own unique way with grain and pasta. Our collection offers just a few.

Try steeping wild rice with Texas game, or concocting Hopping John. Of course, a favorite in San Antonio is Spanish Rice—a delicious combination of chopped onions, green peppers, chile peppers, tomatoes, garlic and cominos.

SPANISH RICE

3 tablespoons bacon drippings
1 cup uncooked rice
1 medium onion, chopped fine
1 garlic clove, minced
1½ cups canned tomatoes
2 tablespoons carrots, minced

2 tablespoons green pepper, minced
1 teaspoon cominos
1 (10½ oz.) can beef or chicken broth
salt and pepper

Brown the rice well in hot bacon drippings. (This is the most important step in the preparation of this dish). Add the remaining ingredients, cover, and cook slowly until all liquid is absorbed, about 25 minutes. (If you prefer the spicier dish, add 1 small chopped chile pepper instead of the green pepper.) Serves 6.

To prepare a speedy and simple Spanish flavored rice dish, saute 1 cup of raw rice until it is golden. Add 1 minced garlic clove, ¼ cup minced onion, 1 teaspoon salt, ½ teaspoon ground cumin, 1½ cups water and ½ (8 oz.) can tomato sauce. Mix well, cover and simmer for 25 minutes. Serves 4.

FORT SAM HOUSTON QUADRANGLE — Paula Shelokov

HOPPING JOHN

1 can condensed onion soup
1 soup can water
1/4 teaspoon salt
1/2 teaspoon Tabasco
  (McIlhenny)

1 package frozen black-eyed peas
1 1/2 cups cooked ham strips
2 tablespoons salad oil
1 1/2 cups water
1 1/2 cups pre-cooked rice

In medium saucepan, combine onion soup, water, salt, and Tabasco. Bring to a boil. Add black-eyed peas, cover and simmer 40 to 45 minutes until peas are tender. Saute ham in oil. Add water, rice, and ham strips to pea mixture. Continue to simmer about 5 minutes until rice is tender and water absorbed. Serves 6.

The origin of such an intriguing name is lost in legend. Perhaps it derived from some strange custom of having the children hop once around the table before being served, or it may have been the name of a sprightly butler.

FROST BROS., SAN ANTONIO, TEXAS

VALENCIA RICE

2 tablespoons butter
2 tablespoons onions, chopped
  fine
2 zucchini cubed (1 1/2 cups)
2 cups raw rice
salt and pepper to taste
1/2 teaspoon thyme
1/2 bay leaf

1/2 package frozen peas, cooked
3 tablespoons butter
3/4 cup peeled tomatoes, cubed
2 cups water
1/2 cup chicken broth
2 teaspoons parsley
2 tablespoons chopped
  pimientos (optional)

Preheat oven to 400°. Melt butter in casserole, add onions and cook until wilted. Add zucchini and tomatoes and stir. Cook until most of the liquid evaporates. Add rice and stir. Add water, salt and pepper, chicken broth, and bring to boil on top of stove. Add bay leaf and thyme and bring to boil again. Bake covered, 18 minutes or until moisture is absorbed and rice is tender. Add peas and butter and mix thoroughly. Serves 8.

MRS. LEO F. DUSARD, JR. (BETTY)

SAVORY RICE WITH PEAS

1 tablespoon olive oil
¼ cup butter
1 small onion, chopped
½ slice bacon, diced
2 cups fresh or frozen peas
¾ cup rice

1¾ cups chicken stock or
  Swanson's Chicken Broth
1 teaspoon salt
pepper to taste
1 tablespoon grated Parmesan

Heat olive oil and butter in a heavy kettle and brown the onion and bacon. Add the peas and cook for 5 minutes, stirring frequently. Add the rice and cook for 3 minutes longer, stirring often, until the grains are well coated with oil and butter. Add the chicken stock, salt and pepper. Cover and cook over low heat for 15 to 20 minutes. The rice should absorb all the liquid and be tender, but not mushy. Toss with the grated Parmesan. Serves 6.

MRS. LAWRENCE A. MARTIN, JR. (DOLORES)

RICE-BROCCOLI CASSEROLE

1 cup long grain rice
2 packages frozen broccoli
1 can cream of chicken soup

1 small jar Cheez Whiz
1 onion, chopped
4 tablespoons butter

Cook rice and broccoli separately. Saute onion in butter. Heat soup and melt the Cheese Whiz in the soup. Layer rice, broccoli and sauce in a casserole. Bake 20 to 30 minutes at 350°. Serves 6 to 8.

GRAHAM B. MILBURN, MD

GREEN RICE

2 cups uncooked rice
2 eggs, beaten
⅔ cup salad or olive oil
2 cups sharp cheese
2 cups cream

3 medium onions
1 clove garlic
1 cup parsley (before grinding)
1 green pepper
salt to taste

Cook rice as directed. Grind or chop other ingredients in a blender. Add beaten egg to oil and milk. Combine and add mixture to rice. Bake in casserole for 1 hour at 350°. Serves 12.

MRS. GERALD W. MASSY III (DOROTHY)

BEAUTIFUL BAKED RICE

5 tablespoons butter
2 cups rice
¼ cup onion, minced
½ teaspoon garlic, minced
3 cups chicken broth

3 sprigs parsley
2 sprigs thyme or ½ teaspoon
　dried
1 bay leaf
pinch cayenne or Tabasco

Melt 2 tablespoons butter in a heavy saucepan or oven-baking dish. Saute onion and garlic, stirring with a wooden spoon, until onion is clear. Add rice and stir briefly over low heat until well coated with butter. Stir in stock. (Make sure there are no lumps in the rice.) Add remaining seasonings. Cover with a tight lid and place in 400° oven. Bake about 20 to 25 minutes. Remove cover and discard parsley and thyme sprigs. Using a 2-pronged fork, stir in remaining butter. Rice may be made up to 2 days ahead and re-heated very slowly in a 200° oven about 1 hour. Serves 8.

MRS. KENNETH GAARDER (MARIE)

CURRY RICE

1½ cups rice
6 tablespoons butter
1 tablespoon mild curry

1 tablespoon hot curry
3 cups chicken broth
1 cup yellow raisins

Brown rice in the butter until straw colored and add curry, chicken broth and raisins. Bring to a boil, cover, and reduce heat. Simmer 15 minutes, or until broth is absorbed. Serves 8.

MRS. H. RANDOLPH BROWN

SAFFRON BAKED RICE

6 cups cooked rice
½ lb. Monterey Jack cheese,
　grated
1 (4 oz.) can peeled green chiles,
　chopped

2 cups sour cream
1 tablespoon saffron
salt and pepper to taste

Combine rice, cheese, chiles, saffron, salt and pepper. Mix lightly. Fold in sour cream. Spoon into an 8 cup mold or deep baking dish. Bake 30 minutes in 350° oven. Serves 12.

GRITS SOUFFLE

1 cup grits
3 cups boiling salted water
4 eggs
1 cup milk

1 teaspoon sugar
1 cup grated New York State
   sharp cheese
2 tablespoons butter

Pour grits slowly into boiling water and cook until thick. Separate eggs and beat egg whites until stiff. With the same beater beat the yolks. Add to yolks, 1 cup milk, sugar and mix well. Stir cooked grits very slowly into the egg yolk mixture until it is well mixed. Add grated cheese, mix well again and fold in beaten egg whites. Melt the butter in the bottom of the baking dish to be used so that it covers generously. Pour in the grits and bake in 350° oven for about 45 minutes.

MRS. ERNST V. KUNZ

UNHUMBLE HOMINY

2 cups canned hominy (liquid
  ½ drained)
1 can mushroom soup
½ cup cream
1 teaspoon Worcestershire
½ teaspoon salt

¼ teaspoon celery seed
⅛ teaspoon cayenne
¾ cup slivered almonds
1 small can sliced mushrooms
1 cup corn flake crumbs
1 stick margarine, melted

Mix hominy, mushroom soup, cream, Worcestershire, salt, celery seed, cayenne, almonds and mushrooms. Pour into buttered baking dish. Combine margarine with corn flake crumbs. Sprinkle over the top of hominy mixture. Bake at 350° for 30 minutes. Serves 6 to 8.

MRS. GEORGE C. VINEY (PEG)

KASHA

¾ cup buckwheat groats
  (medium grain)
1 teaspoon Gaylord Hauser
  Veg-All

2 cups boiling water
1 medium onion, chopped
2 tablespoons butter or Mazola
  margarine

Saute onions in butter or margarine until transparent. Cover and cook over very low heat for 1 hour. In another skillet, toast groats in a dry pan over medium heat, stirring frequently with a wooden spoon.

Combine Veg-All with boiling water. When the groats are a toasty brown, remove from the heat and pour in the boiling water. Cover and allow to stand for at least 20 minutes . Just before serving, mix hot onion mixture with groats. Serve with Texas Beef Neck Bones (see Index), plain, or with any meat gravy. Serves 4.

With a few modern changes, this has been in my family for years. It traveled with them from Turkey to Russia when they were prisoners during a Turkish-Russian war. My grandmother taught it to me.

MRS. LEONARD STERN (JEANNETTE)

LASAGNA

2 lbs. ground beef
2 tablespoons olive oil
2 garlic cloves, crushed
1 (8 oz.) can tomato sauce
1 large can tomatoes
1½ teaspoons salt
½ teaspoon oregano

½ teaspoon pepper
½ lb. lasagna noodles
½ lb. Mozzarella cheese, sliced
1 pint Ricotta cheese or Cottage cheese, well drained
½ cup Parmesan cheese

Brown the beef in a skillet with olive oil and garlic. Drain 1 cup of liquid off the tomatoes and add the tomatoes, tomato sauce and seasonings to the skillet. Cover and simmer 15 to 20 minutes. Cook the noodles in boiling salted water until just tender, about 15 minutes. Drain and rinse. Fill a baking dish with alternate layers of noodles, Mozarella cheese, Ricotta or Cottage cheese, tomato-meat sauce and top with Parmesan cheese. Bake in 375° oven for 15 to 20 minutes until bubbly. This freezes well and can be prepared ahead. Serves 6 to 8.

MRS. MICHAEL J. KAINE (ETHEL)

SPAGHETTI PERFECTION

1 (10 oz.) package vermicelli
1 teaspoon salt
6 quarts boiling water

½ cup butter or margarine
½ cup Parmesan cheese
fresh ground pepper

Bring water to a rapid boil. Break spaghetti in half and add slowly so water continues to boil. When all spaghetti is rapidly boiling, set timer for 8 minutes. Put several ice cubes in a tumbler of water. When timer goes off, immediately pour the iced water into the boiling spaghetti. Drain spaghetti into a colander. Into the cooking pot, add the butter and cheese. Put the drained spaghetti on top and rapidly toss the spaghetti so it is well coated with butter and cheese. Sprinkle with pepper. Serve with your favorite sauce or serve as is as a pasta accompaniment. For extra rich variation, add 1/4 cup commercial sour cream along with cheese and butter. Serves 8.

MRS. CARLOS PERRY (JAN)

GREEN NOODLE CASSEROLE

1 cup butter
2 lbs. onions, chopped
2 lbs. ground beef
1 lb. fresh mushrooms, sliced
1 large can tomatoes
salt, pepper to taste
pinch sugar
Angostura Bitters, dash
1½ cups dry red wine

2 teaspoons basil or oregano
1½ lbs. green noodles, cooked
  and drained
1 cup flour
6 cups milk
1 teaspoon nutmeg
1 teaspoon thyme
1 cup Parmesan cheese, grated

Brown onions in a heavy skillet in ½ cup butter until golden, about 25 minutes. Add ground beef and mushrooms and cook 3 to 4 minutes. Add tomatoes, salt and pepper, pinch of sugar, Angostura Bitters, basil or oregano and wine. Allow sauce to simmer slowly 2½ hours. Cover part of the time, but if too watery, remove cover.

Melt ½ cup butter in a saucepan and stir in flour with a wire whisk. Cook for a few minutes and add milk, stirring until smooth. Add nutmeg, Angostura Bitters, salt and pepper and a pinch of sugar and thyme. Add cheese and stir until smooth.

Put a thin layer of noodles in the bottom of a large, round casserole, 12 inches in diameter. Cover with a thick layer of beef and tomato sauce. Continue layering, ending with a thin layer of noodles. Cover with cream sauce 1½ inches deep. Bake about 30 minutes at 350°. Dish may be assembled early in the day of serving. Tomato beef sauce may be made 1 or 2 days ahead. Serves 12 to 15.

BAYLA BISKIN

CANELLONI

18 manicotti tubes or (6-inch) entree crepes (see Index)
2 tablespoons olive oil
1 medium onion, chopped
1 carrot, chopped
2 lbs. ground beef
1½ teaspoons salt
1 cup red wine, dry
½ cup parsley, chopped
3 cups Mornay Sauce (see Index)

Boil manicotti tubes according to package directions and drain. Saute onion and carrot in oil. Add meat and brown. Add wine, salt and parsley. Simmer for 15 minutes. Stir in ½ cup Mornay Sauce.

¼ cup olive oil
¾ cup onions, minced
2 (8 oz.) cans tomato sauce
2 tablespoons tomato paste
¼ cup dry red wine
½ teaspoon basil
¼ teaspoon thyme
1 teaspoon salt
½ teaspoon pepper

Saute onions in oil until soft. Add remaining ingredients and simmer for 30 minutes.

To assemble Canelloni, pour a little of the Mornay Sauce, (see Index), into bottom of a 9x13 inch baking dish. Stuff manicotti tubes or roll crepes with meat mixture and arrange in a single layer in the dish. Pour remaining Mornay Sauce over the top and spoon on the tomato sauce. Sprinkle with Parmesan cheese. Bake at 350° for 30 minutes or until hot and bubbly. May be made in advance. Serves 8 to 10.

MRS. GEOFFREY P. WIEDEMAN, JR. (SANDY)

SUPER SPAGHETTI SAUCE

3 cloves garlic
2 teaspoons salt
½ tablespoon basil
¼ tablespoon black pepper
2 tablespoons sugar
¼ tablespoon crushed red pepper
2 (15 oz.) cans Hunts Tomato Sauce with Bits
3 tablespoons olive oil
1 cup dry red wine
1½ lbs. ground meat
3 large chicken breasts, cooked and shredded
1 (6 oz.) can tomato paste
1 (6 oz.) can mushrooms
sausage and olives (optional)

Brown 1/2 the ground meat and make small meat balls of the other 1/2 and brown. Crush garlic, salt, pepper, basil, sugar and red pepper with a mortar and pestle. Pour olive oil in a large pot and add crushed seasonings and wine. Simmer 10 minutes. Add tomato sauce and simmer, covered, 1/2 hour. Add tomato paste, mushrooms and simmer 10 minutes. Add ground meat and meat balls, shredded chicken breasts, (olives and sausage if desired) and simmer 30 minutes. Serve over cooked spaghetti. Serves 4 to 6.

MRS. JOE H. FROST

WILD RICE

1 1/4 cups wild rice
1/3 cup butter or margarine
1/2 cup parsley, chopped
1/2 cup scallions, chopped with green
1 cup celery, sliced

1 can beef consomme soup
1 1/2 cups boiling water
1 teaspoon salt
1/2 teaspoon marjoram
1/2 cup Sherry

Wash the rice well in several water changes and allow to stand 1 hour, covered with water. Drain well. Melt butter in a baking dish and saute celery, scallions and parsley. Add rice, consomme, water, salt and marjoram. Cover and bake about 45 minutes in 300° oven or until rice is tender and all liquid is absorbed. Stir with a fork 2 or 3 times while baking. Stir in Sherry and continue baking about 5 or 10 minutes longer. Serves 8.

M. W.'S WILD RICE DRESSING

2 medium onions
2 apples
2 carrots
1 cup bread crumbs
1 lb. pork sausage

1 cup cooked wild rice
3 eggs, slightly beaten
1/4 teaspoon sage
1/4 teaspoon mace
salt and pepper to taste

Rinse the cooked rice with cold water. Grind apples, onions and carrots together and add bread crumbs. Brown the sausage, and if very fat, drain. Combine sausage, rice and bread crumb mixture. Add mace, sage, salt, pepper and eggs. This makes enough dressing to stuff 3 big mallard ducks, 1 big turkey, or 2 chickens. Freezes well.

MRS. WILLIAM STANFORD (MARLENE)

Bread

A basket of fragrant hot rolls or muffins can turn the simplest meal into a memorable feast.

In San Antonio fresh tortillas, bolillos and other Mexican *panes* are available from *south of the border* bakeries. A native Frenchman daily bakes croissants, brioches, and those long delicious baguettes of bread in authentic French ovens for all to see at a local supermarket.

The quick breads—muffins, biscuits and their variations, are just what their name implies—speedy to make. The yeast breads take longer, but are rewarding in their tantalizing aroma and satisfying flavors.

WANDA'S WHITE BREAD

1 cup scalded milk	2 tablespoons salt
1 cup boiling water	1 yeast cake
1 tablespoon butter	1/4 cup lukewarm water
1 tablespoon lard	6 1/2 cups all purpose flour
2 tablespoons sugar	

Soften yeast in lukewarm water. Combine sugar, salt, butter and lard in a large bowl. Add milk and boiling water and allow to cool to luke warm. Add yeast and gradually add flour, mixing by hand or large spoon until dough no longer sticks to the bowl. Turn onto a floured board and allow it to rest for 10 minutes. Knead until it is elastic. Put into the bowl, cover and allow to rise. Punch down, shape into loaves and place into greased bread pans. Allow to rise again and then bake for 40 minutes in a 400° oven until golden brown. Makes 2 loaves.

WANDA LaFOLLETTE

LITTLE CHURCH — LA VILLITA — Margaret Wray

WHOLE WHEAT BRAN BREAD

3 cups warm water
¾ cup honey
3 tablespoons dry yeast
½ cup vegetable oil
2 cups whole wheat flour
3 cups unbleached white flour

½ cup powdered milk
½ cup wheat germ
1 tablespoon salt
2 to 3 cups bran flakes (not cereal, buy in a Health Food Store)

Combine warm water, honey and yeast in a large bowl and allow to stand 5 minutes. Add oil, whole wheat and white flour and mix with an electric mixer. Stir in bran flakes, powdered milk, wheat germ and, if needed, more whole wheat flour to make a stiff dough. Turn onto a floured board and knead until it is smooth and elastic, about 7 minutes. Put the dough into a greased bowl, cover and allow to rise in a warm place about 1 to 1½ hours until doubled in volume. Punch down dough, divide into 3 equal parts, shape into loaves and place in 3 standard size buttered bread pans. Cover and allow to rise in a warm place about 1 hour. Bake in 350° oven for 50 or 60 minutes.

MRS. ROBERT KEAHEY

DILL CASSEROLE BREAD

1 package dry yeast
¼ cup warm water
1 cup creamed Cottage cheese, warmed
2 tablespoons sugar
1 tablespoon instant minced onion

1 tablespoon butter
2 teaspoons dill seed
1 teaspoon salt
¼ teaspoon soda
1 egg
2¼ to 2½ cups all purpose flour

Soften yeast in water. Combine Cottage cheese, sugar, onion, butter, dill seed, salt, soda, egg and softened yeast in a large bowl. Gradually add flour beating well with electric mixer after each addition. Cover and allow to rise in warm place until light and doubled in size, about 1 hour. Stir down dough. Put in a well greased 8 inch round 1½ to 2 quart casserole. Allow to rise in a warm place until light, about 30 to 40 minutes. Bake in 350° oven for 40 to 50 minutes until golden brown. Brush with soft butter and sprinkle with salt. Makes 1 round loaf.

MRS. JOHNSON LEWENTHAL (PAT)

SALT STICKS

1 lb. sifted flour
1 teaspoon salt
1 teaspoon sugar
1/3 stick margarine, softened
1 package dry yeast

1/2 cup instant mashed potatoes
1/2 cup boiling water
1/2 cup milk
1 egg, beaten
caraway seeds

Mix instant potatoes with boiling water. Combine flour, salt, sugar, margarine, yeast and potato mixture in a large bowl. Add milk slowly and knead in the bowl. Cover with a dish towel and allow to rise 1 to 2 hours in a warm place. Turn onto a floured table. Tear off a chunk of dough and roll thin. Cut dough into triangles, 6 inches to each side. Roll triangles into sticks and allow to rest 1/2 hour. Place sticks on a lightly oiled and floured cookie sheet. Brush the sticks with beaten egg, salt generously and sprinkle with caraway seeds. Bake about 30 minutes in 400° oven. To freeze Salt Sticks, bake 10 minutes, wrap 4 or 5 sticks in foil and place in the freezer. When ready to use, place unwrapped, still frozen, in a 350° oven about 15 to 20 minutes.

It is often difficult to find a place warm enough to allow dough to rise, especially in air conditioned houses. An oven, heated to 125° then turned off with the light on, will remain warm enough to do the job.

CORNEL SAROSDY

LEE ANN HAWKINS ROLLS

1 cup shortening
1/2 cup sugar
1 1/2 teaspoons salt
1 cup boiling water
2 eggs, beaten

2 yeast cakes
1 cup cold water
6 cups unsifted flour
melted butter

Pour boiling water over the shortening, sugar and salt. Blend and cool about 10 minutes. Add eggs. Allow the yeast to stand in cold water for 5 minutes. Stir into the sugar and shortening mixture. Add flour, blend well, cover and place in refrigerator and chill. (This will keep in the refrigerator for up to 1 week). Roll out, cut in circles with a biscuit cutter, and dip each in melted butter. Fold in half and place close together in a buttered baking pan. Cover and allow to rise 2 hours. Bake in 350° oven about 20 minutes, or until brown. To freeze the rolls, bake about 10 minutes until set and lightly brown. Allow to cool, wrap in saran and place in the freezer. When ready to use, allow to thaw and finish baking for 10 minutes until puffed and brown. Makes 13 dozen.

MRS. LAWRENCE A. STONE (MARNETTE)

BASIC SCONE RECIPE

2 cups flour   3/4 to 1 cup milk
2 tablespoons butter   1 teaspoon salt
4 teaspoons baking powder

Sift dry ingredients together. Cut butter into the dry ingredients until it looks like bread crumbs. Add liquid gradually, mixing with a knife to a soft dough. Toss onto a floured board and roll lightly 3/4 inch thick. Cut with a biscuit cutter, place on a floured or greased cookie sheet and brush with milk. Bake in a 400° oven for 12 to 15 minutes.

Cheese Scones: Add 1/2 cup grated cheese to dry ingredients and 1/4 teaspoon paprika.

Orange or Lemon Scones: Add 1 teaspoon orange or lemon rind, or place 1 tablespoon marmalade on each scone. Add 2 tablespoons sugar to dry ingredients.

Minced Ham Scones: Roll dough 1/2 inch thick and cut with a biscuit cutter. Brush with melted butter and sandwich together with chopped ham.

MRS. PETER V. WESTON (YVONNE)

DONNIE'S CORN PANCAKES

1/2 cup flour   1 1/2 cups milk
1 cup corn meal   1 heaping teaspoon sugar
2 teaspoons baking powder   1 egg
1/2 teaspoon salt

Combine all ingredients and beat well. Cook on a lightly oiled hot griddle or skillet. Makes 12 to 15 pancakes.

MRS. DOROTHY C. PICKETT

SOUTHERN SPOON BREAD

1 cup white corn meal
1½ cups boiling water
1 tablespoon melted shortening
3 eggs, well beaten

1 cup milk
1 tablespoon baking powder
¼ teaspoon salt

Add boiling water to corn meal. Mix well. Cool. Add melted shortening, eggs, milk, salt, and baking powder. Blend well. Pour into 3x7 inch teflon or greased baking dish . Bake at 375° for 30 minutes. Serve at once. Serves 4 to 6.

MRS. RICHARD H. ECKHARDT

PUMPKIN BREAD

3⅓ cups flour
2 teaspoons soda
1½ teaspoons salt
1 teaspoon cinnamon
3 cups sugar

1 teaspoon nutmeg
1 cup oil
4 eggs
⅔ cup water
2 cups pumpkin

Sift dry ingredients into bowl. Make a well in mixture and add oil, eggs, water and pumpkin. Mix until blended. Put into a greased and floured loaf pan. Bake 1 hour at 350°. Makes 2 large or 3 small loaves.

MRS. WILLIAM H. HAIGHT

CRANBERRY MUFFINS

1 can whole cranberry sauce
2 cups biscuit mix
⅓ cup sugar

1 egg, unbeaten
¾ cup milk
2 tablespoons salad oil

Combine biscuit mix, sugar, milk, egg and salad oil in bowl. Mix only until dampened. Break up cranberry sauce with fork and carefully fold into batter. Fill greased muffin tins ⅔ full. Bake at 425° for 20 to 25 minutes. Makes 1½ dozen muffins.

MRS. HERBERT C. BROOKE

D. Pfannstiel

Desserts

The happy ending to a memorable meal is the dessert. The secret of every good cook is to choose a dessert to compliment the menu—not overpower it.

After a luncheon, a light dinner, or for a dessert party, a rich glamorous treat is in order. But, something simple is the natural follow-up to a elaborate meal.

Try a frozen mousse, a light and airy meringue, or a velvety pudding. And every now and then, the drama of the famous classics, such as Cherries Jubilee or Crepes Suzette, will finish your dinner with a flourish.

CREPES SUZETTE

12 dessert crepes (see Index)	juice of 1 orange
1/2 stick butter	juice of 1/2 lemon
1/4 cup sugar	3/4 oz. Cointreau
peel of 3 oranges, sliced	3/4 oz. Grand Marnier
peel of 1 lemon, sliced	2 ounces Brandy

Melt butter in a large, shallow chafing dish. Add sugar and mix well. Add orange and lemon peels and the juices. Simmer until peels are transparent. Place 3 crepes at a time in this liquid and fold into quarters. Push the folded crepes to the side and continue until all 12 crepes are in the pan. Pour in the Cointreau, Grand Marnier and then the Brandy. Allow to heat a moment and then ignite. Swirl the pan gently until the flame dies out and serve 3 folded crepes to each person. Spoon some of the sauce over each portion. Serves 4.

To make Crepes Suzette in advance: combine 1 stick of butter, 1/4 cup of sugar, grated zest (color only) of 1 orange, juice of 1/2 orange (scant), 1/4 cup Grand Marnier. Beat with an electric mixer

TOWER OF THE AMERICAS — Drusilla Pfannstiel

until light and fluffy. Spread the butter mixture over 18 individual dessert crepes. Fold each one in quarters and place in a lightly buttered flame proof serving dish, overlapping a little. Spread a little butter mixture on the top. Cover and refrigerate. When ready to serve, place in a 350° oven for 15 to 20 minutes. Heat 2 ounces of Brandy, pour over warmed crepes and ignite. Serves 6.

CHERRIES JUBILEE

1 cup Bing cherry juice
1 tablespoon cornstarch
1/4 cup sugar
1/2 cup Bing cherries

1 tablespoon butter
2 tablespoons Kirsch, heated
2 tablespoons Brandy, heated
6 scoops vanilla ice cream

In a chafing dish, bring cherry juice to a boil. Combine cornstarch, sugar and a little of the juice. Add to the boiling mixture. Boil 1 minute and add the cherries. Add the butter and stir until melted. Pour in the Brandy and Kirsch and ignite. When flame dies down, stir and serve over vanilla ice cream. Serves 6.

BLACK AND WHITE MERINGUE FLAMBE

10 egg whites
1/4 cup super fine sugar
1/4 teaspoon cream of tartar

1/4 cup good Brandy
Mocha Chocolate Sauce (see Index)

Put just enough water in a large pan to allow a 12 cup Bundt Pan to sit flat on the bottom of the pan. Remove Bundt Pan and bring water to a boil on the top of the stove. Brush inside of the Bundt Pan with a little melted butter. Beat egg whites, gradually adding sugar and cream of tartar. Beat until standing in peaks. Pour mixture into the Bundt Pan. Place Bundt Pan in the boiling water and bake in a 350° oven for 20 minutes. Allow to cool on a rack in the Bundt Pan. Unmold and pour Mocha Chocolate Sauce, (see Index), decoratively over the meringue. Heat Brandy, ignite and pour over the meringue and sauce. Serves 10 to 12.

This may be made in advance of serving time if allowed to sit on a rack in the Bundt Pan, but it will shrink a little. It is, also, good served with Melba Sauce (see Index).

MRS. GEOFFREY P. WIEDEMAN (CAROLYN)

LEMON MERINGUE NEST

4 eggs, separated   1½ cups sugar
½ teaspoon cream of tartar   3 teaspoons lemon juice
2 pinches salt   1 teaspoon lemon rind, grated
1 teaspoon vanilla   1 cup cream, whipped

Beat egg whites and cream of tartar until foamy. Add 1 cup sugar, sprinkled on with a teaspoon. Beat until meringue forms peaks. Add pinch of salt and vanilla. Slightly grease a 9 inch pie plate. Spoon in beaten meringue and shape into a nest, ½ inch above sides of plate. Bake at 275° for 1 hour, then at 350° for 15 minutes, or until pie shell is lightly browned. Turn off heat and leave in oven overnight. For filling, combine egg yolks, ½ cup sugar, lemon juice, lemon rind and pinch of salt in double boiler. Cook until thickened, about 8 to 10 minutes. Cool overnight. Fold mixture into whipped cream. Spoon filling into meringue shell. Serves 6 to 8.

MRS. H. HOUGHTON PHILLIPS

CRANBERRY CREPES FLAMBE

18 dessert crepes (see Index)   2 tablespoons light corn syrup
1 cup orange juice   1 cup water
¼ teaspoon salt   ½ cup soft butter
1¼ cups granulated sugar   ¾ teaspoon orange extract
3 cups washed cranberries   1⅓ cups sifted powdered sugar
4 tablespoons grated orange peel ½ cup light rum

Combine orange juice, salt, granulated sugar and water in a 3 quart saucepan. Stir over medium heat to dissolve sugar, and then allow to boil, uncovered, for 10 minutes without stirring. Reduce heat, add cranberries, 2 tablespoons grated orange peel and cook, uncovered, for 15 minutes or until sauce has thickened, stirring occasionally. Remove from heat and stir in corn syrup. Set aside.

Combine soft butter, 2 tablespoons grated orange peel, pinch of salt, orange extract and powdered sugar. Beat until light and fluffy. Set aside.

To assemble, spread each crepe with orange-butter filling. Fold into quarters and arrange in an oven-proof serving dish. Cover with foil. When ready to serve, reheat crepes in 300° oven for 20 minutes. Reheat cranberry sauce and pour into a flame proof serving dish, heat rum, ignite and pour over cranberry sauce. Take sauce flaming to the table and serve over crepes. Serves 6 to 8.

MRS. CLIFFORD J. BUCKLEY (HELEN)

HONEY SYRUP BAKLAVA

Baklava Syrup:
2 cups sugar
1½ cups water
½ large lemon rind, grated
5 whole cloves

2 cinnamon sticks
1 cup honey
2 tablespoons rum or Brandy
1 tablespoon rum flavoring
4 tablespoons lemon juice

Combine sugar, water, lemon rind, cloves and cinnamon sticks. Boil until slightly thickened. Remove from heat and add honey, rum or Brandy, rum flavoring and lemon juice. Allow to cool. (If syrup is to be kept for future use, remove the spices.)

Baklava:
1½ lbs. butter, melted
1½ lbs. Phyllo Pastry (see Index)
1 lb. walnuts, coarsely chopped

½ lb. almonds, chopped fine
½ cup sugar
2 teaspoons cinnamon

Combine walnuts, almonds, sugar and cinnamon and divide into fourths. Cut Phyllo leaves to fit a 13x9x2 inch pan. Butter bottom of pan and following the directions for using Phyllo Pastry sheets, place 10 sheets on the bottom of the pan. Sprinkle ¼ of the nut mixture over the Phyllo. Repeat this process until all Phyllo and nut mixture is used.

When all ingredients have been used, cut 2 inch diamonds in the Baklava and pour remaining butter over the dish. Bake for 1 hour in 325° oven. Remove from oven and pour ½ of the cooled Baklava Syrup recipe over the top. Wait 1 hour and pour the remainder of the Syrup over the Baklava. Baklava may be stored in a tightly sealed tin.

CAROLE CALLSEN

GATEAU MIREILLE

1 cup rice
1 cup sugar
3 cups milk
4 eggs, separated

½ to ¾ cup almonds, minced
1 oz. Grand Marnier
whipped cream and strawberries

In saucepan, cook rice, sugar and milk for 30 minutes, or until rice is tender. Add almonds; mix thoroughly, stirring constantly. Remove pan from heat and add egg yolks. Add stiffly beaten egg whites, then the liqueur. Pour mixture into a buttered and floured Charlotte pan. Bake at 350° for 30 minutes. Set aside to cool. Unmold on serving plate. Decorate with whipped cream and strawberries. Serve with warm Brandy Sauce (see Index).

MRS. RALPH ROWDEN (FRANCINE)

MILLIONAIRE PIE

2 cups powdered sugar
1 stick margarine
1 large egg
¼ teaspoon salt
½ teaspoon vanilla

1 baked (9 inch) pie shell
1 cup heavy cream
¼ cup chopped nuts
1 cup canned, crushed pineapple,
   drained

Cream powdered sugar and margarine together. Add egg, salt and vanilla. Mix until light and fluffy. Spoon mixture evenly into baked pie shell and chill. Whip cream until stiff and blend in pineapple and nuts. Spoon on top of pie and chill thoroughly. Coconut may be added with the pineapple.

MRS. KENNETH HOWARD (BONNIE)

LEMON CHESS PIE

1 cup sugar
3 eggs
½ cup light Karo
1 tablespoon corn meal

6 tablespoons sweet or sour cream
1 teaspoon vanilla
juice of ½ lemon
1 (9 inch) unbaked pie shell

Beat sugar and eggs together well and add remaining ingredients. Pour into pie shell and bake in 350° oven until almost firm, about 45 minutes. Serves 6.

MRS. PORTER LORING, JR. (JACKIE)

CHOCOLATE CHIP ANGEL PIE

3 egg whites
1 teaspoon vanilla
1 cup sugar
1 cup graham cracker crumbs
1 cup chopped pecans

1 teaspoon baking powder
½ package chocolate bits
 (semi-sweet)
½ cup whipping cream, whipped
maraschino cherries

Beat egg whites and vanilla until stiff peaks form. Combine cracker crumbs, pecans, sugar, baking powder and chocolate chips and fold into meringue. Spread evenly in greased and floured 9 inch pie pan. Bake in 350° oven for 20 to 25 minutes. Cool and top with whipped cream and maraschino cherries.

GRAHAM B. MILBURN, MD

ITALIAN CREAM CAKE

½ cup margarine
½ cup Crisco
2 cups sugar
5 egg yolks
2 cups flour

1 teaspoon soda
1 cup buttermilk
1 cup coconut
5 egg whites, beaten

Cream well margarine, Crisco and sugar. Add egg yolks, one at a time. Set aside. Sift together flour and soda, and add alternately with buttermilk. Add coconut. Fold in beaten egg whites. Pour into baking pan, 13x9x2. Bake at 350° for 30 to 45 minutes, or until toothpick comes out clean when inserted in center of cake. Frost with Italian Cream Icing, (see Index).

MRS. MIKE MONTGOMERY (GLADYS)

ITALIAN CREAM ICING

½ cup margarine
1 (8 oz.) package cream cheese
1 box powdered sugar

1 teaspoon vanilla
1 cup chopped nuts

Cream margarine and cream cheese. Add remaining ingredients and mix well. Spread on cooled Italian Cream Cake, (see Index).

MRS. MIKE MONTGOMERY (GLADYS)

DARN GOOD DATE CAKE

2½ lbs. dates, halved
2 lbs. pecans
2 cups flour
½ teaspoon salt
3 teaspoons baking powder

1¼ cups sugar
5 large eggs, separated
1½ teaspoons vanilla
1½ teaspoons lemon extract

Mix dates with pecans. Sift flour, sugar, salt and baking powder twice and then sift a third time over the dates and pecans. Mix well. Beat egg whites and set aside. Beat egg yolks well, add vanilla and lemon extract and combine with date-nut mixture. Fold in egg whites and pour into waxed paper lined cake pan. Bake at 300° until done. If the cake browns too quickly, cover with foil and lower the temperature.

MORTON BROWN

BANANA CAKE

½ cup shortening or butter
1½ cups sugar
2 eggs
1 teaspoon vanilla
1 cup mashed ripe bananas
2 cups flour

¼ teaspoon baking powder
¾ teaspoon baking soda
½ teaspoon salt
¼ cup sour cream or buttermilk
½ cup chopped pecans
powdered sugar (optional)

Cream well shortening, sugar and eggs. Add vanilla and bananas. Sift together flour, baking powder, baking soda and salt. Add flour mixture to creamed mixture alternately with sour cream or buttermilk. Sprinkle pecans on top of cake. Bake in 350° oven in a greased and floured pan. (In an oblong pan bake 35 minutes; in a tube pan bake 40 minutes.) Sprinkle with powdered sugar when cool.

MRS. JULIUS WOLFSON

TEXAS PECAN TORTE

3 cups pecans
6 eggs, separated
1½ cups sugar
3 tablespoons flour
1 teaspoon salt

3 tablespoons rum
½ cup whipping cream
2 tablespoons powdered sugar
1 cup chocolate chips
½ cup sour cream

Chop pecans very fine in a blender, 1 cup at a time. Beat egg yolks until light and beat in sugar, flour, salt, 2 tablespoons rum and nuts.

Set aside. Beat egg white until stiff and fold into the nut mixture. Pour into 3 (8 inch) or 2 (10 inch) layer cake pans, buttered and lined with waxed paper. Bake for 25 minutes in 350° oven. Allow to cool. (May be kept overnight). A few hours before serving time, whip cream with powdered sugar and 1 tablespoon of rum. Spread filling between layers. Melt chocolate chips, fold in sour cream and spread over the cake top for icing.

MRS. EDWARD DROSTE

CHRISTMAS PECAN CAKE

2 cups butter
2 cups sugar
6 eggs
1 tablespoon lemon juice
1 teaspoon grated lemon rind
1 tablespoon vanilla

¼ teaspoon salt
1 teaspoon baking powder
3 cups flour
1½ cups golden raisins
4 cups chopped pecans

Cream butter and sugar until light and fluffy. Add eggs, one at a time, mixing well after each addition. Add remaining ingredients except raisins and pecans. Fold in raisins and pecans and bake in buttered tube cake pan for 1 hour and 50 minutes in 300° oven. Allow to cool in pan. Wrap in foil and store in the refrigerator and wait for Christmas.

MRS. WILLIAM H. WALTER III

BROWN SUGAR POUND CAKE

1 box light brown sugar
1 cup white sugar
3 sticks margarine
5 eggs
3 cups flour

1 cup milk
1 teaspoon vanilla flavoring
½ teaspoon baking powder
½ teaspoon salt
1 cup chopped pecans

Cream sugars and margarine. Add remaining ingredients, except pecans, and mix well. Fold in nuts. Bake in tube pan at 325° for 1 hour and 30 minutes. Excellent to serve for morning coffees.

MRS. WILLIAM H. WALTER III

UPSIDE DOWN FUDGE CAKE

1 tablespoon shortening	1 cup flour
3/4 cup sugar	1 teaspoon baking powder
1/2 cup milk	1/2 teaspoon salt
1 teaspoon vanilla	1 1/2 tablespoons cocoa

Cream sugar and shortening together. Add milk and vanilla. Sift flour, baking powder, salt and cocoa into the mixture and mix well. Pour into a greased 8 inch square cake pan.

Topping

1/4 cup cocoa	1 1/4 cups boiling water
1/2 cup white sugar	whipped cream (optional)
1/2 cup brown sugar	ice cream (optional)
1/2 cup chopped nuts	

Combine cocoa and sugars. Spread the chopped nuts evenly over the cake batter and top with the cocoa-sugar mixture. Pour the water carefully over the top and bake for 35 minutes in a 350° oven. Allow to cool. Cut into squares and invert the pieces as you serve. Top with whipped cream or ice cream.

MRS. FORREST M. SMITH, JR. (BETTY)

LEONE'S POPPY SEED CAKE

1 box yellow cake mix	1/2 cup poppy seeds
2/3 cup Wesson oil	1 1/2 cups sifted powdered sugar
2/3 cup apricot nectar	1/3 cup cream or milk
4 eggs	1 tablespoon lemon extract

Mix Wesson oil, apricot nectar, eggs, poppy seeds and cake according to directions on cake mix box. Pour batter into a Bundt pan and bake 45 minutes at 350°. Remove cake from pan and allow to cool. Mix powdered sugar, cream or milk and lemon extract together and pour glaze over cake. This is a light, tart cake and very good for morning coffees.

ANTOINETTE S. BURDETT (MRS. ALLEN M., JR.)

JALISCO POTS DE CREME

1 package Jello Chocolate Creme
  Soft Swirl Dessert Mix
1 cup cold milk

½ cup Kalhua
½ cup whipping cream
2 tablespoons Kalhua

Pour milk into deep narrow bowl. Add dessert mix. Thoroughly blend at low speed on electric mixer. Beat at medium speed for 2 minutes. Add ½ cup Kalhua. Beat 1 minute at medium speed. Spoon into pots-de-creme dishes. Chill. Prepare day ahead or 15 minutes ahead. Whip cream until soft peaks form. Add Kalhua. Whip until stiff. Spoon onto pudding. Serves 6 to 8.

MRS. HARRY BROWN (CAROLYN)

CHOCOLATE POTS DE CREME

6 oz. chocolate bits
2 eggs
1 tablespoon sugar

1 tablespoon brandy
¾ cup milk, heated
whipped cream

Combine all ingredients except whipped cream in a blender and blend for 2 minutes. Pour into pot de creme cups and chill for at least 2 hours. Serve with whipped cream on top. Serves 6.

MRS. STANLEY FRANK

ENGLISH PLUM PUDDING

8 large eggs
4 cups milk, heated
2 cups brown sugar
2 cups flour
1 lb. beef suet, grated
1 lb. bread crumbs
1 lb. raisins
1 lb. currants

1 lb. citron, grated
2 teaspoons allspice, ground
2 teaspoons cinnamon
2 teaspoons nutmeg
2 teaspoons salt
2 teaspoons baking powder
2 teaspoons vanilla
¼ cup Brandy

Soak bread crumbs in milk. Combine flour, allspice, cinnamon, nutmeg, salt and baking powder. Beat eggs and sugar until light. Add vanilla, flour and spice mixture. Mix well and add fruit and suet. Blend well and put in well greased steamer moulds. Allow it to ripen about 12 hours, and then steam the pudding for 4 hours. This will make 2 large or 4 medium size puddings. When ready to eat, heat and serve with Brandy Hard Sauce, (see Index.) To flame, heat brandy, ignite and pour over the hot puddings.

MARY ETTA McGIMSEY

CREAM PUFF CREME PATISSIERE
Dessert Custard Cream

4 eggs, separated
¾ cup sugar
3 tablespoons flour or cornstarch
1½ cups milk, heated
¼ cup whipping cream

1 tablespoon butter
1 tablespoon vanilla, rum or
  Grand Marnier
18 Cream Puff Shells, cooked,
  (Pate A Choux—see Index)

Cream egg yolks with sugar and cornstarch or flour. Beat until mixture is creamy and smooth. Add milk, a little at a time. Cook mixture, over low heat, until thick and smooth, stirring constantly. Add butter, vanilla, rum or Grand Marnier and cream. Set aside to cool. Use the mixture as it is or you may beat the egg whites until stiff and fold into the cream mixture.

Fill 18 Cream Puff Pastry Shells (Pate A Choux—see Index) with this mixture for Dessert Cream Puffs. Arrange on a platter and sprinkle powdered sugar over the puffs. You may also cover the top with Mocha Chocolate Sauce or caramel (see Index).

MRS. RALPH ROWDEN (FRANCINE)

MARGE'S FRENCH CUP CAKES

3 squares bitter chocolate
2 cups powdered sugar
1 cup butter
3 eggs separated

½ cup English walnuts, chopped
1 teaspoon vanilla
10 to 12 vanilla wafers, crushed

Melt chocolate over hot water. Cream butter and powdered sugar. Add egg yolks and melted chocolate. Mix thoroughly at medium speed. Add nuts and vanilla. Fold in stiffly beaten egg whites. Pour into paper baking cups that have been sprinkled with vanilla wafer crumbs. Sprinkle crumbs over top. Chill 8 to 12 hours. May be made in advance. Keeps well. Makes 35 to 40 "midget" cupcakes or 20 to 25 regular size.

MRS. SAM GLASSER

LEMON MOUSSE

3 eggs, separated
1 cup sugar
1 envelope gelatin
¼ cup cold water

½ cup lemon juice
1½ teaspoons grated lemon rind
1 cup whipping cream

Sprinkle gelatin over cold water. In top of double boiler or small pyrex mixing bowl, combine egg yolks, ½ cup sugar, lemon juice and rind. Cook over boiling water until slightly thickened, stirring constantly. Remove from heat, add gelatin. Turn mixture into large bowl and cool but do not allow to set. Beat egg whites until stiff, add remaining ½ cup sugar and beat again. Fold into lemon mixture. Whip cream and fold it in. Pour into decorative mold, 6-cup size or larger. Chill for several hours or overnight. Set mold in very hot water for a second or two and unmold onto serving plate. May be served as is, or with whipped cream and strawberries. This dessert may be prepared in advance, and it may be frozen. Serves 4 to 6.

HELEN HOGAN

MANGO MOUSSE

2 (16 oz.) cans mangoes
  with syrup
8 oz. cream cheese
3 packages lemon Jello

2 cups boiling water
mayonnaise
whipped cream
strawberries

Blend mangoes with syrup and cream cheese in a blender. Dissolve Jello in boiling water and combine with cream cheese mixture. Pour into a mayonnaise lined 2½ quart mold. Chill. If used as a dessert, unmold and add strawberries or other fruits for garnish and whipped cream. If used as a salad, add a dollop of mayonnaise and fruit. Serves 6.

MRS. DONALD JACOBS

LADY FINGER CHOCOLATE FLUFF

3 packages chocolate pudding mix
6 cups milk
2 tablespoons plain gelatin

½ cup cold water
1 pint whipping cream
Angel Food Cake or Lady Fingers

Oil a 4 quart ring mold or Bundt mold. Add milk to mix and stir until smooth. Cook pudding mixture until thick, stirring constantly.

Cool. Soften the gelatin in the cold water. Add softened gelatin to cooled pudding. Line mold with cake pieces or lady fingers. Whip cream. Fold gently into pudding mixture. Pour part or all of pudding cream mixture over cake. (You can alternate mixture and cake in layers if you prefer). Chill in refrigerator at least 4 hours before serving. Unmold on serving platter. Serves 10 to 12.

MRS. H. E. KARREN

STRAWBERRY FLUFF

2 pints fresh strawberries | ¼ cup milk
2 envelopes unflavored gelatin | 4 large egg whites
½ cup water | dash salt
1 cup orange juice | 2 egg whites, sweetened
½ cup sugar | (optional)

Rinse berries in colander with cold water and drain. (Reserve 10 whole berries for garnish.) Remove stems from remainder, place in large bowl and crush well. Set berries aside. Sprinkle gelatin over water in small saucepan and heat over low heat until gelatin dissolves. Add to crushed berries. Stir in orange juice, ¼ cup sugar and milk. Chill mixture until slightly thickened. Beat egg whites and salt until foamy in large bowl of mixer set at high speed. Beat in remaining ¼ cup sugar, 1 tablespoon at a time. Continue to beat until whites are stiff. Fold in chilled berry mixture. Turn into serving dish. Chill until firm. Remove stems of 9 reserved whole berries and cut in half. If desired, spoon 2 additional stiffly beaten, sweetened egg whites in center of Strawberry Fluff. Surround with berry halves and top with whole berry. Serves 8.

MRS. RAY T. WOODHALL (JUNE S.)

SWEDISH BUTTER BALLS

½ lb. butter | vanilla
½ cup chopped pecans | 2 cups flour
½ cup powdered sugar

Cream butter and sugar and add other ingredients. Roll into balls the size of a walnut and place on a baking sheet. Bake at 350° for 30 minutes. Roll in powdered sugar. Makes 30 to 36 balls.

MRS. PETER V. WESTON (YVONNE)

SHORTBREAD

7½ cups sifted flour   1¼ lbs. butter
1⅛ cups superfine sugar

Cream butter well, add superfine sugar and cream again. Mix in flour, then knead very well until it looks like a heavy paste. It may be a bit crumbly, but if pressed together, will hold. Press down firmly into a well-greased 12x18 pan with the back of a spoon or a small rolling pin without handles. Prick all over with a fork and place on middle shelf and bake at 325° for 40 minutes or slightly golden color and shrinks away from pan very slightly. While still hot, cut in fingers about 4x1 inch. Sprinkle with a very fine veneer of superfine sugar. This is in addition to the measured amount in ingredients. (The recipe may be cut in half.) Makes 50 bars.

MRS. PETER V. WESTON (YVONNE)

DATE KISSES

1 cup powdered sugar   1 cup dates, diced
2 egg whites   1 cup pecans, chopped
pinch salt   ½ teaspoon vanilla

Beat egg whites until stiff. Add sugar, salt and beat again. Stir in pecans, dates and vanilla. Drop far apart by teaspoonsful on a buttered cookie sheet. Bake in slow oven until light brown.

MRS. WINFIELD SCOTT HAMLIN

VIENNESE DESSERT BARS

1 cup butter   2 cups flour
1 cup sugar   1 cup walnuts or pecans, chopped
2 egg yolks   ½ cup jam

By hand, mix butter and sugar until fluffy. Add yolks and blend well. Add flour gradually, and fold in nuts. Spoon half of batter into buttered 8 inch square pan. Top with jam, and cover with remaining batter. Bake at 325° for 45 minutes. Cut into bars.

MRS. GEOFFREY P. WIEDEMAN, JR. (SANDY)

AFTER SCHOOL COOKIES

2 cups sugar
3 tablespoons cocoa
1/2 cup milk
1 stick margarine

1 teaspoon vanilla
2 1/2 cups oatmeal
1/2 cup chunky peanut butter

Boil sugar, cocoa, milk and margarine for 2 minutes. Add vanilla, oatmeal and peanut butter. Mix well and drop by teaspoon on wax paper and allow to harden. (May place in the freezer for a few minutes.) Makes 4 dozen.

This is a recipe for mothers with school children. It is possible to have the finished product in youngsters hands in less than 10 minutes.

MRS. WILLIAM J. SIMPSON

GINGERBREAD BOYS

1/3 cup butter or margarine
1 cup brown sugar, packed
1 1/2 cups molasses
cold water
7 cups flour, sifted
1 teaspoon allspice

1 teaspoon ground ginger
1 teaspoon ground cloves
1 teaspoon cinnamon
2 teaspoons baking soda
1 teaspoon salt

In a large mixing bowl, combine butter, brown sugar, molasses, 1/2 cup cold water and blend thoroughly. Combine flour and spices, and add gradually to molasses mixture. Mix well. Dissolve baking soda in 3 tablespoons cold water and stir into mixture. Chill. Roll on floured board until 1/2 inch thick. Use cookie cutter or greased cardboard pattern. Transfer to greased cookie sheet. Use raisins for eyes, nose, mouth, and buttons. Bake at 350° for 15 to 18 minutes. Makes 12 to 18 boys.

This is a Christmas family tradition. My grandmother made gingerbread boys before Christmas, and along with all the other ornaments and candy canes she decorated her tree with fresh gingerbread boys. The aroma of fresh pine and gingerbread brings back fond memories. I have continued this family tradition with my children, and they look forward to the gingerbread boys every Christmas.

MRS. F. DANIEL FOLEY (CARROLL)

CHOCONUT OATMEAL COOKIES

1/2 cup softened margarine
1/3 cup sugar
1/3 cup brown sugar, packed
1 well beaten egg
1/2 teaspoon vanilla
3/4 cup flour

1/4 teaspoon salt
1 teaspoon baking powder
1/4 cup milk
1/2 cup grated coconut
11/2 cups rolled oats
1 cup semi-sweet chocolate chips

Cream margarine with sugars. Add egg and vanilla; mix. Combine flour, salt and baking powder. Add the dry mixture alternately with milk to creamed mixture and blend. Stir in nuts, rolled oats and chocolate chips. Drop by spoonfuls onto lightly greased baking sheet. Bake at 375° for 10 to 12 minutes. Makes 3 dozen.

RICK BIARD

CANDIED WHITE BROWNIES

11/2 cups sifted flour
1/2 teaspoon salt
1/2 cup margarine
2 cups sugar
3 eggs

3/4 cup chopped pecans
2 tablespoons lemon juice
1 teaspoon vanilla
1/4 cup green Glacé cherries
1/4 cup red Glacé cherries

Sift together flour and salt. Cream margarine and sugar together until light and fluffy. Add eggs, 1 at a time, beating well after each addition. Blend flour mixture into egg mixture and beat 2 minutes on medium speed of electric mixer. Blend in nuts, lemon juice and vanilla. Turn into greased 9x13 inch pan. Sprinkle fruit evenly over batter. Bake in moderate oven 350° for 35 to 40 minutes, or until lightly browned. Cool in pan and cut into squares. Makes 21/2 dozen.

MRS. L. S. KARREN

CINNAMON SOUR CREAM COFFEE CAKE

1 cup butter
11/4 cups sugar
2 eggs
1 cup sour cream
2 cups all purpose flour
1/2 teaspoon soda

11/2 teaspoons baking powder
1 teaspoon vanilla
3/4 cup chopped pecans
1 teaspoon cinnamon
2 tablespoons sugar

Combine butter, 1¼ cups sugar and eggs and beat until fluffy. Blend in the sour cream. Sift the flour with soda and baking powder. Add this to the sour cream mixture. Add vanilla and blend well. Spoon ½ the batter into a 9 inch tube pan which has been buttered and floured. Combine pecans, cinnamon and 2 tablespoons of sugar and sprinkle ½ over the batter. Spoon in the remaining batter and top with the remaining nut mixture. Place in a *cold* oven. Set oven at 350° and bake for 45 to 50 minutes.

MRS. WILLIAM K. DOUGLAS (MARIWADE)

GRASSHOPPER PIE

4 tablespoons butter or margarine
3 tablespoons sugar
24 Chocolate Wafers or
  Graham Crackers
24 marshmallows, large
½ cup milk

2 tablespoons Creme De Menthe
2 tablespoons Creme De Cacao
1 cup whipped cream
walnuts or pecans
chocolate shavings

Crush wafers or crackers in a bowl and add sugar and soft butter. Blend well. Press the mixture into an 8 or 9 inch pie plate. Chill 30 minutes, or bake 3 to 5 minutes. Melt marshmallows with milk, stirring constantly, until thickened. Allow to cool slightly and add Creme de Menthe and Creme de Cacao. Fold in whipped cream and pour into the pie shell. Freeze for at least 1 hour. Before serving garnish with additional whipped cream, nuts and chocolate. Serves 6 to 8.

MRS. RALPH ROWDEN (FRANCINE)

FROZEN DATE NUT PIE

2 pints vanilla ice cream
1 (8 oz.) package pitted dates
½ cup water
½ cup sugar
1 teaspoon lemon juice
1 tablespoon plain gelatin

½ cup cold water
¼ cup chopped pecans
1⅓ cup vanilla wafer crumbs,
  finely crushed
¼ cup butter, melted

Cut dates into fourths. Combine with water, sugar and lemon juice. Cover, and cook slowly until dates are soft. Cool. Stir in gelatin which has been dissolved in ½ cup cold water. Add nuts. Combine wafer crumbs with butter. Press into sides and bottom of 9 inch pie plate. Chill. Spread 1 pint ice cream over crust. Cover with date mixture. Top with 1 pint slightly softened ice cream. Garnish with additional wafer crumbs or nuts. Freeze until ready to serve. Serves 8.

DOROTHY L. KATZ

LOTUS ICE CREAM

2⅔ cups light cream
1 cup sugar
⅓ cup lemon juice
⅓ cup chopped toasted almonds

1½ teaspoons grated lemon rind
½ teaspoon vanilla
⅛ teaspoon almond extract

Combine all ingredients in a mixing bowl. Stir until sugar is dissolved. Freeze in a hand-turned or electric ice cream freezer. Note: To ripen ice cream, remove ice to below lid of can; take off lid. Remove dasher. Plug opening in lid and cover inside of lid with several thicknesses of waxed paper; replace lid. Pack more ice and salt around can. Cover freezer with heavy cloth or newspapers. Let ripen about 4 hours. Makes 1 quart.

MRS. EDITH GEROW

MILLIE'S ICE CREAM

8 eggs
½ cup flour
3½ cups sugar
2 packages plain gelatin
2 cups hot milk

3 quarts milk, scalded
4 tablespoons vanilla
2 pints half and half cream
1 pint heavy cream
1½ gallon freezer

Beat the eggs until frothy. Add the flour and sugar and beat again. Dissolve the gelatin in 2 cups hot milk, and stir this mixture into the 3 quarts scalded milk. Slowly pour into the beaten eggs, stirring constantly. Add remaining ingredients. Add enough extra milk, if necessary, to bring up to full line on freezer can. If adding fruit, mash and sweeten before adding to milk mixture, using less milk.

MILLIE KOCUREK (MRS. LOUIS J.)

MINT SURPRISE

1 cup vanilla wafer crumbs
⅔ cup butter
2 cups confectioner's sugar
3 egg yolks
2 squares melted chocolate

1 teaspoon vanilla
3 egg whites, beaten stiff
½ cup chopped nuts
1 quart softened mint ice cream

Sprinkle ⅔ cup of the crumbs in a 9x13 pan. Cream butter and sugar, beat in the egg yolks, and add melted chocolate and vanilla. Fold in the stiffly beaten egg whites. Spread this chocolate mixture over the crumbs, and sprinkle with nuts. Place pan in the freezer for at least 3 hours. Remove from freezer and spread with the softened ice cream. Sprinkle with the remaining crumbs, and store in the freezer. Remove the dessert a few minutes before serving and cut into squares. Serves 15.

MRS. JAMES W. LAURIE

FROZEN CHOCOLATE CREAM

2 squares unsweetened chocolate
1 cup sugar
3 egg yolks, slightly beaten
¼ teaspoon salt

2 cups hot milk
2 teaspoons vanilla
2 cups heavy cream
¼ cup orange liqueur

Melt chocolate squares. Stir in sugar, yolks and salt. Add milk and stir over medium heat for 3 minutes. Add vanilla and chill. Whip heavy cream and fold into chocolate mixture. Add liqueur, place in container and freeze.

MRS. HAROLD O. ATKINSON

BANANAS FOSTER

6 tablespoons dark brown sugar
3 tablespoons butter
3 bananas
1½ oz. Creme de Banana

3 oz. white rum
cinnamon
vanilla ice cream

Melt brown sugar and butter in a chafing dish. Slice bananas lengthwise and add to the dish. Sprinkle with cinnamon. Add banana liqueur and saute until tender. Pour in rum and ignite. Baste bananas with the warm liquid until the flame burns out. Serve immediately over ice cream. (This is also good made with Grand Marnier instead of Creme de Banana.) Serves 6.

MRS. THOMAS A. WACHSMUTH (SUSAN)

PEARS MELBA FLAMBE

2 large cans Del Monte Pear
  Halves
1 small package cream cheese
½ to 1 tablespoon sugar
¼ cup chopped walnuts
whipping cream
1 cup Melba Sauce (see Index)
¼ cup Brandy

Place pears, cut side down, on paper towels to drain for about 1 hour. Mix cream cheese with sugar and add enough cream to make spreading consistency. Stir in nuts. Spread some of the cheese mixture on the flat side of one pear half. Press another half together to make one whole pear. (Try to match pear halves in size and shape.) Set whole pears, large side down, in shallow sided, flame-proof serving dish. Cover with foil and refrigerate for at least 2 hours. Allow to come to room temperature before serving. At serving time, prepare Melba Sauce (see Index) and pour over the pears. Heat the Brandy, ignite and pour over pears and sauce. Serve 1 whole pear per person. Serves 6.

MRS. GEOFFREY P. WIEDEMAN (CAROLYN)

POIRES MAGGIE

2 cups sugar
2 cups water
2 cups apricot nectar
1 lemon, sliced thin
1 teaspoon vanilla
6 unripe, fresh pears
chocolate sauce (see Index)

Combine sugar, water, apricot nectar, vanilla and lemon slices in a saucepan. Bring to a boil and boil for 3 minutes. Peel the pears, cut a slice from the bottom and stand pears, upright, in the syrup. Simmer until they are tender when tested with a toothpick. Place pears on dessert serving dishes and spoon on syrup. Serve hot or cold, topped with chocolate sauce or ice cream, if desired. Serves 6.

MARGARET COUSINS

BERRIES WALTERSPIEL

3 heaping tablespoons blackberries, strawberries, raspberries, blueberries or pineapple
1 scant tablespoon finely diced almond macaroons
vanilla ice cream
Kirsch or orange flavored liqueur
whipped cream

Saturate almond macaroons in a little Kirsch or orange flavored liqueur. Place a generous scoop of ice cream in a dessert dish and sprinkle the top with the macaroons. Cover the crumbs with fruit of your choice and surround with whipped cream, piped through a pastry tube. Serves 1.

LLOYD BENTSEN
United States Senator, State of Texas

FRUITS AU VIN

2 packages Birdseye Quick Thaw Mixed Fruit
1 tablespoon sugar or to taste
dry white or rose wine
lemon juice, to taste
Zabaglione Sauce (see Index)

Thaw fruit and drain thoroughly. Mix the fruit with wine, using only enough to flavor. Add sugar and lemon juice. Chill thoroughly. At serving time, spoon into champagne glasses and top with Zabaglione Sauce (see Index). This sounds too simple, but it's delicious served after a rich meal. Serves 6.

EASY PEANUT BRITTLE

3 cups white sugar
1/2 cup of water
1 cup white Karo
3 cups raw shelled peanuts
3 teaspoons butter
2 teaspoons soda
1 teaspoon salt

Boil sugar, Karo and water until it spins a thread. Add peanuts and stir constantly until it turns a brownish gold. Remove from heat, add butter, salt and soda. Pour on to a buttered cookie sheet to cool.

MRS. PETER J. HENNESSEY, JR.

Sauces, Savories & Sundries

Sauce is *The Sonnet of the Table.* It is the true test of the culinary art of the cook. The simplest dish is enhanced by the accompaniment of a smooth, well-seasoned sauce that lifts it out of the ordinary.

In San Antonio our gardens abound with ingredients for chutney, pickles, jellies and relishes. Pyracantha and jalapeño are Texas specialties. *Picante,* that delicious spicy tomato sauce which originated in San Antonio, is packed into every tourist's home-bound suitcase along with souvenirs of the Alamo.

In this section, we include sauces, eggs, and relishes; side dishes and accompaniments; marinades and miscellaneous mixtures; and a few of the basics plus some of the savories that turn eating into dining!

BECHAMEL SAUCE — Medium Thick White Sauce

2 tablespoons butter
3 tablespoons flour
2 cups milk

¼ teaspoon salt
white pepper to taste

Melt butter over low heat. Add flour and with a wire whisk, stir and cook until mixture begins to dry out a little, about 2 or 3 minutes. Gradually add milk, stirring constantly, until thick. Add salt and pepper. This is a basic cream sauce used in all cooking. May be frozen. Makes 2 cups.

HINT: When making any thickened sauce not to be used immediately, scrape down the sides of the pan with a rubber spatula and cover the top of the sauce with a thin layer of melted butter. This will prevent the top from drying out and the sauce will re-heat smoothly and without lumps.

To make THICK BECHAMEL SAUCE, combine ingredients in the same manner except use 1¼ cups of milk. Simmer the mixture until it has reduced to 1 cup. Use wherever a thick sauce base is required such as souffles and some creamed dishes. You can always add more milk if the sauce is too thick for your recipe.

VELOUTE SAUCE — Chicken, Veal or Fish Stock Sauce

2 tablespoons butter	¼ teaspoon salt
3 tablespoons flour	white pepper to taste
2 cups chicken, veal or fish stock	

Melt butter over low heat. Add flour and with a wire whisk, stir and cook until mixture begins to dry out a little, about 2 or 3 minutes. Gradually add stock, stirring constantly, until thick. This is a basic white stock sauce used in all cooking. May be frozen. Makes 2 cups.

To make SAUCE SUPREME (enriched white stock sauce), combine ingredients in the same manner except use 1½ cups stock, ½ cup whipping cream and add a few drops of lemon juice.

MADEIRA SAUCE — Brown Wine Sauce

½ cup butter	⅛ teaspoon rosemary
1 tablespoon onion, chopped	1 small bay leaf
1 tablespoon celery, chopped	1 tablespoon tomato puree
1 garlic clove, minced	3 cups meat stock or beef bouillon
½ cup flour	2 oz. Madeira
⅛ teaspoon thyme	

Saute onion, celery and garlic in butter for 5 minutes. Add flour and cook a few minutes. Add spices, tomato puree and cook for 5 minutes, stirring constantly. Add stock, bring to a boil, cover and simmer for 1 hour. Strain, add Madeira and heat a few minutes. This is an all-purpose brown meat sauce. May be frozen. Makes about 2½ cups.

MORNAY SAUCE — Cheese Sauce

4 tablespoons butter
4 tablespoons flour
3 cups milk

3/4 teaspoon salt
3/4 cup Swiss cheese, grated

In a saucepan melt the butter. Stir in flour and cook a few minutes. Gradually add milk until smooth. Add salt and Swiss cheese. Makes about 3 cups.

This is a heavy cheese sauce for pasta dishes, etc. If a thinner, lighter cheese sauce is desired for fish, vegetables, eggs, etc., add 1/4 to 1/2 cup grated Swiss cheese, or a combination of Swiss and Parmesan cheese to 2 cups Bechamel Sauce (see Index).

MRS. GEOFFREY P. WIEDEMAN, JR. (SANDY)

SABAYON SAUCE

3 egg yolks
1/2 cup dry white wine
1/2 teaspoon salt

pinch sugar to taste
fresh ground pepper
1 teaspoon lemon juice

Combine all ingredients in the top of a double boiler over just-simmering water. With a wire whisk, beat constantly until sauce is fluffy and doubles in volume. Pour over cooked green vegetables, fish or chicken and serve. Or, you may put the dish under the broiler for a few minutes until lightly browned.

Sabayon Sauce is usually made with more sugar, liqueurs etc., and served as a dessert sauce, (see Zabaglione Sauce). This variation will serve as a vegetable or entree sauce.

MRS. CARLOS PERRY (JAN)

BEURRE MANIE — A Thickening Agent

Combine equal amounts of softened butter with flour until thoroughly blended. Use this mixture as a thickening agent instead of flour and water. After a liquid has been thickened with Beurre Manie, it should simmer for 5 to 10 minutes to eliminate the raw taste of the flour. Beurre Manie may be used immediately; may be stored, covered in the refrigerator; or may be frozen ready to be used as needed.

BLENDER HOLLANDAISE SAUCE

8 tablespoons butter, heated
4 egg yolks
2 tablespoons lemon juice
$\frac{1}{4}$ teaspoon salt
$\frac{1}{4}$ teaspoon Tabasco

Put egg yolks, lemon juice, Tabasco and salt into a blender. Cover and turn on low speed. Immediately remove cover and pour in the heated butter in a slow, steady stream. Turn off motor. This may be kept warm by setting the blender container in a saucepan containing 2 inches of hot water. If it becomes too thick, return container to the blender and add 1 tablespoon hot water and blend briefly. May be frozen. Use with fish, vegetables and egg dishes. Makes $1\frac{1}{4}$ cups.

MRS. SCHREINER NELSON (SHAWN)

BLENDER BEARNAISE SAUCE

$\frac{1}{4}$ cup dry white wine
2 tablespoons tarragon vinegar
1 teaspoon dried tarragon
1 tablespoon shallots or
  green onions, chopped
$\frac{1}{4}$ teaspoon pepper
$1\frac{1}{4}$ cups Blender Hollandaise
  (see Index)

In a small saucepan combine wine, vinegar, dried tarragon, shallots or green onions and pepper. Bring to a boil and cook rapidly until liquid is reduced to about 2 tablespoons. Make Blender Hollandaise (see Index). Add the boiled reduced mixture to the Hollandaise Sauce in a blender. Cover and blend on high speed for 8 seconds. Use over steak, fish, chicken and egg dishes. May be frozen. Makes $1\frac{1}{2}$ cups.

MRS. SCHREINER NELSON (SHAWN)

BOTTLED CLAM JUICE FISH STOCK

$1\frac{1}{2}$ cups bottled clam juice
1 cup water
1 cup dry white wine
1 onion, sliced
6 sprigs parsley
$\frac{1}{4}$ cup fresh mushroom pieces
  (optional)

Combine all ingredients and simmer about 1 hour. Strain and use to make any sauce that calls for fish stock. May be frozen. Makes about $2\frac{1}{2}$ cups.

CANNED BROTH CHICKEN STOCK

½ cup dry white wine
2 cups canned chicken broth
3 tablespoons onions, sliced
3 tablespoons carrots, sliced

3 tablespoons celery, sliced
2 parsley sprigs
⅓ of a bay leaf
pinch of thyme

Combine all ingredients and simmer about 1 hour. Strain and use to make any sauce that calls for chicken stock. May be frozen. Makes about 1½ cups.

BOUILLON SOUP BEEF STOCK

2 cups canned beef bouillon soup
  (do not use consomme—it is
  too sweet)
⅓ of a bay leaf
3 tablespoons onions, minced
3 tablespoons carrots, minced

1 tablespoon celery, minced
½ cup dry red wine
⅛ teaspoon thyme
1 tablespoon tomato paste
  (optional)
2 sprigs parsley

Combine all ingredients and simmer about 1 hour. Strain. It is now an enriched beef stock ready to make any sauce calling for meat stock. May be frozen. Makes about 1½ cups.

COURT BOUILLON — Liquid for Poaching or Marinating Fish

4 cups water
1 cup dry white wine
1 medium carrot, sliced
1 medium onion, sliced
½ bay leaf

2 whole cloves
½ teaspoon thyme
½ teaspoon salt
4 whole peppercorns

Combine all ingredients and simmer for about 1 hour. Strain. Use for poaching fish or for marinating before baking, broiling or frying. May be frozen.

MRS. GEOFFREY P. WIEDEMAN (CAROLYN)

DILLED CUCUMBER FISH SAUCE

1½ cups Bechamel Sauce (see Index)
½ cup cucumber, minced
1 tablespoon shallots, minced
¼ teaspoon crumbled dillweed
1 tablespoon vinegar
salt and pepper

Put minced, unpeeled cucumber into a strainer; sprinkle with salt and allow to drain for about 1 hour. Make the white sauce, combine all ingredients and heat, stirring constantly. Serve warm with any fish.

MRS. GEOFFREY P. WIEDEMAN (CAROLYN)

VERY VERSATILE TOMATO SAUCE

½ onion, minced
1 small garlic clove, minced
2 tablespoons Bertolli Olive Oil
1 (16 oz.) can Italian Plum Tomatoes
½ teaspoon dried basil
½ teaspoon salt
⅛ teaspoon ground pepper
pinch sugar

Saute onions and garlic in oil until soft. Add tomatoes, (coarsely mashed with all the juice), basil, salt, pepper and sugar. Simmer, uncovered, 30 minutes to 1 hour, stirring frequently.

Sauce may be used to spread over chicken breasts, pork chops, eggs, vegetables, baked eggplant halves or almost anything that calls for a tomato sauce topping. Makes about 1½ cups.

MRS. GEOFFREY P. WIEDEMAN (CAROLYN)

WHISKEY BEEF MARINADE

¼ cup whiskey
3 tablespoons A-1 Sauce
2 tablespoons oil
¼ teaspoon pepper
¼ cup soy sauce
2 tablespoons vinegar
½ teaspoon Accent
½ teaspoon thyme or rosemary
½ teaspoon salt
1 onion sliced

Mix all ingredients and marinate large cuts of beef overnight. Use marinade as basting sauce and for making sauces and gravies.

MRS. HARRY BAYNE (MELBA)

MANDARIN BEEF MARINADE

¾ cup Kikkoman Soy Sauce
¼ cup catsup
½ cup salad oil
2 tablespoons sugar
½ cup sherry or red wine

⅓ cup onion, chopped
1 garlic clove, minced
juice and rind of 1 lemon
freshly ground pepper
dash Season-All

Combine all ingredients and marinate cubes of beef for at least 1 hour. Use as a basting sauce and for making gravies and sauces.

MRS. ROBERT DAWSON (JEANNIE)

RUSTY STEAK SAUCE

⅓ cup Worcestershire
½ tablespoon lemon juice
⅓ cup butter
⅓ cup A-1 Sauce

1 tablespoon mustard
1 large can mushrooms, sliced
¼ cup mushroom liquid

Heat Worcestershire sauce, lemon and butter. Add A-1 Sauce, mustard and ¼ cup mushroom liquid. Simmer 15 minutes. Add the sliced mushrooms and cook 15 minutes. Heat when ready to serve.

MRS. JOE H. FROST

SWEET AND SOUR SAUCE
(Benedictine Sisters of Peking Cooking School, Tokyo, Japan.)

¾ cup sugar
¼ cup Kikkoman Soy Sauce
3 tablespoons cornstarch

⅓ cup vinegar
⅔ cup water

Mix all ingredients together and cook over very low heat until thick, stirring constantly. Be careful—it burns easily. This may be assembled in advance, but cook at the last minute. Makes about 1½ cups.

Two Americans, Sister M. Francetta and Sister M. Regia, fled the mainland of China when the Communists came to power. They established a cooking school in Tokyo, specializing in Chinese foods available in the United States. Those Americans, fortunate enough to have known these ladies in their joy of cooking, will remember them with fond memories.

SEAFOOD SAUCE SUPREME

1 cup tomato catsup
2 tablespoons celery, chopped fine
1/4 cup lemon juice
salt to taste
1 teaspoon chopped parsley

1 tablespoon horseradish, or
   to taste
dash of Tabasco
1 tablespoon Worcestershire

Combine all ingredients. Chill well. Serve with seafood.

MRS. WILLIAM BRADFORD BUGG

SOUR CREAM MUSHROOM SAUCE

1 lb. fresh sliced mushrooms
2 teaspoons grated onion
4 tablespoons butter
2 cups sour cream

1 teaspoon salt
1/4 teaspoon pepper
garlic powder (optional)
4 teaspoons flour

Saute mushrooms in butter with onions until tender. Mix sour cream, flour, salt, pepper and garlic powder. Add to mushrooms. Refrigerate. When ready to serve, heat over very low heat for 5 minutes, stirring gently. Serve over steak or roast beef. Serves 4 to 6.

SPICED WATERMELON RIND

3 lbs. white portion of
   watermelon, cubed
5 cups sugar
2 cups cider vinegar
1 cup water
1 tablespoon whole cloves

1 tablespoon whole allspice
1 tablespoon stick cinnamon
   pieces
1 lemon, sliced
1/2 cup salt
3 quarts water

Combine 1/2 cup of salt and 3 quarts of water. Allow watermelon cubes to stand overnight in this water. Drain and cover with fresh, cold water. Bring to a boil and cook over low heat until tender. Drain Combine sugar, vinegar and water. Tie the spices and lemon slices in cheesecloth. Add to sugar mixture. Bring to a boil, stirring constantly. Boil for 5 minutes. Add watermelon, and simmer until cubes are transparent, about 15 minutes. Remove spice bag and pack in hot sterilized jars. Makes about 3 pints.

MRS. JACK C. YOUNG (GERRY)

SPICED PINEAPPLE

1 (20 oz.) can pineapple spears   ½ cup sugar
   or chunks   5 whole cloves
¼ cup vinegar   1 cinnamon stick

Drain pineapple and reserve the syrup. Combine syrup with remaining ingredients and boil 5 minutes. Add pineapple and simmer about 3 minutes. Remove cloves and cinnamon stick. Cool and store in the refrigerator. This is good served with Mexican food. Serves 6.

MRS. JACK C. YOUNG (GERRY)

CURRIED FRUIT

1 (No. 303) can salad fruits   ½ cup brown sugar
1 (No. 303) can pineapple chunks   1 stick butter
1 (No. 303) can apricot halves   2 tablespoons cornstarch
1 cup pecan halves   1 teaspoon curry powder

Drain the fruits, reserving liquid from salad fruits. Combine butter, cornstarch, brown sugar, curry powder, 1 cup of fruit liquid and heat in a saucepan over very low heat. Mix fruits and pecans in a baking dish, add sugar sauce and mix. Bake in 400° oven for 45 minutes, stirring once. This may be prepared in advance and re-heated. It is excellent served with lamb or chicken. Serves 8.

JANET MASSY

FREDERICKSBURG PEACH CHUTNEY

5 lbs. firm, ripe peaches   3 cups sugar
8 oz. raisins   ½ cup candied, crystallized
8 oz. dates, chopped   ginger, chopped (optional)
2 cups apple cider vinegar   ½ cup pecans, chopped
1 lime

Peel and cut peaches into small pieces. Add raisins, dates and vinegar. Slice lime thin and cut slices into quarters. Add to the mixture and cook over medium heat, stirring occasionally, until peaches are soft. Add sugar and cook until mixture is thick, stirring frequently. Add ginger and nuts. Mix well and pour into hot, sterilized jars.

MRS. WYNN D. MILLER

TEXAS FIG PRESERVES

4 lbs. large brown ripe figs   ¼ lemon (less but never more)
2 lbs. sugar

Peel the figs and place them with sugar and thin slices of the lemon in a pan on low heat. Stir until mixture makes a syrup, about 10 minutes. Cook gently for 30 minutes, stirring the last 10 minutes. Pour into sterilized glass jars which have ben warmed in hot water. Seal. Serve on toast for breakfast. Makes 7 half pint jars.

CHARLES G. ORSINGER — KING ANTONIO XLIX

JALAPENO JELLY

1 cup green peppers, seeded   1½ cups white vinegar
1 cup canned jalapeños, seeded   1 bottle Certo
6½ cups sugar

Slice the green peppers and jalapeños as fine as possible and then cut into pieces about ¼ inch long. (Use rubber gloves when cutting the jalapeños.) Put all ingredients, except Certo, into a large kettle and bring to a boil, stirring constantly. Reduce the heat and simmer for 10 minutes. Remove kettle from heat and pour in Certo. Continue to stir the mixture with a wooden spoon until it obviously begins to thicken, about 15 or 20 minutes. It is essential to keep stirring the mixture at this time to prevent a tough "skin" from forming on the top. Pour into sterilized jelly jars and seal with a screw type cap. (Do not use paraffin seals since it may become necessary to invert the jars before the jelly has solidified.)

The trick to making Jalapeño Jelly in this manner is to get the peppers evenly distributed throughout the jelly. It helps to let it stay in the kettle as long as possible, stirring constantly, before pouring it into the jars. If you are lucky, the pieces will be evenly distributed. If they tend to float to the surface, invert the jars for a few minutes and then return them to the upright position. Green peppers which have a large portion of red coloring make a prettier jelly.

If you prefer a smooth jelly, puree the peppers and jalapeños with a little of the vinegar before starting to cook. You may then use the paraffin seal and not worry about pepper distribution.

COLONEL WILLIAM K. DOUGLAS

TEXAS PEAR PRESERVES

8 cups pears   1 lemon
7 or 8 cups sugar $2\frac{1}{2}$ teaspoons ground ginger
$\frac{3}{4}$ to 1 cup water

Peel, core and quarter the pears. Slice lengthwise until you have 8 cups. Seed and remove juice from lemon and cut the rind into thin, round slices. Combine all ingredients and allow to stand in a heavy 5 quart kettle for 2 hours. Bring the mixture to a boil, cover and simmer over low heat for 1 hour, stirring occasionally. Remove cover and continue cooking for 1 to 2 hours, stirring frequently. The cooking time will vary with pot, stove and the desired thickness. When done, the pears should be fork tender and light amber in color. If you like a loose quality preserves, cook until 2 heavy drops of syrup form on the edge of the spoon. If you prefer it thicker, cook until 2 drops of syrup combine. Put in hot sterilized jars and seal tightly. Allow to cool away from drafts and tighten the lids at least twice more while cooling.

This is a good recipe for our Texas pears that never soften. Do not use Bartlett or other eating pears. Select the hard, cooking variety. Do not try to double this recipe, but use 2 cooking pots to make a larger quantity. Makes 4 to 5 pints.

MRS. EUGENE E. MASSY

PYRACANTHA JELLY

7 cups ripe pyracantha berries   7 cups sugar
5 cups water   1 bottle liquid pectin
$\frac{1}{2}$ cup lemon juice   paraffin

Place washed berries in very large pan with water. Simmer uncovered 20 minutes. Strain through a cloth, reserving liquid. Measure 3 cups berry juice, and combine with lemon juice and sugar in large pan. Over high heat, bring to a boil, stirring constantly. Immediately stir in pectin; bring to full boil and boil hard 1 minute, stirring constantly. Remove from heat, skim off foam, and pour into sterilized glasses. Cover with $\frac{1}{8}$ inch melted paraffin. Prepared berry juice may be refrigerated or frozen, prior to making jelly.

MRS. K. W. RICHARDSON

ZABAGLIONE SAUCE

3 egg yolks
3 tablespoons superfine sugar
2 tablespoons sherry

2 drops vanilla
1/4 cup whipping cream
2 tablespoons Grand Marnier

Put egg yolks into a small round-bottom heat resistant bowl and beat slightly. Add sugar, sherry and vanilla. Place bowl over a pan of just simmering water and beat with a wire whisk until very thick. Remove from heat and allow mixture to cool slightly. Whip cream very stiff. Fold into egg mixture and add Grand Marnier. Spoon into sherbet or champagne glasses and serve at once as a dessert. May also be used as a dessert sauce over fresh or frozen fruit, ice cream, cake or meringue. (You may omit whipping cream if using as a dessert sauce.)

BRANDY HARD SAUCE

1/3 cup butter, softened
2 tablespoons whipping cream

1 cup brown sugar
5 teaspoons Brandy

Cream butter and cream until fluffy. Slowly add sugar, beating until light and creamy. Slowly add the Brandy and beat again. Makes about 5 servings. Serve with English Plum Pudding, (see Index).

MARY ETTA McGIMSEY

BRANDY SAUCE

1 cup light brown sugar
1/4 cup butter
4 tablespoons Brandy

2 egg yolks, beaten
2 egg whites, beaten stiff
1/2 cup half and half

Cream butter and sugar and gradually add Brandy. Add egg yolks and half and half. Cook over low heat or hot water until sauce thickens. Fold in the beaten egg whites. Serve warm.

MRS. RALPH ROWDEN (FRANCINE)

MELBA SAUCE

1/4 cup water
1 1/2 tablespoons cornstarch

1 (10 oz.) package frozen
raspberries, thawed

In a heavy saucepan, blend water and cornstarch. Stir in berries. Heat until thickened. Use over ice cream, fruit, or meringue. Makes about 1 cup.

MOCHA CHOCOLATE SAUCE

8 squares semi-sweet chocolate,
  cut into small pieces
½ cup very strong coffee

Cognac or water
thin pat of butter

Melt chocolate with coffee in a double boiler. Add water or Cognac to make desired consistency. Add butter. Serve hot as a dessert sauce over ice cream, fruit, meringue, etc.

QUICK FLAKY PASTRY

1 lb. butter, margarine or
  shortening
½ teaspoon salt

10 oz. boiling water
2 measuring cups, brim full of
  flour

Place butter, margarine or shortening in mixing bowl and break up the pieces with a knife. Pour in boiling water. Allow to stand for a few minutes then stir in the flour, salt and mix thoroughly. Place in the refrigerator until it hardens. Turn onto a floured board and roll once or twice. It appears to be very sticky, but as you roll it, it absorbs some flour. This pastry may be used for quiche and does not need to be pre-baked.

MRS. PETER V. WESTON (YVONNE)

PATE A CHOUX — Cream Puff Pastry for Appetizers
or Desserts

1 cup water
½ cup butter
1 cup all-purpose flour

4 eggs
2 teaspoons sugar
  (omit for appetizer puffs)

Boil water and butter together. Stir in flour all at once. Stir vigorously, over low heat, until the mixture forms a ball, about 1 minute. Remove from heat, add eggs one at a time, beating well after each addition. Continue beating until smooth. (This must be done very quickly as the paste must remain warm while the eggs are being added. You may use an electric beater.) Drop dough, a tablespoon or teaspoon at a time, on an ungreased cookie sheet about 3 inches apart. Bake 20 minutes at 400°, turn oven down to 375° for 10 minutes or until puffs are raised and golden brown. Allow to cool away from drafts. Cut off tops with a very sharp knife and scoop out any soft dough inside.

For dessert puffs, fill with Cream Puff Creme Patissiere (see Index), sweet whipped cream or custard. For appetizer puffs, follow the same procedure, filling the puffs with meat, seafood, cheese or any other suitable cooked mixture. Replace cut off tops. Makes 18 medium size puffs.

MRS. RALPH ROWDEN (FRANCINE)

PHYLLO PASTRY

Phyllo pastry leaves are ready made, tissue paper thin, flat sheets of dough. The sheets are about 12 inches long and 16 inches wide, rolled together, frozen and wrapped in plastic. They are sold in 1 lb. packages and are ready to use. They may be purchased in specialty gourmet shops. Phyllo leaves are used in many Greek recipes, pastries, hors d'oeuvres, and as a covering for many meat and cheese dishes. They may be thawed and re-frozen, and keep for months if well wrapped in plastic.

There is one *IMPORTANT* thing to remember when using Phyllo pastry dough leaves. They *MUST NOT* be allowed to stand open to the air. They become brittle and, literally, disintegrate into nothing. Work with only 1 sheet at a time. Either keep it covered with a damp cloth or buttered generously at all times to prevent it from drying out. Also, keep the unused, plastic wrapped package covered with a damp cloth when not in the freezer.

Phyllo may be used in large sheets, or cut in slices from the un-rolled package to the desired width with a sharp knife. Narrow slices, about 2 inches wide, are used for hors d'oeuvres and appetizers. Large sheets, or slices about 4 inches wide are suitable for main courses and individual servings.

To use slices, cut the desired widths from the whole unrolled pack-age. Unroll each slice, one at a time. Prepare one strip of Phyllo for each hors d'oeuvre or individual serving. Brush it generously with melted butter and place cooked filling, (meat, cheese, etc.) in one corner of the strip. Fold into triangles in the fashion of folding the American Flag. Tuck the edges under and place on a cookie sheet with the folded ends down. Brush with more melted butter and bake in a

325° oven for 30 to 35 minutes or until golden brown. The Phyllo will bake flaky and crisp.

If you use the large sheets, brush each sheet generously with melted butter and stack 2 or 3 sheets together. Spread the desired cooked filling in the center of the top sheet and roll, jelly-roll fashion, tucking in the ends. Place on a cookie sheet and brush with more melted butter. Bake in the same manner as the smaller ones. After the roll is baked, slice thick for serving portions.

You may also cut Phyllo sheets to fit a specific baking dish size with layers of filling in between, such as Baklava. Use several sheets for each layer, brushing each sheet generously with melted butter. Bake according to the recipe directions or until crispy and brown.

After preparing the filled Phyllo, stacked or rolled, it may be frozen. Do not thaw before baking, but allow extra cooking time. If you wish to make a dish using Phyllo ahead of time but do not wish to freeze it, bake immediately after preparing with the desired filling until it is not quite brown. Reheat at serving time and finish browning.

MRS. GEOFFREY P. WIEDEMAN (CAROLYN)

CREPES

¾ cup milk
¾ cup water
3 egg yolks
1 tablespoon sugar

3 tablespoons Brandy
1½ cups flour
5 tablespoons melted butter

Place all ingredients in blender in the order given. Cover and blend at top speed 1 minute. Scrape down any flour that clings to the sides and blend 3 seconds longer. Cover and refrigerate for at least 2 hours. Brush a very hot 4 to 6 inch skillet or crepe pan lightly with oil. Pour 1 or 2 tablespoons of batter in the pan, tilting it immediately so that the batter will spread over the entire bottom of the pan. Cook one side until lightly brown. With a spatula, lift the crepe at the edge and turn it over. Lightly brown the other side. Repeat until all crepe batter has been used. Makes 16 to 18 (5 inch) crepes.

Crepes may be made in advance and freeze well. Place waxed paper in between each crepe, in stacks of 6 or 8. Wrap the stacks in waxed paper and then in foil. Tape the openings. They will keep frozen for months. Allow to thaw, still wrapped, in the refrigerator.

SOUFFLES

There are two kinds of souffles — savory and sweet. Savory souffles are flavored with cheese, seafood, meat, poultry or vegetables. They are served alone or with entrees. Sweet souffles contain sugar and are flavored with vanilla and liqueurs, etc. They are considered desserts.

For the standard 6-cup souffle dish (larger souffles are difficult to make), there are a few simple measurements which hold true for any entree souffle. Combine 1 cup of Thick Bechamel Sauce, (see Index), ¾ to 1 cup flavoring ingredients, 4 egg yolks and 5 egg whites. This will serve 4 or 5 people.

For the same size dessert souffle, there are also some general measurements. Instead of the Thick Bechamel Sauce base, 1 cup of a sweet sauce base made with sugar, flour and milk is used. It is combined with 4 egg yolks. 5 egg whites, 2 teaspoons vanilla and 3 to 4 tablespoons flavoring liqueur (Grand Marnier, Cointreau, etc.).

Souffles should not scare the cook. With a light hand, they are easy and fun to make. Just be sure you are ready to eat the souffle when the souffle is ready to be eaten.

SPINACH SOUFFLE

1 cup warm Thick Bechamel Sauce
  (see Index)
1 tablespoon shallots or
  green onions, minced
1 tablespoon butter
1 cup frozen spinach, chopped
¼ teaspoon salt, or to taste

pepper to taste
4 egg yolks
5 egg whites
¼ teaspoon cream of tartar
⅓ to ½ cup Swiss cheese,
  grated (optional)

Saute green onions or shallots in butter. Add spinach and salt. Stir over high heat to evaporate as much water as possible. Beat the egg yolks into the Thick Bechamel Sauce, and stir in spinach mixture. Add cheese, if desired. Beat egg whites with cream of tartar until stiff, but not dry, and gently fold into spinach sauce mixture. Pour into a

6-cup, buttered souffle dish or Charlotte mold. Place in 400° oven, immediately turn to 375°, and bake 30 to 40 minutes. Serve immediately. Serves 4 or 5.

All vegetable souffles are made in the same manner. Use any finely diced or pureed vegetables, such as broccoli, artichoke hearts, asparagus, mushrooms, etc. You may also use any cooked meat, poultry or seafood — chopped or pureed. The method of preparation is the same.

GRAND MARNIER SOUFFLE

3 tablespoons flour
¾ cup milk
⅓ cup sugar
4 egg yolks
2 tablespoons butter

5 egg whites
1 tablespoon sugar
¼ teaspoon cream of tartar
2 teaspoons vanilla
3 to 4 tablespoons Grand Marnier

Combine flour, sugar and milk in a saucepan. Cook until thick, stirring constantly. Allow to cool slightly. Beat in egg yolks one at a time, and then butter. Beat egg whites with 1 tablespoon of sugar and cream of tartar until stiff, but not dry. Add vanilla and Grand Marnier to the sauce and gently fold in the beaten egg whites. Pour in a generously buttered 6 cup Charlotte mold or souffle dish which has been sprinkled with sugar. Place in a 400° oven, immediately turn it to 375°, and bake 30 to 40 minutes. Serve immediately. Serves 4 or 5. (All dessert souffles are made in the same manner.)

CHEFSE SOUFFLE

1 cup warm Thick Bechamel Sauce
   (see Index)
¾ to 1 cup cheese, grated
4 egg yolks, well beaten

5 egg whites, well beaten but
   not dry
¼ teaspoon cream of tartar

Melt cheese in Thick Bechamel Sauce (see Index). Beat in the egg yolks, carefully, to prevent curdling from the heat of the sauce. Gently fold in egg whites which have been beaten with cream of tartar. Pour into generously buttered 6 cup Charlotte mold or souffle dish which has been sprinkled with cheese. Place in a 400° oven, immediately turn it to 375°, and bake 30 to 40 minutes. Serve immediately. Serves 4 or 5.

MEDICA — Seasoned Sicilian Bread Crumbs

1 cup bread crumbs
1/3 teaspoon salt
1 garlic clove, chopped very fine
  (optional)

1 tablespoon Romano cheese,
  grated
1 tablespoon parsley, chopped
black pepper to taste

Combine salt and garlic. Add bread crumbs, cheese, parsley and pepper. Use with Eggs Medica (see Index), vegetables, or wherever seasoned bread crumbs and cheese are desired.

MRS. VICTOR ALESSANDRO (RUTH)

AVOCADO OMELET

4 egg yolks
4 egg whites, beaten stiff
1/2 teaspoon salt
fresh ground black pepper
1 tablespoon butter
2 diced avocados

lemon juice
2 tablespoons butter
2 tablespoons flour
1 cup milk
1/2 teaspoon salt
1/3 cup sharp grated cheese

Sprinkle avocados with lemon juice and salt and set aside. Beat salt, pepper and 1/4 cup cold water with yolks and fold in the beaten egg whites. Melt 1 tablespoon butter in skillet; add the eggs and cook 2 to 3 minutes over medium heat. Then put the skillet in a 350° oven to bake for 10 to 15 minutes, or until set on top. While this is baking, make a sauce by melting 2 tablespoons butter in saucepan, blending in flour, then milk and salt. Cook until thick. Add cheese and stir until melted. Add avocado. Spread half of omelet with sauce. Fold over and top with the remaining sauce. Serves 2 to 3.

MRS. BURLESON SMITH

MOM PORRECA'S RICOTTA OMELET

2 lbs. Italian sweet sausage
2 lbs. Ricotta cheese
6 eggs
1 teaspoon salt

1/2 cup chopped parsley
1/2 teaspoon baking powder
several teaspoons milk

Cut sausage into 1 inch pieces. (If you prefer a hot sausage, you may use part Italian hot sausage; but, use no more than 1 lb.) In a large ovenproof skillet, cook sausage pieces thoroughly and drain well. Scrape the bottom of the pan so it is smooth and arrange the sausage pieces in one layer on the bottom of the skillet. Combine baking powder and milk and beat together with eggs and salt until light and fluffy. Fold in the Ricotta cheese until all large lumps are broken. Do not mash. Pour egg and cheese mixture over the sausage and cook very briefly until it just starts to bubble. Immediately place in a 375° oven and cook about 20 minutes or until mixture is set. Test with a knife in the center of the omelet. Cut into wedges and serve. This makes an excellent brunch dish. Serves 8 to 10.

MRS. JOSEPH J. JOHN (CUPE)

EGGS BENEDICT

4 English muffins
8 slices Canadian bacon or ham,
   cooked
8 eggs, soft poached

3 cups Hollandaise Sauce (see
   Index)
butter

Split English muffins in half, toast and spread with butter. Place a slice of Canadian bacon or ham on each muffin half. Top with a poached egg. Pour Hollandaise Sauce over each one and garnish with parsley. Serve with broiled tomatoes. Serves 8.

To prepare Eggs Benedict in advance, poach the eggs exactly 3 minutes. Immediately slip them into a shallow pan of ice cold water. This will stop the cooking process. Cover and place the pan in the refrigerator until ready to serve. At serving time, transfer the eggs to a pan of boiling water for exactly 1 minute. This will finish the cooking process.

MONTEREY EGGS

6 slices sour dough bread, toasted
   and cut into cubes, about 4 cups
4 oz. natural Cheddar cheese,
   grated
4 oz. Monterey Jack cheese,
   grated
9 eggs, slightly beaten

4 cups evaporated milk
1 teaspoon salt
1/8 teaspoon pepper
1 teaspoon prepared mustard
10 slices bacon, cooked crisp
   and crumbled
1/2 tablespoon chives, chopped

Spread bread cubes evenly on the bottom of a greased baking dish, 13 1/2x8 3/4x1 3/4 deep. Spread the Cheddar cheese and then the Monterey

Jack cheese over the bread. Blend the slightly beaten eggs, milk, salt, pepper, mustard and chives together and pour over cheese and bread mixture. Bake at 325° until egg mixture is set, about 25 to 30 minutes. Crumble bacon and sprinkle over eggs for the last 10 minutes of baking. Bread and cheese may be prepared in advance. Serves 10.

MRS. JAMES B. COUCH

QUICHES

A delicious hot quiche makes an impressive away-from-the-table first course—tart and aromatic. It is also a handy and easy luncheon dish. It may be made in individual quiche dishes or cut pie-shape from a larger shell. It freezes well and may be prepared in advance. To freeze, bake 10 minutes less than directed in the recipe. Cool thoroughly, wrap in foil and freeze immediately. When ready to serve, unwrap, but do not allow to thaw. Place in a 325° oven for 25 minutes or until hot and golden brown.

QUICHE AU FROMAGE

½ lb. Swiss or Gruyere cheese, grated
1 tablespoon flour
1 (9 inch) pie shell, baked
4 eggs
¼ teaspoon salt
dash nutmeg
2 cups light cream
2 tablespoons butter or margarine

Toss the cheese with the flour and spread on top of the pie shell. Beat the eggs, salt and nutmeg, and then beat in the cream. Slowly pour into the baked pie shell. Dot with butter. Bake in 375° oven on the middle shelf for 25 minutes or until a knife inserted in the center comes out clean. Cut into wedges. May also be made in individual quiche dishes. Serves 6 to 8.

MRS. PETER V. WESTON (YVONNE)

SHRIMP QUICHE

3 eggs
1 cup milk
3/4 teaspoon salt
dash of dill weed
dash white pepper
1 1/2 cups Swiss cheese, grated

1 (5 oz.) can shrimp, drained
3 tablespoons green onion, chopped
2/3 cup California walnuts, chopped
16 pastry lined tart pans

Beat eggs lightly and combine with milk, salt, dill weed and pepper. Stir in cheese, shrimp, onion and walnuts. Spoon into small pastry lined pans and set on a baking sheet. Bake at 375° about 20 minutes or until filling is set and pastry is done. Serve warm or cold. Makes about 16 quiches in 4x2 1/2x3/4 inch dishes.

MRS. PETER V. WESTON (YVONNE)

CRAB QUICHE

1 cup shredded Swiss cheese
9 inch pastry shell, unbaked
1 cup cooked fresh or (7 oz) can crabmeat, drained
2 green onions, sliced with tops
3 eggs, beaten
1 cup light cream

1/2 teaspoon grated lemon peel
1/2 teaspoon salt
1/4 teaspoon dry mustard
dash mace
1/4 cup almonds, sliced
parsley

Place cheese evenly over the bottom of the pastry shell. Top with crab meat. Sprinkle with green onions. Combine eggs, cream, lemon peel, salt, dry mustard and mace. Pour evenly over the crab. Top with almonds and bake in 325° oven about 45 minutes or until set. Allow to stand 10 minutes before slicing. Garnish with parsley. Serves 6.

MRS. RICHARD H. ECKHARDT, JR.

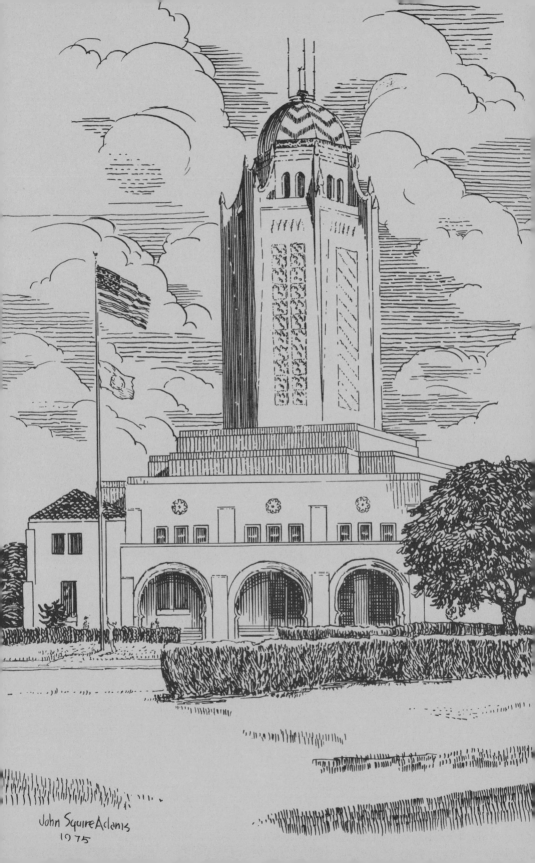

John Squire Adams
1975

The Tables of San Antonio

Dining Delights from Outstanding
San Antonio Restaurants

The stranger may think of San Antonio as a middle-sized Texas town well-known for its famous landmark, The Alamo. It has been romanticized for generations in the folklore and legends of wandering cowboys, western dime novels, Hollywood scripts, Plaza Chili Queens and "San Antonio Rose".

However, San Antonio is more than just a romantic image of the past. With justifiable pride, the city clings to her history and heritage and actively strives to preserve them. At the same time, it's a thriving, modern metropolis shouting "Today!" with every whispered echo of yesterday.

Ours is a cosmopolitan city of nearly a million people. Its ethnic groups are as varied as those of other major American cities. The customs and backgrounds of many lands flow through every cultural expression, be it music, art, dance, drama or food.

The restaurants of San Antonio reflect that variety. Without question, the authentic flavors of Mexico have always been an important part of our dining delights. They are the SPICE OF SAN ANTONIO! Many famous Mexican dishes originated here, cabrito and chili — to name only two. But a host of fine restaurants, from the New York-type Italian eating establishment to the gourmet intimacy of haute cuisine cater to all our tastes. Whether you are resident or visitor, you are sure to enjoy the charm and diversity of dining in San Antonio.

This section of SAN ANTONIO COOKBOOK II is devoted to just a few of those outstanding restaurants . We regret that space does not permit including more. We are indebted to each of them and to the chefs who shared their secrets with us. Their community support of the San Antonio Symphony is appreciated by all our citizens.

RANDOLPH AIR FORCE BASE — John Squire Adams

BILL TASSOS' BARN DOOR, originally a stage coach stop on the road to Nacogdoches, has been the scene of many a family birthday party since he opened it in 1953. The homey family-style restaurant has lost none of its warmth during its extensive expansion over the years. For the browser there are all sorts of collections . . . jugs and bottles, bills, posters, calling cards, even farm equipment. The North Party Room has been added for the use of private groups. Charcoaling is the specialty of the house, be it steak, chicken or fish, and the homemade salad dressings are superlative.

BILL TASSOS'
BARN DOOR GARLIC DRESSING

4 eggs	4 garlic cloves, minced
1 teaspoon salt	5 sprigs parsley, chopped
1 teaspoon dry mustard	4 green onions with tops, chopped
4 cups salad oil	3 celery stalks, chopped
4 hard boiled eggs, minced	½ cup lemon juice and vinegar

Beat eggs on low speed in a blender. Add salt and mustard. While eggs are blending, add salad oil VERY SLOWLY in a steady stream. Add lemon juice and vinegar, mixed to taste, and then add the remaining ingredients. Allow dressing to remain in the refrigerator in a covered container for a few hours and mix well before serving. This improves with age and makes 1 quart.

CASA RIO, certainly a part of "The Spice of San Antonio," has introduced thousands of tourists since 1946 to the adventure of Mexican flavors — San Antonio style. The original fireplace, walls and cedar beams give atmosphere to this mid-19th century building, but the block long, umbrella patio by the river's edge is the main attraction. Proprietors are Franklin Hicks and Bill Lyons, a son-in-law of the originator and pioneer of river development, A. F. Beyer, whose family holds the land title which dates back to 1771.

CASA RIO AVOCADO SALAD OR DIP

1 large ripe avocado
small curd cottage cheese
fresh tomato slice
lemon juice

small hot green chile pepper
 or Tabasco sauce
onion salt
garlic salt

Mash avocado until creamy. Add enough cottage cheese to make smooth but not to change color. Puree tomato in blender and add avocado mixture. Finely chop a small, firm green chile pepper and gradually blend enough into avocado to make flavor hot or picante. Tabasco may be substituted. Mixture should be creamy, firm and smooth, with ingredients completely blended. Add garlic and onion salt to enhance flavor, lemon juice to preserve color. Serve on tomato slice and lettuce with French dressing. Serves 2. Good as a dip.

CASEY'S JOHN CHARLES RESTAURANT came into being in 1961 for personal reasons—to give John Casey the fine prime beef and wines for which he had developed a taste during years in New York. His offerings now include not only superb charcoal-broiled steaks but an array of flaming tableside specialties, a 26,000 bottle wine cellar, and dancing in the tiered Rill Room. He shares with us his epicurean philosophy: select food to go with the wine YOU enjoy, for your own body chemistry causes an individual reaction between your palate and the wine.

If you select a light, not too dry white wine such as Mosel or Rhine, serve it with chicken, pork, sauced fish, bland white cheeses and dried or sweet fruits. Match the dry white wines such as Chablis, Pouilly Fuisse or Pouilly Fumé with oysters, non-sweet sauced fish, rich chicken dishes, turkey, veal, cold Beef Wellington, even meat loaf and cold cuts, and sharp white and orange cheeses.

Try a red Bordeaux or a light Italian wine, Chianti or Valpolicella, with red meat, turkey, game, dark-meated fish, ham, orange and rich white cheeses (especially Roquefort), and tart fruits. If you prefer a robust, less dry Burgundy, serve it with intricate sauced meat dishes. It goes well with lamb, beef, ham, roast game, very sharp orange cheeses or a flamboyant white cheese. As for Rosé, everything goes. John Casey strongly recommends that you diary your choices.

EL QUETZAL STEAK HOUSE, a mirrored balcony of the Hilton Palacio del Rio, provides a bird's-eye view of river activity from a sophisticated hideaway. Its theme is the exotic quetzal, a Central American bird of iridescent plumage and a brilliant 2 foot tail. Mariachis provide entertainment for cocktailing or dining from the varied menu which includes Coquilles Saint Jacques, Filet Mignon with Truffle Wine Sauce and an exquisite Chocolate Mousse.

EL QUETZAL
SPIRITED PEPPERCORN STEAK

2 tablespoons white or black
  peppercorn
2 strip steaks, 10 oz. each
  (¾ to 1 inch thick)
3 oz. butter

1 oz. brandy
3 oz. heavy cream
1 teaspoon Lea & Perrins
pinch of salt
1 teaspoon chopped parsley

Crush peppercorn thoroughly with a pestle. Dry the steaks on a paper towel. Rub and press the pepper into both sides of the meat. Cover with wax paper and let stand for at least ½ hour. Heat 2 oz. butter in a skillet until it foams. When the foam subsides, saute the steaks 4 to 6 minutes on each side. Set the steaks on a platter and keep warm. Pour off excess liquid from skillet. Add remaining butter. When it foams, add brandy, reduce heat and simmer. Add cream, salt and Lea & Perrins. Stir for 3 minutes and add parsley. Pour sauce over steaks. Serves 2.

THE FIG TREE, a century-old La Villita house on the Paseo del Rio, is today a gourmet treat of haute cuisine. Dine at leisure with the past amidst red-flocked elegance at intimate tables set with fine crystal and china. The house attracted so much admiration that the Phelps family gave up this private residence for the enjoyment of all. A fig tree rising two stories from the dining patio bears continuous fruit, hence the name.

FIG TREE LAMB

lamb tenderloin (8 oz. strip)   1 oz. liver pate
whole rosemary   bacon slice

Sprinkle lamb with rosemary. Place liver pate on one end of strip. Roll up from pate end. Wrap with bacon slice and secure with tooth-picks. Broil to desired doneness. Serves 1.

Fig Tree Mint Sauce

4 oz. water   1 oz. sugar
2 oz. cider vinegar   1 tablespoon fresh chopped mint

Bring water, vinegar and sugar to a boil. Remove from heat, add mint and steep. Serve a small amount with each portion.

THE GAZEBO provides the pleasures of luncheon in the sun nestled in the midst of the flowers and greenery of Los Patios — an extraordinary garden nursery. John Spice is the originator and president of this unusual complex. He does not call his food gourmet, but where the fork falls, there is delight. The Sunday buffet is outstanding. This popular garden restaurant is a lovely spot for parties and weddings or just for meandering among the galleries and boutiques along the Salado Creek.

GAZEBO CHEESE SOUP

½ stick butter or margarine
3 chopped green onions
3 stalks of celery, chopped
   with some leaves
2 grated carrots
2 (10¾ oz.) cans chicken broth
3 (10¾ oz.) cans Heinz
   potato soup

8 oz. grated yellow cheese
parsley flakes
few drops of tabasco
salt
coarse ground pepper
8 oz. sour cream
3 tablespoons Sherry

Melt butter over low heat and saute onions, celery and carrots. Add chicken broth, cover and simmer 30 minutes. Add potato soup, cheese, parsley, Tabasco, salt and pepper. Stir in sour cream, simmer for 15 minutes, add Sherry and stir. Makes 10 cups. This recipe is contributed by Margaret Coffey Saegert, Food Consultant.

La Fonda Mexican Restaurant on Main, the original of four La Fondas, is run by Bill Berry. The 1910 Mexican Revolution forced his mother's family to flee Mexico. With the help of Angela Martinez, Mrs. Berry reconstructed recipes from the family kitchen of her youth. These are the fine dishes served at La Fonda today. Opened in 1932, it prospered in spite of the depression and many a World War II transplanted Yankee is grateful for her introduction to a favorite food.

LA FONDA CHILES RELLENOS

2 tablespoons shortening
1 onion, chopped
2 medium tomatoes, chopped
1/2 cup raisins
1/2 cup pecans, chopped
1 clove garlic, minced

1 teaspoon comino
1/2 lb. pork, chopped
2 large Bell peppers
2 egg yolks, beaten
2 egg whites, beaten stiff
cooked tomato sauce

Saute in shortening next 6 ingredients with salt and pepper. Simmer 15 minutes, stirring constantly. Add pork, cover and simmer till done, stirring often. Roast peppers at 375°, turning often. Remove, wrap in towel for 5 minutes and peel. Slit peppers, remove seeds and stuff with meat. Fold yolks into egg whites. Roll peppers in salted flour, dip in egg mixture, fry in hot oil, basting often, until brown. Drain on towels and serve covered with tomato sauce of sauteed chopped onions, green peppers and tomatoes.

LA LOUISIANE, one of only six restaurants in the nation to merit the Holiday Magazine Award for twenty-five consecutive years, typifies the charm and imagination of French cooking at its best. Max Manus created a culinary oasis in 1935 which is now internationally known for its haute cuisine and fine wines. Still family-directed under George Darreos, it has expanded from a small dining room to five beautiful rooms in Louis XIV decor. You may dance to a fine orchestra in the Fountain Room.

LA LOUISIANE
RED SNAPPER A LA GEORGE

4 red snapper filets	Juice of 2 lemons
3 tablespoons butter	salt and pepper
sliced fresh mushrooms	Worcestershire sauce
artichoke hearts, canned	

Skin serving size pieces of red snapper, dredge in flour and shake off excess. Brown butter in skillet, then saute filets until well done on one side. Turn and lightly salt and pepper them to taste. Add enough sliced fresh mushrooms and artichoke hearts to cover tops of filets when done. Cook until mushrooms and artichokes are thoroughly heated. Sprinkle all the lemon juice over this, then lightly sprinkle on Worcestershire sauce. When blended, remove from skillet and place mushrooms and artichoke over filets. Add a little water to the juice remaining in the skillet, heat, and pour over filets. Serves 4.

The LITTLE RHEIN STEAK HOUSE, popular with symphony-goers, is a dining delight on the Paseo del Rio. This circa 1847 building, owned by the Conservation Society, was one of the first two-story buildings in San Antonio. Its past has been colorful and of sometimes questionable repute. Frank Phelps has retained the character while converting to respectability. Stone walls are adorned with old mementoes and the large bar came from a local saloon. The discovery and excavation of a silt-filled lower level in 1959 created the Davy Crockett and Jim Bowie rooms. Enjoy dining on the river terrace.

LITTLE RHEIN BLACK EYED PEAS

2 lbs. dried blackeyed peas
5 oz. celery, diced
5 oz. green pepper, diced
1/2 cup red peppers, diced
1 teaspoon black pepper
1 tablespoon salt

3/4 teaspoon ground comino seed
3/4 teaspoon garlic powder
3/4 stick margarine
3 1/4 teaspoon Seasonal
1/5 teaspoon cayenne pepper
pinch MSG

Cover the peas with water and soak overnight. Drain, add remaining ingredients and cover with water. Place in the oven at low temperature and simmer, covered, for at least 2 hours. Add more water if necessary. At the Little Rhein, the peas are served cold in individual dishes as a relish with small loaves of bread and butter.

NAPLES, often starred in gourmet magazines, offers consistently delectable dishes, well attested to by its huge clientele. Neapolitan-born Ralph Branchizio is Italy's loss and San Antonio's gain. He arrived in New York in 1926 and came to this city in 1950, opening his first Broadway restaurant. He moved to the present location in 1959 and has since expanded. His family-learned recipes from the kitchens of southern Italy enhance the delicate flavors of seafood, especially squid and shrimp. A fine selection of wine is available, with emphasis on the Italian.

NAPLES VEAL SCALOPPINE MARSALA

3 slices of veal or yearling about
   2 inches (in diameter)
4 oz. butter or margarine
¼ cup mushrooms, canned or
   fresh cooked

1½ oz. Marsala wine or Sherry
salt and pepper
stock
Kitchen Bouquet

Pound scallops to ¼ inch thick. Salt and pepper them and dust lightly with flour, shaking off excess. In a skillet brown the scallops quickly in butter. Add the drained mushrooms and wine, then simmer. After the wine dissolves, add stock or water and a few drops of Kitchen Bouquet for color. Simmer a bit and place the veal on a warmed serving dish. If the sauce is too thin, a pinch of flour may be added. Stir to thicken. Pour the sauce over the veal. Serves 1.

The Kitchens of San Antonio

We acknowledge the generosity of all who graciously shared their treasured recipes with us and regret that each recipe contributed could not be included. Unsigned recipes are presented for your dining pleasure with the compliments of the entire SAN ANTONIO COOKBOOK II Committee.

RESTAURANT CONTRIBUTORS

SIMPLIFIED METRIC CONVERSION

For simplicity, we have used the nearest convenient measurement converted from our cup, spoon and pound. This is sufficiently accurate for most recipes. For greater accuracy, use parenthesis. Consult metric conversion tables for precise measurements.

LIQUID OR DRY MEASUREMENTS
1 liter = 10 deciliters = 1000 milliliters (liquid)

4 cups ....32 ounces................1 liter (0.946 liter)
    (plus 1/3 cup = 1 liter)
1 cup................................. 8 ounces................1/4 liter
    (plus 1 1/4 tablespoons = 1/4 liter)
1/3 cup .... 3 ounces................1 deciliter (0.088 liter)
    (plus 1 tablespoon = 1 deciliter)
1 tablespoon (15 grams) ....1/2 ounce................15 milliliters
2 teaspoons (10 grams)....................1/3 ounce................10 milliliters

WEIGHT MEASUREMENTS
2.2 pounds = 1 kilogram = 1000 grams

1 pound (454 grams) ....16 ounces................500 grams
1/3 pound (152 grams) ....5 ounces................150 grams
1/4 pound (114 grams) ....4 ounces................125 grams
1/16 pound (28.3 grams) ....1 ounce ....30 grams
                        1/3 ounce .... 10 grams

Index

- 274 -

- 286 -

San Antonio Cookbook II

P. O. Box 17412 - N. Broadway Station
San Antonio, Texas 78217

Enclosed is check or money order for .... copies of
SAN ANTONIO COOKBOOK II at $ 9.95 per
Total including handling and postage 10.95 per
Total including handling, postage and state tax
for Texas Delivery 11.50 per

Please send to: ☐ free gift wrap if des

Name ....

Street ....

City .... State .... Zip ....

San Antonio Cookbook II

P. O. Box 17412 - N. Broadway Station
San Antonio, Texas 78217

Enclosed is check or money order for .... copies of
SAN ANTONIO COOKBOOK II at $ 9.95 per b
Total including handling and postage 10.95 per b
Total including handling, postage and state tax
for Texas Delivery 11.50 per b

Please send to: ☐ free gift wrap if desi

Name ....

Street ....

City .... State .... Zip ....

San Antonio Cookbook II

P. O. Box 17412 - N. Broadway Station
San Antonio, Texas 78217

Enclosed is check or money order for .... copies of
SAN ANTONIO COOKBOOK II at $ 9.95 per book
Total including handling and postage 10.95 per book
Total including handling, postage and state tax
for Texas Delivery 11.50 per book

Please send to: ☐ free gift wrap if desired.

Name ....

Street ....

City .... State .... Zip ....